MARKETING MANAGEMENT

MARKETING
MANAGEMENT

A RELATIONSHIP
MARKETING PERSPECTIVE

CRANFIELD SCHOOL OF MANAGEMENT

St. Martin's Press
New York

MARKETING MANAGEMENT
Text copyright © 2000 Cranfield School of Management
Foreword copyright © 2000 First Direct

St. Martin's Press, Scholarly and Reference Division,
175 Fifth Avenue, New York, N.Y. 10010

First published in the United States of America in 2000

Printed in Great Britain

ISBN   0-312-23186-5

Library of Congress Cataloging-in-Publication Data
Marketing management: a relationship marketing perspective / Cranfield School of Management.
p.   cm.
Includes bibliographical references and index.
ISBN 0-312-23186-5 (cloth)
1. Marketing—Management. I. Cranfield School of Management.
HF5415.13 .M35232 2000
658.8 — dc21
                                                                              00-021419

CONTENTS

CONTENTS

LIST OF FIGURES

LIST OF FIGURES

LIST OF TABLES

PREFACE: INTRODUCTION TO MARKETING MANAGEMENT: A RELATIONSHIP MARKETING PERSPECTIVE

The need for effective marketing is as strong as ever in today's highly competitive and global business environment. The challenge for academics and practitioners alike is how best to apply the principles of marketing to secure strategic advantage. In an unprecedented achievement, *Marketing Management: A Relationship Marketing Perspective* illustrates the process of creating effective marketing through the management of a complex web of relationships.

The concept of Relationship Marketing (RM) has gained currency in recent years across all sectors as it offers a realistic and relevant approach to developing greater competitive advantage through relationship-based strategies. RM represents a paradigm shift in marketing philosophy and contrasts sharply with the focus on a series of individual transactions that has traditionally characterized marketing management.

Based on the theory developed by Christopher, Payne and Ballantyne, and evolved through the research of the wider Marketing & Logistics Group at Cranfield School of Management, this novel marketing approach is the subject of this informative, insightful and instructive text. The profile and mechanics of RM are set out in five cross-related sections, escorting the reader through a practical explanation of the application and implementation of RM, and culminating in a focus on how RM both serves and reinforces market orientation.

PART I

The role of relationship marketing in business is introduced in the context of the field of marketing and in relation to the concept of market orientation. *Chapter 1* examines the connection between organizations that demonstrate a high level of market orientation and those that excel at relationship marketing: successful companies usually perform well on both counts. RM involves having a 'market orientation' that is actively translated into the delivery of superior customer value on a continuing basis. Like any marketing strategy, it is founded on the twin pillars of internal culture and organizational structure. However, RM's winning formula additionally recognizes the significant contribution of people and how their attitudes, actions and interactions critically impact the business agenda.

Chapter 2 examines the growing trend away from the conventional transactional approach to business towards a concentration on building relationships both externally and internally. Adopting a relationship-based perspective of marketing requires marketers to abandon the traditional view of dealing with only one market and to identify a number of relevant markets that may be managed simultaneously. Target audiences may extend beyond customer markets to include all stakeholders, comprising internal markets, suppliers, employees, shareholders, and so on. The challenge for marketers, therefore, becomes one of managing multiple markets.

Chapter 3 concludes the first section with a discussion on the range of diagnostic tools available to marketers to help them in managing multiple markets and competing business demands.

PART II

Part II tackles the huge issue of actually *doing* marketing, through an examination of the customer relationship audit. The aim of this section is to describe the processes which provide the marketer with an understanding of the customer market, whether the business of the organization is in the provision of goods and services for consumers or other businesses. *Chapters 4 and 5* are devoted to the fundamental ingredient of RM: that is, understanding both consumer and organizational buyer behaviour.

Chapter 6 outlines the process of segmenting the market to develop a typology of the customer or market segment so that marketing efforts may be focused on the most promising opportunities and customer value may be delivered through the dynamics of the supply chain. *Chapter 7* follows through with an overview of the purpose and process of market research, the findings of which determine the direction and dimension of marketing strategy.

Chapter 8 rounds off the section with an in-depth discussion on the direct relationship between customer retention and profitability that lies at the heart of relationship marketing. The need for a strategic approach to keeping valuable customers and to overcoming present and potential causes of customer defection is emphasized.

PART III

Part III of the book is concerned with creating customer value through the expanded marketing mix. Traditionally, the marketing mix has been popularly described in terms of the '4 Ps': Product, Price, Place and Promotion (this final element has more recently been referred to as the communications mix). *Chapters 9, 10, 11 and 13* consider each of the four marketing elements from a relationship marketing perspective, getting to grips with the differential advantage provided by each of the individual components. *Chapter 12* brings these essential elements together under the auspices of 'added value': that which gives credence to the brand and its competitive position. However, adopting a complete relationship marketing approach means expanding the traditional marketing mix.

Chapter 14 soundly argues the importance of incorporating three additional marketing mix elements: Customer Service, People and Processes. The tenets of RM are shown to support the belief that marketing relies on more than the creation of customers and the generation of sales; it depends on enduring relationships born of trust and mutual benefit.

PART IV

Part IV of the book competently covers planning and organizing for RM. *Chapter 15* presents customer marketing planning as a logical and sequential series of steps following on from the setting of marketing objectives.

Chapter 16 takes up the challenge with a detailed discussion of the organizational requirements inherent in RM. The point is firmly made that it is not enough for organizations simply to be convinced of the value of adopting a market orientation and appreciating the potential of RM: new types of structure which serve to enhance customer relationships must be explored, as traditional organizational forms generally mitigate against the successful implementation of RM.

Chapter 17 closes the section with an examination of Key Account Management, a natural development of customer focus and relationship marketing in business-to-business markets. Based on Cranfield research which demonstrates how the buyer–seller relationship moves through observable phases, the chapter provides a practical framework for better understanding and practising Key Account Management.

PART V

Chapter 18 concludes the book by drawing together the preceding four parts under the banner of RM as an effective means of tapping the power of marketing. The chapter stresses the importance of adopting an integrated approach to marketing as advocated by RM, and highlights the imperative for marketing to be better understood within business in order that its true potential can be realized.

The book's intention is not to promise a 'quick fix' solution to problems of initiating or implementing RM, but to offer a viable and valuable route to resolving marketing difficulties where the application of relationship marketing is appropriate and where it is applied properly. *Marketing Management: A Relationship Marketing Perspective* takes us a welcome step forward on the pathway to achieving a marketing approach that can realistically confer sustainable, competitive advantage.

Finally, I would like to thank my colleagues for their leading role in progressing our understanding of RM and to recognize Margrit Bass for her contribution in editing this collaborative work.

SUSAN BAKER

LIST OF ABBREVIATIONS

ACORN	A Classification of Regional Neighbourhood Groups
ATM	automated teller machine
CAPI	computer aided personal interviewing
CATI	computer aided telephone interviewing
CEO	Chief Executive Officer
CRM	Customer Relationship Management
CSF	critical success factor
DMP	decision-making process
DMU	decision-making unit
DPM	Directional Policy Matrix
EDI	electronic data interchange
EDLP	everyday low price
EDP	electronic data processing
EPOS	electronic point-of-sale
GM	genetically modified
HHCL	Howell, Henry, Caldecott, Lury
HRD	human resource development
ICT	information and communications technology
IMC	integrated marketing communications
IT	information technology
JIT	just-in-time
KAM	Key Account Management
KPI	key performance indicator
NPD	new product development
NPV	net present value
P&G	Procter & Gamble
PC	personal computer
PEST	political, economic, social, technological
PIP	Pilkington Innovation Process
PLC	Product Life Cycle
P/T	part-time
R&D	research and development
RM	relationship marketing
ROI	return on investment
RSPB	Royal Society for the Protection of Birds
SBU	Strategic Business Unit
SFA	Sales Force Automation

SIC	Standard Industrial Classification
SPV	special purpose vehicle
SWOT	strengths, weaknesses, opportunities, threats
TQM	Total Quality Management
USP	unique selling proposition
VMI	Vendor Managed Inventory

FOREWORD

First Direct is delighted to be supporting Cranfield School of Management by writing this foreword, thus contributing to what we believe to be yet another important piece of work from this institution.

While some may be of the attitude that **relationship marketing** is simply the latest fashion in the marketing world, we would cry that this could not be further from the truth. The fact is that in all markets customer relationships are absolutely key; indeed, they are the cornerstone of **brands**. Why? Simply because how a customer feels about an organization is at the very essence of what brands are all about.

At First Direct our whole approach is about developing relationships with our customers; banking is a commodity market, where all products are basically the same, and frankly most people quite understandably feel that banking and finance is somewhat of a dry topic, to say the least. With this in mind, it is obviously extremely important to pay a huge amount of attention to how the customer feels about utilizing the brand. How do they feel about telephoning First Direct, what do they feel when they are banking via the Internet, for example, and, critically, how do they feel when they have finished interacting with us? None of this is about different types of bank accounts, credit cards or insurance, but much more to do with emotional benefit.

Relationship marketing is really, as Levitt described so well, marketing speak for creating and retaining customers. When one thinks about the implied logic, it really does make a great deal of common sense. The fact is that people want to be recognized for what they are – that is, they are different from everyone else. The reality for marketers is that modern technology means that organizations can now think much more about offering their customers tailored offers, based on what those customers have actually told them, and communicating those offers to large numbers of people, while retaining a feel of individuality and difference.

Of course, the big irony about all of this, whether one talks about relationship marketing, micro marketing or any other description, is that this concept has been practised for many years without being named as such. One hears about a golden age of customer service, when shopkeepers knew all their customers by name, and provided levels of service that have never been repeated since. While it is probable that such an age never quite existed as such, it would be true to say that relationship marketing would embrace these ideas.

At First Direct we pride ourselves on having the most satisfied banking customers in the UK, and the bank is actually recommended once every six seconds. People do not join First Direct because it is a telephone bank or even because it offers other channels such as Internet and mobile phone delivery; they actually join because it makes them feel just a little bit better about life, by putting them in control of their banking with a quick, efficient and friendly (what, from a bank?!) service.

And the real benefit? They can then get on with something more exciting in their lives!

MATTHEW HIGGINS

Marketing Innovations Manager

First Direct

ACKNOWLEDGEMENTS

The authors and publishers are grateful to the following for permission to reproduce copyright material: AC Nielsen, Headington, Oxford, for Figure 12.7 'Own-label grocery share'; American Marketing Association for Figure 5.2 'Buyer behaviour matrix', from Rangan *et al.*, 'Segmenting customers in mature industrial markets', *Journal of Marketing*, New York, October 1992, vol. 56, no. 4, pp. 72–83; *Financial Times* for Case Study 1: a move towards central purchasing, on page 68, adapted from 'Living life to the max – PepsiCo has combined an ambitious promotion with a plan to squeeze suppliers', *Financial Times*, 29 September 1994; First Direct for Foreword, and quotes in Case Study 1: the one-to-one future – First Direct Bank, on pages 178–81; Interbrand, Newell & Sorrell Limited, London, for their list of the top twenty brands 1999, on page 170; Pearson Education Limited for Figure 13.1 'Estimated UK communications mix expenditure', from Chris Fill, *Marketing Communications, Contexts, Contents and Strategies*, 2nd edn, © Prentice-Hall Europe 1999, with information supplied by the Advertising Association (1995); Pret A Manger (Europe) Limited for Figure 15.2 'Pret A Manger's logo and mission statement'; United Biscuits (UK) Limited for Figure 12.8 'McVitie's Go Ahead!® brand at launch', ® Registered Trade Mark of United Biscuits (UK) Limited. Every effort has been made to contact all the copyright-holders, but if any have been inadvertently omitted the publishers will be pleased to make the necessary arrangement at the earliest opportunity.

PART I

THE ROLE OF RELATIONSHIP MARKETING IN BUSINESS

1 A MARKET ORIENTATION

Mike Meldrum

In this chapter:

- The multidimensional nature of market orientation
- The significance of market orientation for relationship marketing
- Market orientation and issues of implementation
- The difficulties of establishing a market orientation

MARKETING RECAST

The case for marketing being a valuable contributor to organizational performance no longer needs to be made. Most managers now recognize that the ability to win sales and repeat orders requires more than just good sales techniques. However, all too often, people within organizations lose sight of this 'extra' requirement and become transfixed by the immediate return – the imperative of the next sale. Their marketing reaction is to reach for the traditional transaction-based approach, with its measurable but myopic systems. Marketing was never meant to be this.

In its true version, marketing is defined as a business process which seeks to match an organization's human, financial and physical resources with the wants and needs of its customers within the context of its overall competitive strategy.

Customers rarely want simply to be sold to; they want to be valued. They want their circumstances to be acknowledged and their needs to be satisfied. This demand for a matching of the supplier's offer to the customer's need is something greater than the resultant transaction: it resembles some kind of higher order business relationship.

This move beyond the traditional realm of transaction marketing has led to a new emphasis in marketing, with a focus on relationships and the development of the notion of relationship marketing (RM). Marketing is recast as a matter of relationship management. It does not abandon the fundamental principles of marketing, but builds them into something more powerful and more relevant for the fiercely competitive markets of today's global market place. This re-conceptualization of marketing forms the basis of the way in which marketing is thought about, taught and practised at Cranfield, and is what has led to the creation of this book.

One of the concepts underpinning the development and implementation of successful relationship marketing strategies is that of *market orientation*.

Organizations that implement RM well – those that embrace and practise the RM approach – usually exhibit a high level of market orientation.

Organizations that are inclined, in principle, policy and practice, towards meeting and anticipating the needs of markets are said to be market-oriented. This business focus on markets aims to maximize the match between supply and demand, and to minimize the likelihood of inappropriate outputs and wasted inputs. Organizations that actively seek to identify and solidify relationships with the people that buy their goods and services, be they end consumers or business-to-business customers, are pursuing RM. The connection between the attitude that inspires the aim (market orientation) and the activity that delivers the aim (RM) forms the context of this chapter and the crux of RM management.

One route to achieving more sophisticated and integrated RM activity is to look at this connection the other way round: if a business can develop or improve its degree of market orientation, then it should be able to obtain better levels of RM.

Using market orientation as the basis for implementing RM raises a number of thought-provoking questions. How is the concept of market orientation best addressed? Which particular aspects of an organization should reflect or determine its degree of market orientation? What are the differences between an organization that has a market orientation and one that has not? What changes must be made if an enterprise is to become more market-oriented? In order to answer these fundamental questions, we must first consider what is meant by market orientation.

DEFINING MARKET ORIENTATION

Although the term 'market orientation' has been in common usage for some time, it does not possess a universally accepted definition. That market orientation is not confined to an 'official' meaning and is used in variety of capacities by academics and practitioners alike is evidence of the concept's utility and versatility. To appreciate its crucial significance to the marketing agenda in general, and RM in particular requires a sound understanding of the ways in which the term is applied.

To begin with, there is the consideration of whether a 'market' orientation is something distinct from a 'marketing' orientation, and whether or not being 'customer focused' or 'competitively aware' is also the same or something different again. Some would argue that using the term market or customer, instead of marketing, draws attention away from internal organizational issues and overemphasizes external activities. The danger is that, although firms need to be in tune with their markets, customers and competitors, an excessive focus on external matters can distract from the achievement of the returns required for long-term business survival. For many organizations, these returns are measured as profits of one form or another, while for others they may be the achievement of social, charitable or artistic objectives.

Internal factors that affect profitability or the achievement of other types of objective, so the argument goes, should consequently have an equal influence on the practice of marketing. Thus marketing managers must have an appreciation of such areas as resource availability, cost generation and organizational capability, as well as an in-depth knowledge of customer wants and needs. Without the former, it becomes difficult to gauge the attractiveness of different marketing opportunities; without the latter, the business is unfocused.

An alternative approach to understanding the term market orientation recognizes that the rationale for raising the topic of market, marketing or customer orientation is one and the same: namely, being more effective in the market place. Trying to distinguish between these and similar terms is, accordingly, a waste of valuable management time. The debate adds little to the way in which marketing is practised or relationships are developed, and detracts from the need to 'get on' with the business of business.

The terms that are used and the ways in which they are depicted do, however, reveal telling characteristics of the market-oriented business. These can be listed as:

- A concern for customers
- An interest in the business environment
- A focus on competitors
- Curiosity about the future
- An entrepreneurial spirit
- A desire for action

From a practitioner's point of view, the important point is not whether a market orientation is something distinct from a marketing orientation (and so on), but that a management team is able to draw on the marketing principles involved and to agree a direction for the business. In this sense, it is important that marketing theory is able not only to support actively the determination of strategic business decisions, but also their implementation. For many commentators, therefore, the various terms are used synonymously.

To be consistent with modern writers, this book uses the expression 'market orientation' as a generic term for the organizational attributes that together comprise the features of a market, marketing or customer-focused enterprise. The number of closely related terms which can be collected under the umbrella of 'market orientation' indicates the multidimensional nature of the concept, rather than any serious disagreement about the fundamentals of its meaning.

This multidimensional quality of market orientation can be illustrated by reference to the ways in which different writers have gone about explaining and exploring the concept (see Figure 1.1). For some, market orientation is essentially a *philosophy*, representing a body of thought that can be applied to an organization or used to underpin the way in which a business is conceptualized or run. Others view market orientation as an aspect of organizational *culture*, where attention is focused on the values, attitudes and beliefs collectively held

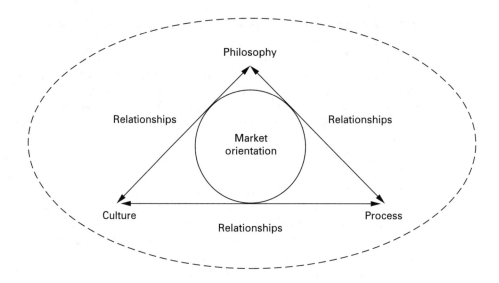

Figure 1.1   Market orientation as a multidimensional construct

by an organization's members. Still others conceive the concept as a *process*: a series of actions or activities that constitutes the heart of what it means to be market-oriented. Each of these three perspectives is dealt with in more detail later in the chapter.

Given this diversity of perception, one way of moving towards a better understanding of market orientation is to identify common themes within the various usages of the term. What becomes strikingly apparent from such an exercise is the emphasis each approach places on the interaction between an organization and its external environment, and the myriad of relationships that this interaction generates. Thus, while the substance of a market orientation may vary from one observer to another, the object of a market orientation remains the same. Market orientation, therefore, embodies:

> The ability and willingness of an organisation to take account of external factors which will affect the possibility of it developing profitable exchanges (however profit is defined by the organisation), both now and in the future, and the ability and willingness of the organisation to take action as a result of these factors to strengthen important relationships.

This definition of market orientation acknowledges the constraints placed on organizations by internal factors (their 'ability and willingness' and their need for certain outcomes or 'profit') and emphasizes the key activity of effective marketing organizations: understanding and acting upon the dynamics of the markets in which they operate and concentrating on critical relationships.

Describing market orientation in this way implies that market-oriented organizations will be particularly interested in understanding how a number of different factors will affect future sales (or exchanges), and what profits or outcomes might be gained from them. According to the existing array of texts dedicated to marketing and competitive strategy, these factors include:

- Customer perceptions and preferences, both existing and potential
- Political, legal, economic, social, technological and institutional trends
- Competitors, both existing and potential
- Opportunities (neglected and/or new needs and wants), both existing and potential
- Relationships, and how they impact on marketing effectiveness

Market-oriented organizations will therefore be interested in the acquisition of intelligence about these areas. More importantly, they will also be interested in the response this intelligence suggests and the actions that it prompts.

A market orientation can thus be seen to incorporate a number of sub-orientations, which together form its substantive elements. Collectively, these sub-orientations emphasize the need for an external focus and make the concept more explicit, 'fleshing out' what is otherwise a difficult concept to define. Importantly, they stress the prevalence and prominence of relationships in marketing.

THE IMPORTANCE OF MARKET ORIENTATION IN RELATIONSHIP MARKETING

As the ultimate goal of marketing is profitable exchanges, market orientation is about laying the foundations for the establishment and growth of relationships that will deliver these exchanges. Market orientation, RM and marketing implementation, therefore, go hand in glove.

Indeed, for many writers, the term market orientation is taken to mean the implementation of RM. The more market-oriented a business, the better it is at implementing the development of marketing relationships. It is hard to conceive of an organization that has a high level of market orientation, but which fails to implement strategies developed in a truly market-oriented fashion and carried out by people working from a market-oriented perspective. Problems with relationships are more likely to stem from organizational inadequacies, such as shoddily conducted market research or poor relationship management, rather than from deficiencies associated with being market-oriented.

Consider, for example, the many instances where managers want their organizations to become more market-oriented and to enjoy better customer relationships, but who adopt insufficient or inappropriate measures to ensure their realization. Popular initiatives such as the 'smile campaigns' used by service businesses represent superficial attempts at substantive change and improved relationships. While the intentions behind them may be worthy, they are unproductive in the long term. Creating better customer relationships requires real organizational commitment, achieved through courses of action that do more than simply create the visible manifestations of a market orientation.

CONVENTIONAL WISDOM

In addition to highlighting the importance of having a market orientation, the need to find better ways of implementing marketing has also led to a number of propositions about how to conceptualize market-oriented organizations. There is no one orthodoxy on the subject and three distinct schools of thought prevail. Each theory has been developed from a particular conventional wisdom about what is important for organizational effectiveness in terms of marketing capabilities. In turn, each has influenced the way a market orientation has been conceived and adds its own depth to the discussion.

Market orientation as a philosophy

In its philosophical sense, market orientation is used to describe a particular approach to the way in which an enterprise is conceived or conceptualized. Theodore Levitt was one of the first proponents of this idea. In his seminal work, he draws attention to the importance of viewing a business in a way that is appropriate to the markets in which it operates. His classic example was the railroads, which defined themselves as being in the railway business, rather than in the transportation business: 'The railroads did not stop growing because the need for passenger and freight transportation declined. That grew. The railroads are in trouble today not because the need was filled by others (cars, trucks, aeroplanes, even telephones), but because it was not filled by the railroads themselves.'[1]

Levitt contrasted the railroads with companies such as DuPont, which saw their activities in a very different light. Instead of defining themselves in terms of their products, the companies concentrated on finding 'customer-satisfying' applications for them. They did not abandon the search for technical excellence, but combined it with an awareness of its relevance to market needs. As a result, these companies continued to thrive while direct competitors steadily lost custom and declined.

The significance of these examples is the way in which the different self-perceptions focus attention on contrary aspects of the business. Seeing oneself as being in the railroad business implies that knowing, understanding and being proficient in running railways is the key to successful business management. If, however, the business is seen as finding the best means of transporting people and freight from one location to another, business management takes on another dimension. The priority then becomes not running a railway, but providing transport and communication services.

As better, cheaper, faster, more effective ways of providing customer benefits appear, the transport business takes advantage of them to compete for custom. The organization that regards itself as being in the business of running railroads, on the other hand, tries to compete by running the railroad better. In those areas where alternative technologies can cost-effectively outperform the railroad, the business will never compete profitably and its future will become uncertain.

A similar example is provided by a luxury ocean cruise company whose business performance was greatly enhanced by the realization that it was closer to being in the hotel business than in the business of running cruise ships. Applying the principles of customer focus and understanding customer perceptions, the company devoted more effort to achieving service excellence than it did to merely improving the efficiency of getting from one destination to another. As a result, it delivered much higher levels of customer value.

At a philosophical level, market orientation is about giving meaning to an enterprise's activities. It provides a set of principles for the management of a business. These principles require operations to be performed in the context of market needs. As has long been acknowledged, the purpose of the organization becomes the acquisition and retention of customers, and the value that is created for customers becomes the measure of business performance.[2]

While strategically supportive in principle, market orientation as a philosophy offers little in the way of practical guidance. It is easier to extol the virtues of being a market-oriented organization than it is to apply them in a meaningful manner.

Market orientation as an organizational culture

One approach to linking market orientation as a philosophy to more practical issues is to look at it as an aspect of organizational culture. Organizational culture refers to the collection of values, attitudes and beliefs that dominate an enterprise. Its value lies in its ability to provide a guide for behaviour and to legitimize certain types of action over others. The power of organizational culture is illustrated by the phrase 'the way things are done around here', which implies accepted standards of approach and action. As one prominent writer notes, a marketing culture is one in which the philosophical principles of market orientation rule, in policy and in practice.[3]

Implementation of effective relationships is achieved in a market-oriented culture because the value systems of the organization are translated into an operational environment that supports and encourages behaviour that contributes value for the customer and profit for the company. However, as the following example shows, the culture of an organization can be a formidable force and may counteract philosophical tenets. Having an appropriate philosophy about the business may not be enough to ensure a market oriented culture.

The example concerns a UK national retail banking organization. Following the introduction of automated teller machines (ATMs), the bank received complaints from infuriated customers who were reliant on the machines to obtain cash outside bank opening hours. The problem was that the machines sometimes ran out of cash. Understanding that their business was all about customer service, the bank's central marketing function issued an instruction that ATMs should be monitored more closely and imposed a system of penalties on branches which experienced 'cash outs'.

In a number of branches, the prevailing culture tended towards isolationist values based on a feeling of alienation from central policy-making. The predominant belief was that senior managers were intent on getting as much work out of branch employees as they could without paying for it. Therefore, the main concern of branch staff was to prevent 'cash outs' being reported, rather than to find ways of keeping sufficient cash reserves in the tills. As a solution, many branches came up with the idea of folding the last note in the machine, which had the effect of jamming the ATM before it could run out of cash. In this way, no 'cash outs' were ever reported, but the policies developed from good marketing principles were not satisfactorily implemented.

Thinking of market orientation in terms of culture focuses attention on inherent social forces, which can discourage as well as encourage the implementation of marketing principles. While creating the right cultural environment is key to the successful implementation of marketing and the nurturing of good relationships, the complex and intangible nature of organizational culture can make this a difficult task, especially on an organization-wide basis.

A further difficulty is that creating a particular culture relies on the absence of other values, attitudes and beliefs in order to be effective. Thus, organizations and their representatives may espouse market-oriented values, but these may be countered by attitudes and assumptions that are at odds with the essence of a marketing culture. A business may support the notion that customers and customer relationships are important, but may tolerate employees, at whatever level, who abuse behavioural guidelines, such as staff who prefer to finish a personal conversation instead of attending to a waiting customer. Without proper organizational reinforcement, a market-oriented culture is inadequate as a means of ensuring the implementation of marketing.

Market orientation as a process

The difficulties associated with achieving a market orientation have led recent writers to take a systems approach to the topic.[4] By focusing on the tangible manifestations of a market orientation, they have endeavoured to identify a set of activities that indicate the extent of its existence within an organization. Rather than try to understand the way the business defines itself or maps organizational culture, they have concentrated on input/output relationships as a way of assessing the degree of market orientation. This approach features the processes required for a business to be market-oriented.

The starting point for examining market orientation as a process is, naturally enough, the market place itself. From a process point of view, the main element of the exercise is the systematic collection and collation of market intelligence. Since marketing is about the attainment of profitable exchanges, market factors that influence the ability and willingness of customers to engage in such exchanges form an important input to organizational processes. The regular collection, analysis and dissemination of market information provides an effective basis for measuring and improving activities that promote market orientation.

The communication of this information throughout the organization is crucially important, for an organization's relationship with its market depends on more than just the activities of its marketing department. Employees from almost every function can have an impact on the experience of an organization's markets and customers. It is, therefore, imperative that every member of the organization operates from similar understandings of the market place and customers' needs, and responds accordingly.

From a process perspective, market orientation becomes the generation and dissemination of, and organization-wide response to, market information. The degree of market orientation will depend on the extent to which these processes occur.

Research in this area has identified three key influences, sometimes termed antecedents, on the degree of market orientation within an organization.

1. *Senior management factors.* This encompasses the extent to which senior managers are themselves convinced of the value of a market orientation and how actively they communicate their commitment to more junior employees. As senior managers help generate the organizational climate, it is important that they encourage the 'right' processes.
2. *Inter-functional relations.* This refers to the degree of conflict or cooperation between different functions within an organization. Barriers derived from, say, feelings of self-importance by one group are likely to impede the flow of information around a business and inhibit coordinated responses to it.
3. *Organizational systems.* This concerns the ability of decision-making and reward systems to foster the generation and dissemination of market information and market responsiveness. Many organizations have found themselves hampered by, for instance, bonus systems that reward volume, rather than relationships, or an emphasis on acquiring new business, rather than retaining existing customers. The administrative aspects of an organization need to be in line with marketing principles if they are not to obstruct market orientation processes.

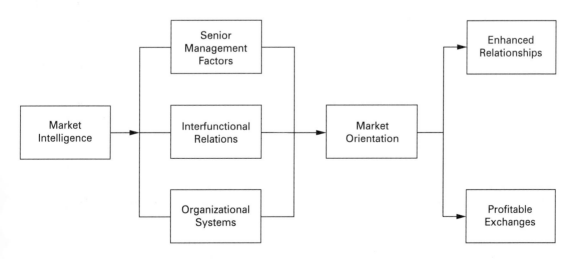

Figure 1.2   Market orientation as an input/output system

Regarding market orientation as a process is beneficial in that it provides a structured view of what issues need to be addressed to achieve a market-oriented organization. However, it is lacking in not linking these actions to a cultural context or to the behavioural requirements needed to ensure the quality and effectiveness of processes. A process approach thus enriches our understanding of what it means to be market-oriented, but leaves us wanting in respect to its role in achieving better marketing relationships.

CURRENT TRENDS IN IMPROVING MARKET ORIENTATION

Current trends in improving market orientation reflect the strengths and weaknesses of market orientation as a philosophy, a culture and a process. They are also a consequence of general developments in marketing thought which seek to address changes in business demand, capability and expectation. One of these trends is the advent of quality initiatives under the banner of Total Quality Management (TQM). Another is the growing interest in internal marketing as a missing link in developing market-oriented businesses. Yet another is the appearance of marketing competencies as a means of identifying the skills required to achieve a market orientation.

Total Quality Management

Although quality management and marketing may, at first sight, appear to be different animals, they have a number of important similarities. In particular, they have both been described in philosophical, cultural and process terms. Like market orientation, TQM can be regarded as a philosophy in that it entails a set of principles that give meaning to (in this case) quality issues within a business. As with market orientation, TQM can also be seen in a cultural light since it implies that a set of values, attitudes and beliefs must be present in an organization for people to implement policies that promote quality standards. In addition, both market orientation and TQM can be approached from a systems perspective, as demonstrated by the existence of standards such as BS 5750 and ISO 9000.

A more important connection between the two concepts is their shared interest in customer perceptions. Under modern approaches to TQM, the definition of quality moves away from 'conformance to specification' to something which 'meets customer requirements'. Such similarities have led to speculation that the success experienced in achieving better levels of quality may have some parallels for the improvement of marketing practice.

Where the development of marketing capabilities has been studied in the light of experiences of introducing TQM, recommendations have usually been couched in terms of 'success factors' of one form or another. These criteria include:

- Having senior managers who lead rather than control
- Removing barriers between the different parts of the organization and taking a holistic view of the business

- Pushing responsibility for achieving quality/marketing improvements down the organization to obtain bottom-up redesign
- Providing training in both the discipline being developed and the skills associated with the new way of working, such as teamworking or benchmarking
- Measuring, rewarding and publicizing achievements
- Making information relevant to decisions freely available
- Employing methods for analysing and understanding situations, such as customer needs or competitor positions

While these factors do not ignore issues of culture or organizational structure, they tend to focus on systems and processes, emphasizing the need to incorporate such thinking into the development of a more market-oriented business. On closer examination, however, many of the factors identified here are similar to those advocated within the different schools of thought about market orientation.

Internal marketing

An alternative approach to TQM in developing a more market-oriented organization is the emerging concept of internal marketing. This is based on the idea that the skills and abilities that marketing professionals use to gain advantage in the market place can also be used to good effect within the organization itself.

Internal marketing involves regarding members of staff as customers. In applying a customer focus internally, the needs, wants and desires of employees are identified and programmes are constructed to encourage and enable them to engage in exchange activities with colleagues. The resulting collaboration not only enhances internal morale and operational efficiency, but also improves service levels to the external customer, therefore progressing the marketing campaign.

One of the vehicles for putting such an idea into practice is marketing planning. The implication is that planning for any marketing activity encompasses two strands: an external focus and a parallel internal focus. Traditional approaches to marketing planning have concentrated on the development of an external position and how internal resources should to be used to achieve it.

The logic of internal marketing is inescapable. If marketing principles make sense for external customers, then they should make equal sense for anybody else who can be regarded as a customer. Adopting the perspective that members of the organization are also customers of the organization can provide useful insights into the management of interfunctional relations and the coordination of marketing effort.

In practical terms, however, internal marketing is limited in what it contributes to the wider issues of organizational culture, since it too often defaults to a communications exercise. Selling the need to value relationships with customers is a far more complex issue than just letting people know what is going on.

Competencies for the marketing professional

A further trend has seen the development of a market orientation based on the cumulative capabilities of individuals to carry out marketing tasks effectively. It implies a direct relationship between the possession of marketing competencies and the achievement of a market orientation. The implication is that an organization's marketing activities can be improved if greater levels of competence in marketing-related skills can be acquired.

Considerable investments have been made to identify and codify the skills and abilities required of competent staff and marketing managers. Of particular interest has been the idea that measurable competencies will enable the identification of skills gaps, inherent in both individuals and organizations. This has generated long lists of essential attributes that purport to encapsulate the essence of high performance in marketing.

Naturally enough, many of the skills identified reflect areas of expertise associated with the elements of the marketing mix: product, price, promotion and so on. At a higher level, they also encompass advanced skills such as analysis, planning and decision-making.

In general, competencies of this form tend to be activity-based and related to specific actions, such as the production of a marketing plan or the influencing of others in reaching strategic decisions. This is especially true where competencies are used as a basis for appraisal and advancement. Skills and abilities that can be objectively described and observed are felt to provide a fairer basis for judging a person's job performance.

One of the drawbacks to breaking competencies down into their component parts for this purpose is the tendency to oversimplify matters. As a result, lists of marketing competencies often ignore many important 'higher order', or 'meta', competencies that are increasingly being recognized as essential for effective management, and marketing management is no exception. An example in marketing might be the ability to engender trust in other people (an attribute of great importance for the management of relationships with customers or when presenting market research data to, say, field sales personnel).

The development of comprehensive sets of competencies is certainly useful for identifying training needs and technical deficiencies. They are also helpful in efforts to 'professionalize' marketing in the same way that accountancy, law and engineering are considered to be professions. Where the identification and promotion of marketing competencies fall short is in addressing the higher order behaviours that encourage organizational philosophy, culture or processes to be more in line with marketing principles.

SUMMARY

This review of the concept of market orientation highlights a number of different organizational features that are crucial to the development of a market orientation and effective RM. While none of the approaches discussed here provides a total solution to the problem of how to achieve effective RM, they do collectively suggest the fundamental issues that need to be acknowledged and addressed. Managers intent on developing their organization's capacities in RM must bear in mind not only the principles and approaches discussed in the rest of this book, but also the wider organizational issues of market orientation and the activities it implies.

Notes

1. T. Levitt, 'Marketing Myopia', *Harvard Business Review*, July/August 1960.
2. P. Drucker, *The Practice of Management* (New York: Harper & Row, 1954).
3. C. Webster, 'A Note on Cultural Consistency Within the Service Firm: The Effects of Employee Position on Attitudes Towards Marketing Culture', *Journal of the Academy of Marketing Science*, vol. 19, no. 4, pp. 341–6.
4. The key work here was done by A. K. Kohli and B. J. Jaworski, 'Market Orientation: The Construct, Research Propositions and Managerial Implications', *Journal of Marketing*, vol. 54 (April), pp. 1–18.

RELATIONSHIP MARKETING: MANAGING MULTIPLE MARKETS

Adrian Payne

In this chapter:

- The role of relationship marketing
- The key elements of relationship marketing
- The relationship marketing multiple markets model
- The difference between transactional marketing and relationship marketing
- How to plan for multiple markets

THE ROLE OF RELATIONSHIP MARKETING

Over the past 15 years, RM has become a topic of great interest to many organizations. It has its origins in industrial and business-to-business markets. However, since the early 1990s, interest in RM has extended to service markets. In the past five years, many consumer goods companies have started to seek ways to develop stronger relationships with their final consumers, in addition to building traditional business-to-business relationships with their immediate customers. Thus all sectors – industrial, service and consumer – are now increasingly examining ways to gain greater competitive advantage through relationship-based strategies.

Many marketing authors have concerns about the relevance of much of traditional marketing theory, with its inherent short-term transactional emphasis. Customary marketing practices have been found to be lacking, especially in business-to-business marketing where establishing and maintaining long-term relationships with customers is critical to the organization's success.

The traditional marketing approach emphasizes the management of key marketing mix elements within a functional context. The new RM approach, while recognizing that these key elements must be addressed, reflects the need to create an integrated, cross-functional means of marketing: one which stresses keeping as well as winning customers. Current marketing focus is shifting from customer acquisition to customer retention, and is ensuring that the appropriate amounts of time, money and managerial resources are directed at *both* these key tasks.

The new RM paradigm reflects a marked change from traditional marketing to the market orientation described in Chapter 1. Hence the term RM embraces an organization-wide perspective of marketing, rather than a narrow, functional focus. Although the term RM is now widely adopted, perhaps a better term to describe the emphasis on cross-functional activities might be relationship management, for RM involves a pan-company approach to managing market relationships.

Our approach to RM is derived from the work of Christopher, Payne and Ballantyne,[1] who developed a broad theory of RM. The key elements of their marketing theory involve:

- Emphasizing a relationship, rather than a transaction, approach to marketing
- Understanding the economics of customer retention and thus ensuring the right amount of money and other resources are appropriately allocated between two tasks (retaining and attracting customers)
- Highlighting the critical role of internal marketing in achieving external marketing success
- Showing how the principles of RM can be applied to a range of diverse market domains, not just customer markets
- Recognizing that quality, customer service and marketing need to be integrated in a much closer manner than has previously been the case in many organizations
- Illustrating how the traditional marketing mix concept of the four Ps (Product, Price, Promotion and Place) does not adequately capture all the key elements which must be addressed in building and sustaining relationships with markets
- Ensuring that marketing is considered in a cross-functional context

This broad concept of RM is depicted in Figure 2.1. The diagram illustrates the transition from transaction marketing to RM. The move to cross-functional

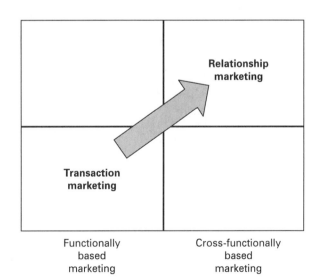

Figure 2.1   The transition to RM

marketing reflects the difficulties encountered by traditional hierarchically-structured and functionally-oriented organizations that adopt a departmental or functional approach to marketing. RM highlights the organization of marketing activities around cross-functional processes as opposed to organizational functions. This cross-functional approach to customer management has become a major theme in RM.

The RM philosophy also stresses the need to change from employing marketing strategies that are based mainly on customer acquisition to those that focus on customer retention. Customer retention lies at the heart of RM and is discussed in greater detail in Chapter 8.

ADDRESSING MULTIPLE MARKETS

The outstanding feature of our RM approach is that it recognizes a diversity of key 'markets', or 'market domains', that organizations need to consider. Figure 2.2 illustrates one such expanded view of marketing: the RM multiple markets model. This model has been applied with great success in many diverse sectors. The framework is constructed of typical key market domains where organizations should direct marketing activity and where the development of detailed marketing strategies may be required. Apart from customer markets, these main focal points might include: referral markets; supplier and alliance markets; recruitment markets; influencer markets; and internal markets.

Figure 2.2   The RM multiple markets model

To achieve success in the complex and fast-paced market place of today, it is increasingly being acknowledged that a number of key market areas need to be addressed. The multiple markets model enables a diagnostic review to be undertaken of the key market domains that may be of importance to any given organization. As a result of such a diagnosis, a number of key groups will be identified which are of special importance. The exact number of markets to be focused on by any given organization will vary. Thus some organizations will need to focus significant emphasis on relatively few, while others will have a much greater number to take into account. Let us now consider each of the exemplar markets in turn.

Customer markets

Customer markets are central to the multiple markets model. Customers must, of course, remain the prime focus of marketing activity; however, marketing activities need to be directed less at transactional marketing with its emphasis on the single sale and more on building long-term customer relationships.

Transactional marketing exhibits a number of specific characteristics, including:

- Focus on single sales
- Orientation to product features
- Short timescale
- Little emphasis on customer service
- Limited customer commitment
- Moderate customer contact
- Quality is primarily a concern of production

RM, by contrast, displays the following attributes:

- Focus on customer retention
- Orientation to customer value
- Long timescale
- High customer service emphasis
- High customer contact
- Quality is the concern of all

While it is clear that a relationship focus has been fully adopted by some businesses, it is noticeably absent in others. Many companies still take the transactional route where the attention given to winning a new customer, once successful, is immediately transferred to the next prospect. Little effort is expended in keeping the existing customer.

As competition intensifies, it becomes imperative for organizations to recognize that existing customers are easier to sell to and are frequently more profitable. Managers may agree intellectually with this view, but the practices within their organizations often tell a different story. Frequently, much greater emphasis and resources are placed on attracting new customers, while existing customers are taken for granted. It is only when some breakdown in service quality occurs and the customer leaves or is on the point of defection that the spotlight is focused on the existing customer.

The experience of a large city firm of solicitors provides a good illustration of how marketing effort can be dangerously misdirected. In this firm, two events occurred within a short period of each other. The first incident involved the acquisition of a contentious piece of litigation work from a new client. This work, worth around £200 000, was likely to be a one-off contract as the client's regular legal advisers were unable to handle it due to a conflict of interest. The law firm's partners were delighted with the litigation partner's brilliant coup in winning this new client.

Six weeks later, another partner in the firm persuaded an existing client, a large corporation that had dealings with several law firms, to give his law firm all the company's conveyancing work. Prior to this moment, the city firm had served the client in only one area of law. The appointment represented additional work worth about £300 000 in the first year, with the expectation that it would provide an ongoing and growing source of future income. As such, it represented, in net present value (NPV) terms, perhaps five times as much profit as the piece of litigation work, yet news of the conveyancing assignment received little attention in the firm.

This illustration is not meant to suggest that new customers are not important, for indeed they are vital to the future success of most organizations. However, a balance needs to be achieved between the effort that is directed towards winning new customers and that which is given to serving existing customers. All too often it is the existing customer who receives insufficient attention.

Referral markets

What is the best form of marketing? One view is that the best marketing for your organization is that which is undertaken by your own customers. Customer referrals provide a formidable means of marketing at little cost to the company, and thus the creation of customer 'advocates' is vitally important. But existing customers are not the only type of referral market: many other groups can refer business to organizations. These other referral markets include intermediaries, connectors, multipliers, agencies, and so on.

Let us consider an example from a bank to illustrate this point. Referral sources for the bank included insurance companies, real estate brokers, accountancy and law firms, as well as existing customers and the bank's employees. The bank commissioned an internal review to identify the amount of business (both historic and projected) generated through referral sources. The study served to confirm that referral sources accounted for significant business volume, although the bank had traditionally made little effort to promote custom from this direction.

Shortly after undertaking the study, the bank held a strategy retreat. The programme included a discussion on referral sources as well as presentations from several of them – in this case, important intermediaries. The bank was surprised at the criticism it received from these intermediaries, which reinforced the research finding that the bank's referral markets were being neglected. Equipped with an enhanced understanding of the value of referred business, the bank then established a task force to develop better relations with referral sources and to design a marketing plan incorporating referral markets. These measures produced a continued improvement in the business generated by the bank's referral sources.

Most organizations need to consider both existing customers and intermediaries as sources of future business. Therefore, both present and prospective referral sources should be identified and a plan developed for allocating marketing resources to them. Efforts should also be made to monitor the cost benefit. However, it should be noted that the benefits of increased marketing activity in this area may take some time to come to fruition.

Supplier and alliance markets

Organizations' relationships with their suppliers are undergoing fundamental change. The old adversarial relationship – where a company tries to squeeze its suppliers to its own advantage – is, in many instances, giving way to one based much more on partnership and collaboration. This trend represents good commercial sense. Manufacturers, for example, typically spend over 60 per cent of total revenue on goods and services from outside suppliers.

The new 'cooperative' relationship with supplier markets is being described under a number of different names. At AT&T, it is known as 'vendorship partnership', while at the European electronics group, Philips, it is called 'co-makership'. In the USA, it is referred to as 'reverse marketing'. Whatever term is used, the aims of this new business relationship are closer cooperation between customer and supplier from a very early stage, mutual concentration on quality, commitment to flexibility, attainment of lowest costs, and achievement of long-term relationships.

A feature of the 1990s was the increasing importance of various forms of strategic alliance. Alliances are a potential source of supply of capital, managerial skills, market position, global coverage, technological skills, and much more.

Recruitment markets

The scarcest resource for most organizations is no longer capital or raw materials: it is skilled people. An appropriately trained and experienced workforce is perhaps the most vital element in customer service delivery. Global economics and the changing nature of employment have not helped to enlarge the recruitment pool, even if unemployment levels are climbing to historic levels. The basic reason for the current lack of skilled workers is demographic trends. In the USA, the percentage of people aged between 16 and 24 is expected to fall from around 20 per cent in 1985 to 16 per cent in 2000, with a projected decline in the 25–34 age group from 23 per cent to 19 per cent over the same period. This broad pattern of reduced population growth exists in most western countries.

Obviously, these age groups represent key markets of new skilled workers entering the labour market. If attracting the best quality recruits is important to business success then this market will become a priority. The following brief example demonstrates the kinds of improvements that can be made to recruitment processes.

A large and well-known accountancy practice was having difficulty attracting newly qualified recruits. The reasons were not hard to discover. Its recruitment literature was old-fashioned and lacking in visual impact. On visits to university campuses – a traditional source of recruits – the company was represented by an old and uninspiring partner, and disinterested administrative staff. The firm then instituted a marketing plan to try to improve the situation and this involved redesigning recruitment literature (with the help of recent graduates), sending the brightest partners on university visits accompanied by managers with interesting experiences to recount, and sponsoring awards and prizes at target universities. As a result of the recruitment marketing campaign, the firm's 'offers to acceptances' ratio increased dramatically.

Influencer markets

Influencer markets include a range of markets, which tend to vary according to the type of industry concerned. In the context of RM, members of the influencer market include individuals or groups that directly or indirectly impact on the organization. For instance, companies involved in selling infrastructure items, such as communications or utilities, will place government departments and regulatory bodies high on their lists of important influencers. Companies registered on the stock exchange interface with a diverse financial community, including brokers, analysts, financial journalists, and so on, who together comprise a powerful influencer market. Other influencer markets include the media, shareholders, standards bodies, consumer associations, and environmental control authorities.

MCI Communications Corporation in the USA provides a good example of the need to identify target influencer markets. William G. McGowan, who some years ago was Chairman and Chief Executive of MCI Communications, faced some key marketing tasks with respect to influencer markets in the early days of MCI. These influencer markets included:

- Venture capitalists – McGowan had a business start-up that was a capital-starved communications company and he had to raise sufficient finance from venture capitalists
- Regulators – McGowan had to convince the regulators that he could construct and satisfactorily operate a long-distance telecommunications network
- Lobbyists – members of MCI had to become skilled lobbyists to get past the strict regulations of the Federal Communications Commission, which was dominated by AT&T (it was for this reason that the company established their headquarters in Washington, DC)

- Litigators – in challenging AT&T's domination of long-distance telephone lines by way of a private anti-trust case, MCI became involved in a complex lawsuit where relationships with law firms and lawyers were critical

To grow the company, MCI had to focus on its important influencer markets as well as its original mission. This suggests that involvement in other activities outside the scope of core business operations may be necessary to protect and progress the core business.

While such activities are often carried out under the heading 'public relations' or 'corporate affairs', it is important that they be recognized as an essential component of RM and that they be allocated sufficient and appropriate resources.

Internal markets

Internal marketing encompasses many issues in management, but has only two main aspects. The first is the idea that every employee and every department in the organization is an internal customer and/or an internal supplier. The objective here is to optimize the operations of the organization by ensuring that every individual and department both provides and receives excellent service.

The second aspect is making certain that all members of staff work together in a manner befitting the organization's stated mission, strategy and goals. The importance of achieving this internal alignment is particularly apparent in service firms where there is a close interface with the customer. In this context, internal marketing aims to ensure that staff provide the best representation of the organization in all telephone, mail, electronic and personal contacts with customers.

Internal marketing is regarded as an important activity in developing the market orientation discussed in Chapter 1. In practice, internal marketing is concerned with communications, and with developing responsiveness, responsibility and unity of purpose. The fundamental objectives of internal marketing are to develop internal and external customer awareness and to remove functional barriers to organizational effectiveness. Further, internal marketing plays an important role in employee motivation and retention.

While relatively little research has been undertaken into internal marketing practices, it is clear that a consideration of internal markets is essential to overall business success. Where internal marketing is concerned with the development of an improved market orientation, the alignment of internal and external marketing ensures coherent RM.

IDENTIFYING GROUPS OR SEGMENTS WITHIN EACH MARKET DOMAIN

The identification of the key groups or segments in each market domain is the first step in applying a multiple markets framework to an organization. In this section, we will consider this initial step in relation to the customer market domain, as it is the most critical market within the RM multiple markets model. A similar approach can be used for each of the other five market domains.

The customer market domain may be concerned with up to three broad groups: direct buyers, intermediaries and final consumers. To define these groups, let us consider the situation of a washing machine manufacturer. The manufacturer sells washing machines to a number of approved wholesalers, who in turn sell them to retail outlets. The retail outlets then sell the appliances to individuals. In this example, the wholesaler is referred to as the 'direct buyer', the retailer who buys from the wholesaler is called the 'intermediary', and the individual who purchases the appliance from the retailer is the 'consumer'. In this example, the description of 'customer' applies to all three groups. (In some industries, there may be further intermediaries who represent additional steps within the distribution channel.)

Market segmentation needs to be undertaken at all levels of the customer market domain, not just with the organization's direct buyer. As market segmentation and distribution channels are discussed in detail in subsequent chapters (Chapters 6 and 10 respectively), we will comment on them only briefly here.

A market segment is a group of customers with the same or similar needs. Market segmentation is the process of dividing a generic market into a number of smaller groups, or market segments, so that an appropriate offer can be created and presented to each group. For example, a manufacturer of consumer durables, serving many international markets, may segment its direct buyers (the wholesalers to which it sells directly) in terms of country, size, volume, level of sophistication, ownership, and so on. The manufacturer can also segment the retailers (the intermediaries to whom the wholesalers sell) according to relevant segmentation criteria. Finally, the manufacturer can segment the final consumers (to whom the retailers sell). In the process of segmenting these customers, the manufacturer should develop a detailed understanding of the needs and preferences of customer segments.

Once the relevant segmentation base (or bases) has been determined, the market segments or sub-groups at the direct buyer, intermediary and consumer levels of the distribution chain can be identified. The opportunities presented by each of these segments can then be examined, providing an indication as to which are the most attractive segments and what are the most appropriate strategies for exploiting them.

The failure of many manufacturers to develop constructive relationships with their final consumers is fairly common. Many readers will have had disappointing experiences in terms of purchasing durable consumer products such as motor cars. They might have been motivated to purchase a certain vehicle by the appeal of promotional activities, only to be disappointed by the subsequent lack of service provision by the vendor dealer. They might have been further upset when their attempts to obtain redress directly from the manufacturer were met with total disinterest or disregard.

Within the automotive sector, radical changes in both distribution and RM practices, such as the innovative approach being adopted by Daewoo, are now causing other motor car manufacturers to question what can be done to develop closer relationships with final consumers.

A similar approach to that employed in the customer domain can be used to identify the target relationships in each of the other five market domains. For example, Figure 2.3 lists the key markets and market segments for a property company. It should be emphasized that, within a multiple markets model, any one group may play a role in a number of these markets. For example, customers may participate in: the customer market where the interaction is between the firm and its customers; the referral market where the interaction is between an existing customer and a prospective customer; and the influencer market where they may be part of a user group which interacts with the firm.

Customer Markets

Existing
- airlines
- utility services
- freight forwarders
- cargo handlers
- hotels

New
- off market airlines
- new airlines
- international airports
- logistics / integrators
- development around airports

Internal Markets

- marketing 'property' to group

Referral Markets

- existing satisfied customers
- other airport people
- business advisers / surveyors
- property consultant / surveyors

Recruitment Markets

- employment agencies
- headhunters / search firms
- graduates
- internal transfers

Supplier Markets

- framework suppliers
- consultants
- contractors
- international suppliers

Influencer Markets

- shareholders
- city analysts / stockbrokers
- business press
- general press and media
- regulator
- government
- local authorities

Figure 2.3   The key markets for a property company

DETERMINING MARKET EMPHASIS IN RM

Once the broad groups and the segments within them have been identified for each market domain, we can proceed to assess the present and desired levels of marketing emphasis for each of the market domains. To consider these levels of emphasis for each market, a RM network diagram (also known as a 'spidergram'), as shown in Figure 2.4, can be used.

This diagram has seven axes: two for customers (existing and new) and one for each of the other five relationship markets discussed earlier. The scale of one (low) to ten (high) reflects the degree of emphasis (cost and effect) placed on each relationship market. The division of customers into 'new' and 'existing' reflects the two critical tasks within the customer domain, that of customer attraction and customer retention. A group of managers within a firm can then make an assessment as to the current and desired levels of emphasis on each market domain by means of a jury of executive opinion and place these on the RM network diagram.

This approach to reviewing relationships within the key markets can be illustrated by a reference to the illustrative RM network diagram for The Royal Society for the Protection of Birds (RSPB), a leading conservation charity, as shown in Figure 2.5. This diagram is based on the views of a number of people, including former executives at the RSPB, and represents an external assessment of developments in that organization.

In the mid-1990s, the RSPB might have considered a number of issues regarding relationship markets, as delineated in '1995/6' in Figure 2.5. These issues include:

- Greater attention on retaining existing members (the RSPB has placed much emphasis on member acquisition. Should more attention now be directed towards existing members?)
- Reinforcement of customer care and service quality issues within internal staff
- Stronger focus on influencer markets

This identification of the relationships within the key market domains represents the first stage of the marketing diagnostic process. The second stage of analysis examines the groups or segments within each market domain in terms of present and desired marketing emphasis. Useful network diagrams, or spidergrams, can then be developed for each market domain. For example, Figure 2.6 shows a spidergram for referral markets of an accounting firm.

PLANNING FOR MULTIPLE MARKETS

The foregoing two stages of market analysis serve to identify the key groups or segments in each market domain and to provide an initial view of the existing

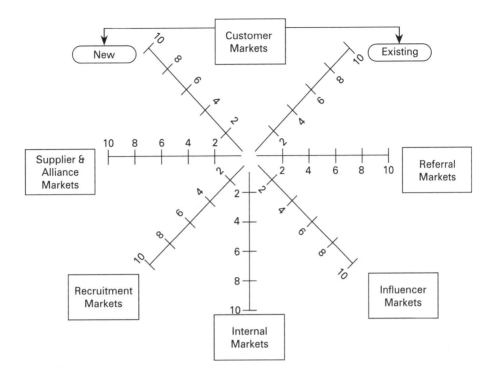

Figure 2.4 RM network diagram

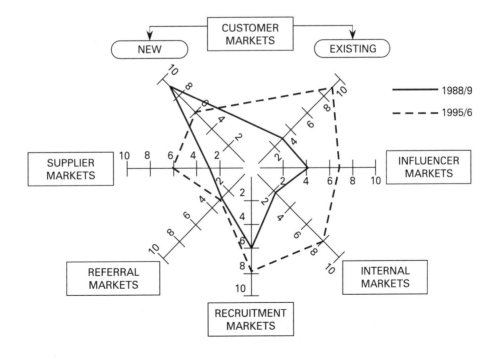

Figure 2.5 RM network diagram for the RSPB

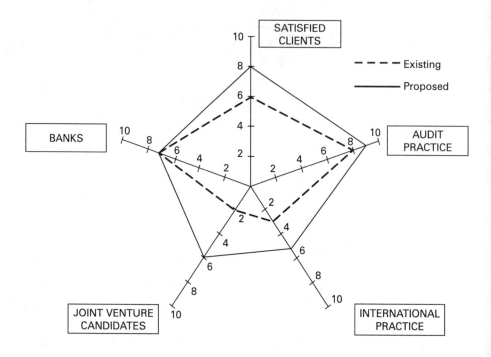

Figure 2.6   Referral markets for an accounting firm

and potential levels of marketing emphasis directed at them. The final two steps in the marketing planning process involve researching the expectations and needs of the key segments, and then determining the appropriate market strategies, including which segments require a detailed marketing plan.

The marketing planning process for customers is discussed in Chapter 15 and the same process can be applied to each of the other five main markets. The market domains do not always require their own formal written marketing plan, although many organizations may find it useful to develop them. However, some form of marketing strategy must be developed for each one.

In addition to the obvious benefits that it provides within the customer market domain, a rigorous marketing planning process can potentially deliver a superior relational approach to all the segments within the five 'non-customer' market domains. For example, in the influencer market, this structured and relational approach to marketing planning surpasses the methods of market communication and persuasion advocated by so much of public relations and corporate affairs literature.

The marketing planning process follows four phases as discussed in Chapter 15. These phases are: goal-setting, including the establishment of specific market objectives for each segment; situation review, including research on segment expectations and needs; strategy formulation; and resource allocation and monitoring. The constituent steps within these phases of the marketing planning process enable the objectives of each segment to be achieved.

SUMMARY

RM extends the marketing concept beyond traditional marketing and embraces the entire supply chain to achieve greater customer value at every level in the chain. Unlike the transactional, functionally-oriented approach, RM is a cross-functional process concerned with balancing marketing efforts among key markets. A critical issue within the customer market domain is to ensure that appropriate emphasis is devoted to customer retention as well as customer acquisition.

The RM multiple markets model shows that organizations can manage a network of relationships in different market domains through the identification of the particular groups, or market segments, within them. Appropriate, but complementary, strategies and plans need to be developed for each market and market segment. The multiple markets framework can also be applied in a range of other marketing contexts. Chapter 12, for example, explains how companies' brands can impact across the markets to improve customer retention and profitability.

The adoption of the RM philosophy is as important to business success as the written strategy, or marketing plan. For instance, a formal marketing plan for an internal market is of little value if front-line staff are not motivated and empowered to deliver the quality of service required. The needs of all relationship markets should be addressed in exactly the same way as customer markets, for high levels of service quality are essential in establishing and maintaining any market relationship.

Since its development in 1991, the multiple markets model has been used by more than 50 organizations to develop plans for each of their market domains (and market segments), and to demonstrate the benefits of adopting the RM perspective. This approach has proved a robust tool in enabling organizations to recognize and respond to their networks of target markets.

This chapter has stressed that RM activities directed at customers are necessary, but not sufficient in themselves to influence RM. Organizations must also address the other relevant market domains and the segments within them. Successful RM involves an informed and integrated approach to all of these market domains in order to achieve competitive advantage.

Note

1. M. G. Christopher, A. F. Payne and D. Ballantyne, *Relationship Marketing: Bringing Quality, Customer Service and Marketing Together* (Oxford: Butterworth-Heinemann, 1991).

Further reading

L. L. Berry, 'Relationship Marketing', in Leonard L. Berry, G. Lynn Shostack and Gregory D. Upah (eds), *Emerging Perspective on Services Marketing* (Chicago: American Marketing Association, 1983), pp. 25–8.

E. Gummesson, *Total Relationship Marketing* (Oxford: Butterworth-Heinemann, 1999).

P. Kotler, 'It's Time for Total Marketing', *Business Week Advance Executive Brief*, 2 (1992).

A. F. Payne (ed.), *Advances in Relationship Marketing* (London: Kogan Page, 1995). This chapter is based on an updated version of a Cranfield School of Management working paper appearing on pp. 29–52 of the 'Advances' book. Sections of this current book are reproduced here with the permission of the author.

H. Peck, A. F. Payne, M. G. Christopher and M. K. Clark, *Relationship Marketing: Strategy and Implementation, Text and Cases* (Oxford: Butterworth-Heinemann, 1999).

MARKETING DIAGNOSTIC TOOLS

Roger Palmer

In this chapter:

- Product/market strategy and differentiation
- Marketing diagnostic tools
- The Product Life Cycle
- The Ansoff Matrix and the Boston Matrix
- The Directional Policy Matrix
- Case studies using the Boston Matrix and Directional Policy Matrix

INTRODUCTION

The product or range of products is the tip of the marketing iceberg, being the most visible thing connecting the supplier to the customer. Products encapsulate a company's response to the market place, balancing perceived customer needs against the company's ability to satisfy those needs. Products also form the source of all revenue and profits, and factor significantly in commercial prosperity.

While marketing managers as functional specialists may not have direct line authority and profit responsibility, their influence on profitability through the product range and its relationship to the market can be considerable. This relationship between product/market strategy and business success is reflected in the fact that marketing managers' performance is often measured in terms of market share, profitability, customer acquisition and customer retention.

Put simply, product/market strategy is the totality of the decisions taken within an organization concerning its target markets and the products it offers to those markets. Few companies offer just one product, for the simple reason that a number of different products are required to maximize the volume of customers with which the company can successfully do business. Planning the product portfolio, therefore, begs the fundamental question, 'What is the optimum number of products at any given time?'

We live in a dynamic world and as external market pressures change – interest rates and competitor activities, for example – so too does the definition of what is an optimal product portfolio. Thus managing the product range to effectively respond to existing and potential market demands is a key marketing activity, and one which has a direct impact on business development in both the short and long term.

DIFFERENTIATION

A simple economic model characterizes successful marketing and this is given in Figure 3.1. The demand curve describes the relationship between price and quantity. Except in rather special circumstances, as the price of a product goes up, the quantity demanded by customers goes down. Intuitively we understand this, for the more expensive a product becomes, the less likely we are to buy it.

However, our individual tastes and price thresholds vary greatly. Not all customers want exactly the same thing and some are prepared to pay more if the product delivers better value. The factors that determine a product's estimated worth, desirability or utility are difficult to measure, being a complex mix of numerous intangibles. It stands to reason that by offering a range of products, we can increase our chances of appealing to customers' varying needs and value systems. This notion underlies the concept of the product range and introduces another important issue for the marketer: differentiation.

Selecting the most suitable strategies for our products is what product management is all about. The creation of *differential advantage*, or perceived added value, lies at the heart of strategic marketing. By providing products which are in some way superior to competitive offers and to similar products within the same range, we not only extend consumer choice in terms of product features, but also in terms of product benefits, or what the product promises to deliver.

It is an old saying in marketing that 'People don't buy products, they buy benefits'. In other words, the customer purchases a product because of what it can do for them and not because of its technical aspects. Theodore Levitt,

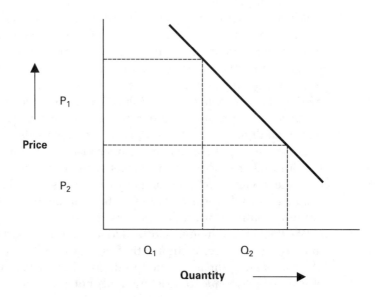

Figure 3.1 Micro-economic model of marketing

a marketing guru, neatly captures the distinction between features and benefits in his famous remark that, 'customers don't buy ¼ inch drills, they buy ¼ inch holes'. Successful marketing relies on selling solutions to perceived problems, rather than on selling a set of product features.

Marketing a range of products involves identifying customer needs and responding in terms of customer benefits. Undertaking careful market research to obtain an understanding of the 'problems' that customers seek to solve can assist the process of achieving differential advantage. Selling products by way of a 'benefit proposition', rather than a technology boast, focuses on the customer's requirements and is therefore more likely to close a sale.

Products within the same range are differentiated not only by benefit, but also by price. Pricing is an important consideration as it reflects a product's commercial viability as well as its market position. The price charged on a product must secure a financial return at least equal to its base cost, including the costs of any additional features. If the customer does not recognize, appreciate or value the benefit being offered, then there is no justification for a price premium.

While it is perfectly feasible to increase prices in the short term, such action may be taken at the expense of market share, as customers will defect to competitors who offer better value for money. Short-termism therefore runs the risks of short-sightedness; a solution to this year's nagging headache may stimulate severe migraines in the future. Encouraging customers to become price conscious, and most need little encouragement in this respect, is a two-edged sword: customers may be won or lost. Regaining lost customers can result in a price war, loss of margin, and narrowing or loss of price differentials within the product range. To effect both short-term gain and long-term security, product/market strategies must be skilfully and realistically devised.

REQUIREMENTS FOR TOOLS

The marketing manager has the complex task of managing the product range to ensure that customer needs are met, that products are properly differentiated and that appropriate price differentials are established. The longevity of the customer relationship and the sustainability or growth of profit depend upon these objectives being achieved collectively and consistently. To meet this challenge the marketer must exercise analytical ability, strategic skill and sound judgement.

A range of diagnostic tools is available to help in marketing decision-making and planning, and these are discussed in turn. The techniques are primarily analytical in purpose, serving to enhance our understanding of current and potential product/market trends in order that we can maximize opportunity and minimize risk. It must be emphasized that they are not a substitute for the marketer's expertise, but an aid in making product performance profiles and projections.

When using any of the analytical tools presented here, it is important to be clear about what we mean by a 'product' and to define the unit of analysis carefully. For example, it is easy to confuse a 'product' with a 'brand'. A brand can have an almost indefinite lifespan, while a product can undergo numerous permutations and modifications: changes in pack size, distribution channels, colour or flavour, for example. The unit of analysis can range from the SBU (Strategic Business Unit, or profit centre) to classes of products or individual products.

THE PRODUCT LIFE CYCLE

The Product Life Cycle (PLC) is a generic description of the way a product behaves in the market place, from the point at which it is launched through to peak, decline and withdrawal. This recurrent series of product states, as depicted in Figure 3.2, is a useful way to visualize how a product progresses through the market, adopting different strategic priorities and management implications at each successive stage.

Unlike the human life cycle – where the only certainties in life are taxes and death – the PLC does not necessarily reach a natural end. The life cycle curve can be prolonged through careful management and investment, or indeed, hastened to an early demise by poor management at the cost of wasted resources. The PLC demonstrates how products move and are manipulated in the market place, extending from the introductory phase through to the typical stages of rapid growth, maturity, saturation and finally decline as the product is overtaken by other products that better fulfil customers' needs.

Both the shape and duration of the PLC can vary. For example, the life cycle for fashion items and fad products can be steep, but short-lived, whereas the life cycle of aircraft can run to many years. There is a recognized propensity for life cycles to become shorter as the rate of technological innovation increases and the expectations of customers heighten. The mechanical typewriter, for instance, may have enjoyed a life cycle of a decade or more, while its latter day equivalent, the word processing program, may have a life cycle measured in months.

The level of sales plotted on the vertical axis is usually given in unit or revenue terms. For marketing purposes, it is often of more value to measure

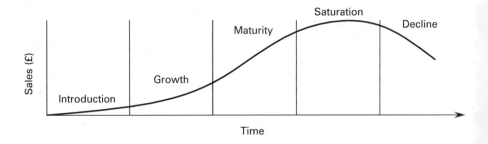

Figure 3.2 The PLC

sales against the growth in the market as this gives a better indication of the product's competitive ability and attractiveness to the customer. Of course, absolute sales volumes are also important as they determine revenue and profitability.

The PLC can be used in a number of ways.

1. The PLC can be a *predictive* device, forecasting how products may behave in the future and allowing corrective action to be taken. It can help us to understand how products relate to markets and, as shown in Figure 3.1, to appreciate where certain elements of the marketing mix may be more appropriate to particular PLC stages.
2. The PLC can be a *comparative* device, warning of any significant deviations from the market norm or enabling a strategic balance to be achieved among products within the same range.
3. The PLC can be a *formative* device, assisting the design of future product/ market strategies based on sales performance in combination with experience and additional analysis. It can provide clues about what are the most appropriate strategies to use at different stages of the life cycle.
4. The PLC can be a *manipulative* device, indicating when short-term strategies might be used to 'distort' the life cycle to our advantage.

While the PLC is an effective aid to understanding how products behave in markets, it is not without drawbacks. The PLC model is not especially adept at examining a range or portfolio of products as the life cycle may vary from one product to another. Also, the life cycle has limited value as a predictive tool. Once the product has run its course, the PLC does not enlighten strategy for new products in new markets: it is relevant only to existing products within existing markets. To assist where the PLC falls short, there are additional analytical devices, generically known as matrix tools. The three most widely known and important of these are the Ansoff Matrix, the Boston Matrix and the Directional Policy Matrix.

THE ANSOFF MATRIX

Developed by Igor Ansoff in the 1960s when he worked with the General Electric Company in the USA, this marketing diagnostic tool was originally designed for use with the SBU unit of analysis (see Figure 3.3). Because of its simplicity and versatility, the Ansoff Matrix has wide application and is particularly helpful in structuring future product and market opportunities.

The Ansoff Matrix has two axes, representing *products* and *markets*. In this context, the product could be service-based. Each axis is divided into *existing* and *new* poles to give a simple four box structure. In reality, there are many gradations between these two extremes. One of the advantages of using matrix tools is that they can reduce complexity, aiding a clearer understanding of product behaviour and market dynamics.

In considering our future strategy, the Ansoff Matrix suggests a number of options, each with varying degrees of risk. Obviously, our current position is

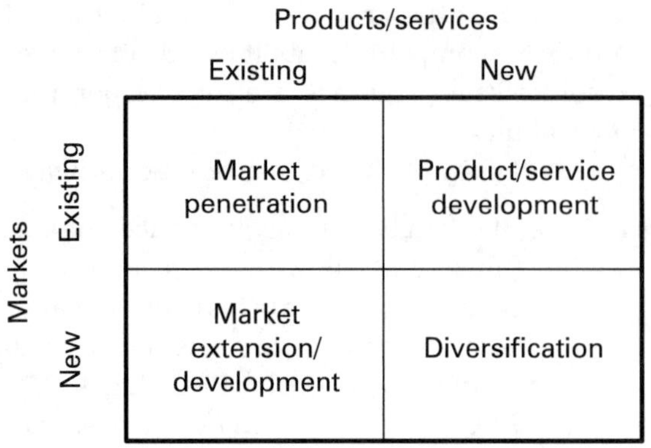

Products/services

	Existing	New
Markets — Existing	Market penetration	Product/service development
Markets — New	Market extension/ development	Diversification

Figure 3.3   The Ansoff Matrix

located in the top left-hand corner, where our products are competing in established markets and where we have greatest knowledge and experience. This quadrant therefore represents the lowest level of risk. As we move out of this comfort zone, so the level of risk increases, but so do the opportunities. Of course, profit is the reward for risk, but how much risk versus how much profit? The Ansoff Matrix helps us to understand these relationships better and to arrive at more informed judgements about our present position and proposed future direction. The combination of options provided in the Ansoff Matrix gives rise to the following broad strategies.

1. *Market Penetration* – to grow our business, we should consider ways in which we can gain more customers for our current product offering: for example, by seeking routes to alternative markets in order to reach customers we do not currently serve.
2. *Product Development* – it may be that our customers buy products elsewhere that are complementary to those we sell. By developing our product range and thus augmenting our product benefits, we can build on established customer relationships and buying patterns. However, this move may require an investment in product development, which in itself carries inherent risks.
3. *Market Development* – this approach can be applied in a number of ways. More market research may enable us to find and address unsatisfied customers or segments within our current area of operations. Alternatively, there may be opportunities to expand geographically into other domestic or export markets. It is reasonable to assume that potential customers have satisfied their needs to a greater or lesser extent, and that entering new markets may involve significant risks attributable to high investment costs and dealing with the unknown.
4. *Diversification* – this strategy embodies greatest risk, since both markets and products are new. We are furthest from our area of expertise and

encroaching upon the territory of a competitor, who will almost certainly have the advantages of greater market knowledge and acceptance. Even buying our way in through product acquisition offers no guarantee of success as this means that the established player places a lower value on the business than we do; otherwise they would not be tempted to sell.

THE BOSTON MATRIX

The Boston Matrix was developed by the Boston Consulting Group and its founder Bruce Henderson, and was introduced to the business world in the early 1970s. Originally designed as a financial management tool, it now has an accepted role in marketing and strategic planning. The technique's popularity rests in its ability to capture a number of concepts simply and to offer strategic guidelines for future action. Boston Matrix terminology has become part of everyday business language. Again, it is a simple four box matrix, as illustrated in Figure 3.4.

The axes of the Boston Matrix consider products in two dimensions: *relative market share* and *market growth rate*. The measure of market share is not absolute market share, but is relative to the largest competitor. This is important because it reflects the degree of dominance enjoyed by the product in the market. For example, if the industry leader has a market share of 30 per cent and our product claims a share of only 15 per cent, then this represents a ratio of 0.5:1 in the other company's favour. However, if we were the market leader with a share of 30 per cent and our main competitor had only 15 per cent, then the ratio would be 2:1 and we would be in a market dominant position. Market dominance has both financial and marketing advantages in that our 'share of

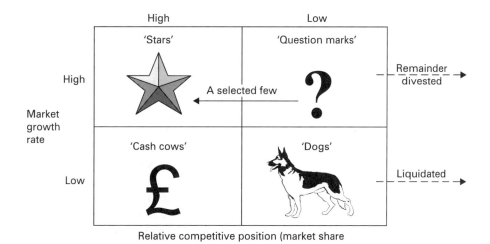

Figure 3.4 The Boston Matrix

mind' is highest and we have the greatest opportunity to achieve a low cost position. The definition of high relative market share is generally taken to be ratio of 1:5 or more. The vertical axis denotes market growth rate, the extent of the scale being dependent on prevailing circumstances within the industry concerned. However, the cut-off point for high, as opposed to low, market growth is often seen as 10 per cent.

While the Boston Matrix is simple in concept, it begs questions such as, 'Who are the main competitors and what are their shares?' or 'What is the definition of the market and how do we find out the market growth rate?' Despite its inability to address these issues, the Boston Matrix is an appealing tool because it takes into account a number of important factors affecting the ability of products (or whatever unit of analysis is used) to compete and generate profits.

The Boston Matrix uses four boxes to categorize the generic nature of the product being described. The *Question Mark*, sometimes referred to as the 'problem child', does not hold a dominant market position and thus has low market share, but is in a high growth market. Question Marks are often recently introduced products, which run a high risk of failure. They may not progress through to the *Star* box, building market share as sales improve. As the PLC indicates, the period of rapid market growth eventually subsides and the product then enters the *Cash Cow* box. Here, the product has a high relative market share of a low growth market and is thus regarded as a mature product. As market share declines, the product passes into the *Dog* box. Bruce Henderson is unequivocal in his view that there is no room for Dogs in the product portfolio and they should be deleted from the product range.

The Boston Matrix is based on the principle that cash – not profits – drive a product from one box of the matrix to another. Understanding the distinction between cash flow and profits is crucial. At least as many businesses go bankrupt due to lack of cash or liquidity as due to poor performance in relation to factors such as low sales. When cash flow is managed effectively, the viability of the business improves, as indicated in Figure 3.5.

In financial terms, the quadrants of the Boston Matrix may be summarized as follows.

1. *Question Mark* – strong cash consumer, requires large amounts of cash to fund product development and introduction costs.
2. *Star* – cash neutral, generating cash as volume and revenue builds rapidly, but requiring substantial funding to support promotion, product range development and expansion costs.
3. *Cash Cow* – cash generator, providing the funds needed to support other parts of the business. The danger here lies in excessively milking the cow, causing it to lose market presence and share.
4. *Dog* – cash neutral or cash consumer. At one time probably a strong performer in the product range, but now substantially declined, generating a poor cash flow and perhaps even consuming cash due to the costs of maintaining the product in the range. It is characteristically difficult to cost out the time and resources required to manage such products, and thus Dogs can impede or destabilize overall business progress.

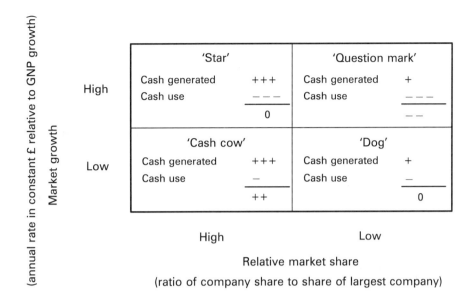

Figure 3.5   The Boston Matrix: cash management

The function of the Boston Matrix is to aid forward planning by suggesting strategy for the future development of the range: selectively invest in Question Marks; invest in and grow Stars; maintain Cash Cows; and critically examine Dogs and delete them as appropriate.

Case Study 1: using the Boston Matrix

Integra Building Products is a German based company with subsidiaries in most European markets. It makes a range of modular wall and ceiling products that are used to provide flexible office layouts.

Integra experienced a serious problem with its range of ceiling tiles. Over the years, the tile range had grown substantially until there were nine different styles and textures, each of which were available in up to a dozen colours. The company found, however, that it was rather better at making ceiling products than selling and marketing them. Excess stocks of slow selling lines and unpopular colours were fast taking up valuable storage space, prompting an urgent rationalization of the product range.

To address this problem, Integra carried out a comprehensive audit of its products, examining the historical sales figures for each range of products in terms of product colour. This information was used to construct summary tables of trend data for each market, showing which ranges were growing, declining or remaining static, and highlighting the most popular colours. The PLC was then applied to the tables to determine which products were failing to justify their position in the range against a set of agreed financial criteria. This yielded a 'first cut' view of those products which could be safely deleted from the range.

More detailed analysis was carried out using the Boston Matrix, where growth rates in each of the markets were determined and product range performance as measured by sales growth and market share was calculated. It was planned that a breakdown by colour of separate product ranges should also be plotted on the matrix. However, by this stage, the diagnosis was sufficiently detailed and the company felt confident to reduce the colour options available without further product analysis.

Integra's study revealed that the company should reduce colour options, rather than the range of textures, although the latter could also be rationalized to a worthwhile extent. As a result of the product review, strict guidelines were put in place to help regulate the introduction of new products in order to prevent a recurrence of the problem of excess stocks.

THE DIRECTIONAL POLICY MATRIX

Building on the success of the Boston Matrix, the Directional Policy Matrix (DPM) was developed as a further sophistication of the matrix tool technique. McKinsey, an international firm of management consultants, in conjunction with General Electric in the USA and Shell in Europe, designed it as a multi-factor approach to portfolio management.

The DPM is similar in construction to the Boston Matrix, as shown in Figure 3.6. It was originally introduced as a 3×3 matrix, rather than the more conventional 2×2 structure, and is today used in either format. The major difference between the two matrices, however, lies in the way the axes are constructed.

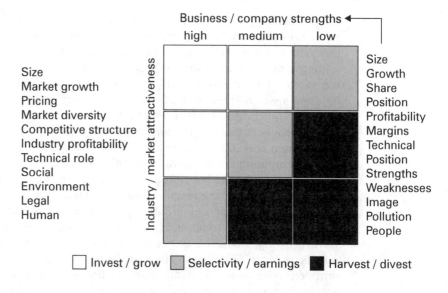

Figure 3.6   The DPM

The Boston Matrix uses only two factors to analyse performance: market growth rate and relative market share. While these factors are very important to product and business success, they are not the only contributing variables. The DPM attempts to provide a more comprehensive picture by widening the scope of the axes to embrace *market attractiveness* and *business strengths*. The criteria defining these broad headings may include:

Market Attractiveness	*Business Strengths*
Growth rate	Market share
New channels developing	Flexible production capacity
Premium pricing opportunity	Trained sales force
Export opportunities	Technical service network
Weak competitors	Established distribution system
Increasing quality requirements	Research and development (R&D) skills

Once the axes criteria are established, they can be weighted in terms of importance and ranked against those of competitors or other products to provide a comparative view. It is worth reiterating here the importance of clearly defining the unit of analysis to be used.

The DPM technique can be demonstrated by selecting a few of the criteria listed under Business Strengths, and weighting and scoring them accordingly.

	Weight (%)	*Ourselves* Score ($\times$ weight)	*Competitor A* Score ($\times$ weight)
Market share	35	$6 \times 0.35 = 2.10$	$4 \times 0.35 = 1.40$
Flexible production capacity	25	$8 \times 0.25 = 2.00$	$7 \times 0.25 = 1.75$
Trained sales force	25	$4 \times 0.25 = 1.00$	$8 \times 0.25 = 2.00$
Technical service network	15	$9 \times 0.15 = 1.35$	$3 \times 0.15 = 0.45$
Overall Score		6.45	5.60

DPM Terminology

Criteria	A list of factors considered critical relative to the market and unit of analysis.
Weight	Based on allocation of 100 percentage points.
Score	An assessment on a 1–10 scale of performance against the criteria.
Overall Score	Weight multiplied by score for each criteria, added together to give the overall score on a 1–10 scale for the axis. This is then plotted on the appropriate axis of the matrix.

The DPM can then suggest appropriate marketing strategies, as outlined in Figure 3.7.

1. INVEST FOR GROWTH – Businesses that are relatively high in business strengths and market attractiveness. Apply or use resources to promote profitability.

2. MANAGE FOR SUSTAINED EARNINGS – Businesses with medium strength in markets of medium to low attractiveness. Maintain a strong position in moderately attractive markets, but do not invest in increased market share.

3. MANAGE FOR CASH – Businesses with a relatively weak position in a relatively unattractive market. Harvest for current profitability or divest.

4. OPPORTUNISTIC – Businesses with low business strength and high market attractiveness or vice versa. Three options are available:

    (a) Invest and develop if resources are available, but check extent of possible diversification and cash availability

    (b) Maintain a holding position and continue to monitor

    (c) Divest to a buyer able to exploit the opportunity, or consider a joint venture or alliance

Figure 3.7 The DPM: prescriptive strategies

Case Study 2: using the Directional Policy Matrix

American International Chemicals (AIC) is a multinational chemicals and plastics business with a major presence in Europe. It has manufacturing facilities in the UK, Belgium and Italy, and distributes products through national subsidiaries and a wholesale/retail chain. As gross margins were squeezed, AIC found that the cost of working with a large number of intermediaries became increasingly untenable. The company had to reduce supply chain costs without losing access to the volume markets. The challenge, therefore, was to identify the distributors who will continue to grow as the industry rationalizes.

To resolve this issue, AIC hired a firm of consultants with particular expertise in supply chain management. The consultants interviewed AIC staff in all of the subsidiaries as well as a range of distributors, from low to high performers and international companies through to family firms. From the data obtained, the consultants elicited a series of factors that contributed to volume and particularly margin growth. Some of these factors were inherent within the products. Obviously, a unique product still within patent would attract a high margin due to this factor (a product 'value-add', as they termed it). Conversely, they were also interested to identify distributors who could add value to products, rather than just 'shift kit' (a distributor 'value-add').

Employing these isolated factors, the consultants created a matrix with two axes, identifying value-added factors related to products and those related to the type of distributor. These factors were weighted in terms of importance and then ranked on both axes. Local staff in each country did the scoring, but the consultants moderated the process to ensure that there was comparability across subsidiaries.

> In this way, a DPM was constructed as a basis for deciding future distribution policy. The DPM technique clearly identified the few distributors who were able to sell in volume and contribute added value to the product through technical and sales support services. These high performers formed the basis of a revised distribution policy. The majority of distributors, who generated low margins and did not maintain the product value perception, were the obvious starting point in the rationalization of the distribution network.

To further refine the use of these matrix tools, each product or other unit of analysis can be delineated by a circle representing turnover, margin or some other measure. With the DPM, for example, the market size can be represented as a circle proportionate to sales or unit volumes with a with a pie slice portraying market share. By projecting to a desired future market position, matrix tools can be used to encapsulate product strategy. A range of proprietary software tools is available.

SUMMARY

A critical task of the marketing function is to manage the introduction, development and, ultimately, deletion of products to meet company requirements for profitability and customer needs for product or service solutions. This task is undertaken in the context of a highly competitive and constantly changing environment.

Marketing diagnostic tools assist marketing planning and decision-making by reducing and digesting market complexity. The PLC provides a framework for understanding how individual products behave in the market place. The Boston Matrix and DPM are useful in examining complex interactions between products and markets, and in developing marketing strategy. The Ansoff Matrix helps in forecasting the future market position of products, and thus the options for product strategy and portfolio management. While these analytical tools represent valuable marketing aids, successful marketing relies on the judgement and creativity that only the marketer can provide.

References

G. S. Day, 'The Product Life Cycle: Analysis and Application Issues', *Journal of Marketing*, Fall 1981, pp. 60–7.

A. Morrison and R. Wensley, 'Boxed Up or Boxed In: A Short History of the Boston Consulting Group Share/Growth Matrix', *Journal of Marketing Management*, 7 (1991), pp. 105–29.

P. Kotler, *Marketing Management; Analysis, Planning and Control*, 9th edn (Englewood Cliffs, NJ: Prentice-Hall, 1996).

PART II

THE CUSTOMER RELATIONSHIP AUDIT

CONSUMER BUYER BEHAVIOUR

Susan Baker

In this chapter:

- A model of consumer buyer behaviour
- The factors influencing consumer buyer behaviour
- Types of consumer buyer behaviour
- The consumer purchase decision-making process

INTRODUCTION

A knowledge of consumers is critical for developing successful RM strategies. It is, after all, consumers who make up markets. Understanding how and why consumers choose from among the plethora of products or services on offer encompasses a wide variety of factors.

This chapter explores the dynamics of consumer buyer behaviour and thus links market segmentation (see Chapter 6), market research (see Chapter 7), branding (see Chapter 12), and marketing communications (see Chapter 13). The factors that influence consumer buyer behaviour are identified and discussed in detail, providing an outline of four types of characteristic buyer behaviour. Finally, a model of the consumer purchase decision-making process is presented to relate the understanding of consumer conduct with the actual purchasing activity that takes place. As discussed later in Chapter 6, consumers are not always the buyers and this chapter adopts the definition of consumers as being the end users of the product or service.

Understanding buyer behaviour is essential for developing consumer relationships. In trying to comprehend why people buy what they buy, marketers have to make judgements about the importance that they ascribe to consumers' expressed beliefs about certain products and services. All over the world people form attachments to different products and services, and research suggests that they do not purchase strictly on the basis of performance alone. In the purchase of a washing machine, for example, the decision to buy may depend on how well the appliance cleans clothes, its ease of use or its reliability. Alternatively, the buyer may be persuaded by the machine's appearance, the sound of the door as it shuts, the excellent after-sales service or the brand name.

It is an accepted fact that consumers buy certain brands for valid non-functional reasons which have to do with emotional values or associated services and benefits (best described as the 'augmented brand': see Chapter 12). It is the job of the marketer to assess which of the product's/service's attributes weigh most heavily in the purchase decision and to exploit this knowledge.

In the opinion of Katherine Hamnett, a well-known clothes designer, designer logos 'can make people think that success can be theirs through acquisition, they believe that Nike can change their world, that Tommy Hilfiger can bring them wealth'. She supports the notion that an intangible value is ascribed to products by consumers, describing how clothes might make people feel rich or look rich. 'It's all about dreams, and people buy crap and think those dreams have been fulfilled.'

These observations raise questions about the impact of brands on consumers. While the power of the brand is explored in greater detail in Chapter 12, it is necessary at this juncture to raise the following questions: if consumers believe that one brand delivers more benefit than another, then is it not only logical that they are prepared to pay more for it? Can consumers be described as 'irrational' when brand attributes unrelated to performance predominate in the purchase decision-making process? Consumer buyer behaviour may well be shaped more by perception than reality – as Hamnett highlights – and it is imperative that marketers take this truth on board.

A MODEL OF CONSUMER BUYER BEHAVIOUR

Buyer behaviour within markets has to be understood before RM strategies can be developed. However, constructing a standard model of consumer buyer behaviour can be somewhat problematic. While the inputs and the outputs of consumer purchase decision-making can be readily identified and, to a certain extent, measured, the intangible element which concerns buyer characteristics and choice determinants is often more elusive. At best, it can be described as a 'black box'.[1] Predicting consumer buyer behaviour may be an imprecise science, but some simple models have been created to assist marketers in gaining a deeper understanding of consumers in order that their custom can be both acquired and retained.

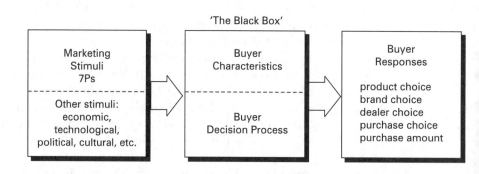

Figure 4.1   Model of consumer buyer behaviour

The inputs in Figure 4.1 can be distinguished between internal stimuli that the marketer has control over – the elements of the expanded marketing mix: product, price, place, promotion, people, processes and customer service (also known as the 7Ps) – and external stimuli. These latter influences tend to be of a political, economic, social or technical nature. In making a purchase decision, consumers respond to the stimuli deployed by the selling company. The greater the company's knowledge is about the reactions these stimuli elicit, the greater the competitive advantage will be for that company.

Outputs refer to buyer responses. Outputs can be identified and assessed in terms of the purchase decision, such as the choice of brand, the place of purchase, the quantity purchased, and the terms and conditions of purchase.

A comparison of the inputs and the outputs raises questions about who buys and how they buy. These issues have led researchers to examine buyer characteristics closely in order to identify the critical drivers in the purchase decision-making process.

INFLUENCING FACTORS

Part of the process of understanding consumer buyer behaviour involves appreciating the context in which consumers make their purchase decisions. Pervasive social influences can be viewed on two levels: the macro level and the micro level. Macro influences embrace culture, subculture and social class, while micro influences comprise the consumer's more immediate social environment of reference groups and family. Let us consider each level in turn, as portrayed in Figure 4.2.

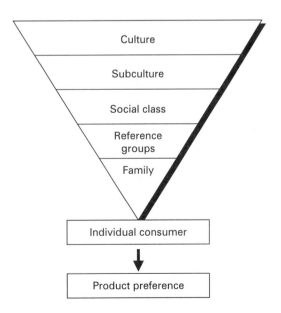

Figure 4.2   Social influences on consumer buyer behaviour

Macro social influences

Macro social factors play a role in shaping the values, beliefs, attitudes and behaviours of individual consumers, and provide useful bases upon which to segment markets. They have direct implications for designing effective RM strategies, especially where management of the marketing mix spans national boundaries. The annals of international marketing contain numerous examples of companies, many of them respected brand owners, who have failed to manage their product/service portfolios successfully because their marketing efforts have neglected to take into account the respective cultures concerned. For example, General Motors' marketing of the Nova car in Spain was destined to bring disappointment, for 'nova' literally means 'won't go' in Spanish. As Simon Anholt, founder of World Writers, put it at a Marketing Society event in October 1997:

> Culture is the things that people think, it is the things they believe in, it is the things that motivate them, it is the things that make them what they are. Language is just the way they say it, and if you get the culture right, then the language is sure to follow.

Culture

Culture can be defined broadly as 'a complex of learned meanings, values and behavioural patterns'[2] that is shared by a society. The relationship between the consumer and the product, often described as the 'product/self relationship', is culturally specific and thus of great interest to marketers seeking to identify the factors which influence purchasing and consumption. As the saying goes, the devil is in the detail.

Consider the Christmas holiday. It appears on the calendars of many countries, yet differences occur in the minutiae of each celebration. For example, the manufacturer of a major chocolate brand was caught out in the first year of trying to manage a pan-European Christmas marketing campaign because it failed to appreciate that Christmas is celebrated differently across the continent. In Holland, Sinterklaas visits on 6 December, while in the UK, Father Christmas arrives on 24/25 December. Epiphany in Greece and Russia is celebrated as the annual main event in early January.

Eurodisney also experienced a number of teething problems when it first opened outside Paris in 1992. Research revealed, among other things, that while Americans prefer 'grazing' (or snacking) all day as they tour the theme park, Europeans want a full meal between 12 noon and 2 p.m. Not recognizing this difference in eating patterns, park caterers were faced with big unexpected queues for food in the early afternoons. To redress this situation, the company had to create more suitable eating opportunities for visitors. In addition, the two main daily parades of Disney characters had to be rescheduled for 11.30 a.m. and 4 p.m. so as not to clash with the luncheon period.

Cultural influences play as important a role in domestic markets as they do in international markets. However, because marketers operating within their home countries tend to be very familiar with the prevailing culture, they may find it harder to recognize the significant cultural factors that influence domestic buyer behaviour.

Subculture

A subculture is a cultural group within a larger culture that has beliefs or interests that are at variance with those of the larger culture. Many types of distinction are used to classify subcultures, including ethnicity, religious or political affiliation, age, and so forth.

Taking age as an example, marketers often distinguish categories of consumer in terms of their age group. People within certain age ranges frequently behave similarly, but in ways which set them apart from other consumers. The youth market, for instance, is described in terms of life stage characteristics. Young people are noted for their willingness to experiment with new identities. They exhibit a tendency to seek peer approval constantly, to be preoccupied with sex and to find conflict with their parents. In terms of lifestyle, today's teenagers are the first computer literate generation. They are comparatively well-travelled, possess unprecedented assertiveness, and are concerned with world issues and global perspectives. Young people currently have the highest earning power ever recorded for their age group, and outward manifestations of their subculture, such as accessories of music and apparel, are exceedingly important to them. These easily identified and insatiable consumers represent every marketer's dream!

Interestingly, youth subculture is not restricted to the UK's 3.5 million strong membership, for it is found in countries across the world. Teenagers comprise the most global market of all. Their tastes, language and attitudes are converging and, as consumers, they purchase a relatively common portfolio of products. The teenager's bedroom is often 'a universal shrine' to pet products and icons, most of which are American in origin. The number of consumers in this market is staggering, totalling 57 million in Mexico, Brazil and Argentina; 42 million in Japan, Korea, Singapore and Vietnam; 28 million in the USA; and 50 million in Europe. It is obvious that the opportunities for marketers with the right products and the right approaches to marketing them are immense.

Social class

The concept of social class is drawn from sociology, where a social group is organized according to a recognized hierarchy based on the individual's status within the group. While the impact that social class has on consumer behaviour is a topic of some debate, marketers favour social class as a form of shorthand to describe their typical consumers. In the UK, consumers have traditionally been classified into six social classes as determined by the occupation of the head of the household, and this is given in Table 4.1. This method of classification has remained in use for a number of years, despite unease at its decreasing relevance to current society.

Table 4.1   **UK socio-economic classification scheme**

Class name	Social status	Occupation of head of household
A	Upper middle	Higher managerial, administrative, professional
B	Middle	Intermediate managerial, administrative or professional
C1	Lower middle	Supervisors or clerical, junior managerial, administrative or professional
C2	Skilled working	Skilled manual workers
D	Working	Semi-skilled and unskilled manual workers
E		State pensioners or widows, casual or lower grade workers of subsistence level

These systems of consumer classification tend to be culturally bound, having been developed on a parochial basis. They do not lend themselves to international comparison. Within Europe, there have been attempts to use a harmonized set of demographics, which focus on the terminal education age of the main income earner in the household, their professional status, and the average net monthly level of household income. However, collecting this kind of data from across European markets can prove problematic in countries such as the UK, where it is common practice for survey respondents to think in terms of their gross annual salary, rather than the net monthly income of their household. The issues surrounding the difficulties of market research are discussed further in Chapter 7, but are mentioned here to illustrate the importance of aligning a classification scheme to the prevailing culture.

The need to find a more appropriate method of defining social class in the UK has been the driving force behind the recent unveiling of a revised classification scheme by the UK government. This is described in the following case study.

Case Study 1: climbing the social classes

Since before the First World War, UK government statisticians have ranked people in terms of their employment: professional, managerial and technical, skilled non-manual, skilled manual, partly skilled, and unskilled. These six social classes were redefined in 1998, some 87 years after their introduction by the Office for National Statistics, during a three-year project that was jointly sponsored by the Economic and Social Research Council. The project report highlighted the fact that changes in the nature and structure of both industry and occupations had rendered the distinction of social class based on skills outmoded and misleading. The new social classifications more accurately reflect current employment conditions, such as reduced job security and greater career uncertainty.

The revised eight major social classes can be sub-divided as follows:

1. higher managerial and professional occupations
   1.1 employers and managers in larger organizations
   1.2 higher professionals
2. lower managerial and professional occupations
3. intermediate occupations
4. small employers and own account workers
5. lower supervisory, craft and related occupations
6. semi-routine occupations
7. routine occupations
8. people who wish to work but who never have.

Updating the social classification system has had the effect of elevating the rank of working women and public sector employees. Teachers and police officers also have been regraded; teachers now belong to Class One, while police officers, who were previously on a par with skilled workers, are now classed as 'associate professionals'.

Micro influences

Purchasing decisions are also influenced at the micro level by the people closest to the consumer, namely family, friends, extended relatives and peers. These people feature significantly in the consumer's immediate social environment and can be grouped into two types of influencer: reference groups and family. Their effect on consumers' attitudes and purchasing behaviour can be considerable.

Reference groups

Reference groups are made up of people who share the consumer's social circumstances and who are personally relevant to the consumer: they influence the way that the consumer thinks, feels and behaves in respect to choosing between different products and services. Classic examples of reference groups are school or college friends and peers. The fixation of young people to own certain brands of footwear, for example, is highly likely to be driven by the desire to conform to the norm for their peer group.

Some companies use reference groups explicitly in their marketing activities. For example, companies such as Tupperware that use in-home selling techniques actively encourage reference groups to exercise their power in the purchasing decision. It is also common practice for health and fitness clubs to build their client registers through special promotions where current members are encouraged to recommend or recruit new members. In this case, reference group endorsement is used to market the clubs' facilities.

Family

Market research traditionally uses the individual consumer as the unit of analysis, but there are types of purchasing decision where the family becomes the decision-making unit. Studies into this phenomenon attempt to describe the various roles played by family members and the complexity of interactions that take place in reaching a collective decision. For example, the choice of restaurant for a family's meal out may well be influenced by the children within the family whose motivation may stem from the appeal of a promotional offer. McDonald's, for instance, is one of the largest toy retailers in the world, tying in promotional give-aways with the release of blockbuster Disney movies.

In fact, it is estimated that, in the USA, children prompt purchases amounting to a staggering $260 billion per annum. This power exerted by children in the market place, directly through the purchases made by immediate family members and indirectly through gifts received from wider family and friends, is technically known as 'pester power'.

In seeking to understand the dynamics of the family decision-making unit, two issues are key: demographic changes in 'the family' and the family life cycle. Family statistics are altering in response to changes in the composition of the household and the nature of child rearing, increased female employment, and lower birth rates. This has necessitated a move away from the traditional picture of the family unit, that of two married parents where the mother is at home bringing up the children and father is out at work. These demographic trends have profound implications for marketers, who face the increasing challenge of identifying and satisfying families' needs without having any firm idea of what the 'family' is.

Present trends indicate that families will continue to be smaller, more affluent, and more geographically mobile. Children today enjoy the highest ever level of material goods and this record is set to continue, presenting tremendous scope for youth-oriented brands. Additionally, opportunities are opening up as people become increasingly willing to pay for services that maximize their use of time: for example, the home delivery of groceries, after-school clubs for children, and so on.

A popular tool for analysing family purchasing behaviour is the family life cycle, which describes the typical changes that take place in the family unit over a period of time. Traditionally, the family life cycle has concentrated on life stage events such as marriage and the arrival of children, and schooling and the departure of children (often referred to as the 'full nest' and 'empty nest' life stages). However, given the evident changes in demographics, the family life cycle is no longer a straightforward linear model, but something resembling a complex network of life patterns that may be connected by tangent, non-traditional or repeated life stages.

The traditional family life cycle is:

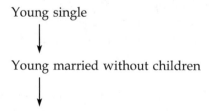

Young single

Young married without children

Young married with children

Middle aged married with children

Middle aged married without dependent children

Older married

Older unmarried

It is crucial that marketers are able to recognize changes at each of these life stages in order that they can re-evaluate the positioning of existing products and services, and identify opportunities for new products and services. For example, the marketing of 'white goods' is generally targeted at young couples who are likely to require domestic appliances in setting up a home together.

Consumer

Influencing factors that have a more direct impact on consumer behaviour are those concerned with the individuals themselves. They include personal attributes, such as age, stage of life, occupation, economic circumstance, lifestyle, personality type, and psychological forces in respect of beliefs, attitudes and motivations. For example, the same individual may display distinctly different buyer behaviour when purchasing a bottle of wine for home consumption as compared to as a gift for a dinner party. Equally, consumers may display a completely different set of purchase motivations and preferences when faced with a so-called 'distress purchase', such as buying petrol when the petrol gauge in the car hits zero as compared to simply topping up a half-full tank.

Market research data on consumer buyer characteristics can be presented to marketers in the form of a typology of buyers for a particular set of products or services. These consumer profiles, with their memorable labels such as 'sporting thirties' and 'young survivors', can be quickly assimilated into marketing strategies. They offer an abbreviated method of expressing a complex set of consumer characteristics and typical buyer behaviours.

The following case study of a typology of British shoppers shows how the personal attributes of consumers can be summarized in a way that is meaningful to marketers.

Case Study 2: a typology of British shoppers

Bluewater, Europe's largest and newest shopping complex opened in Kent, to the east of London, in 1999, at a cost of £350 million. The centre incorporates more than 320 shops, in addition to restaurants, cafés, a crèche, a 12-screen cinema, a boating lake, a picnic area, mountain bike trails and numerous cash points. Approximately 80 000 customers are expected to visit the complex each day and, with an estimated average spend of £25, it is anticipated that Bluewater will become a valuable business for its Australian owners, Lend Lease.

No aspect of the Bluewater project has been left to chance. For five years, researchers have investigated consumer buyer behaviour using a variety of methods in order to create psychographic profiles of anticipated shoppers for the shopping centre planners. The research has been directed by a pyschotherapist with a background in marketing, and has resulted in the identification of seven definitive types of British shopper. These include:

County classics	House-proud; shop at John Lewis and Jaeger; interested in success, concerned about what others think of them and cynical about fashion; numerically the largest cluster
Club executives	BMWs and Boss suits are part of their iconography; career oriented; expect service to be efficient
Sporting thirties	Interested in sports; exhibit a disruptive tendency, really don't want to shop – prefer the bar instead
Home comfortable	Mature customers with traditional tastes; like to be served by people their own age
Young fashionables	In search of an identity; interested in cosmetics, personal grooming and outward appearance
Young survivors	Want low cost amusement; may use shopping to boost their self-esteem
Budget optimists	Don't need to have their egos massaged; looking for a sense of trust in their transactions

Bluewater's research into consumer behaviour was designed to ensure that the shopping centre's offerings would be aligned to shoppers' needs. Attention has been devoted to making every aspect of the shopping experience customer-friendly and customer-focused. Shoppers enter the complex through hotel-style 'welcome' halls, where they are advised by concierges who will do everything from escorting them to a particular shop, to carrying their bags and reminding them where they left their car in the 13 000 space car park.

Bluewater's investigations also identified gender issues common to certain groups of shoppers. These traits have been addressed through special measures such as ensuring that stores such as Marks & Spencer, which the shopping psychologists reported 'is where men tend to get bored and want to go home', are conveniently placed next to gadget shops like Dixons or the bar of a TGI Friday's.[3]

TYPES OF CONSUMER BUYER DECISION

Understanding the actual purchase decision-making process as a fundamental part of creating a relationship with consumers requires an examination of the role and interaction of two important dimensions: the concept of involvement and the degree of difference which consumers perceive to exist between competing brands. These are important elements in both the acquisition and retention of consumers.

'Involvement' is a term used to describe how personally meaningful the purchase is to the consumer. It implies that the act of purchasing will be a conscious activity and that an element of effort will have been invested in making the final choice. The role of consumer 'involvement' refers to the factors listed in Figure 4.3.

❑ high degree of risk (performance, cost, psychology)

❑ high degree of brand differentiation

❑ hedonism and pursuit of pleasure

❑ lifestyle products

❑ special interest products (hobbies and leisure pursuits)

Figure 4.3 The role of consumer 'involvement'

Purchases with high involvement are made by consumers who perceive there to be a high degree of risk. Risk may be judged on the basis of performance (will it work?), cost (is the price too high?) or psychology (is it right for me?). Generally, a high involvement situation is where the purchase is strongly linked to the pursuit of pleasure, as with a hobby or lifestyle product, or an infrequent purchase, such as a bed. Conversely, purchases with low involvement involve little risk and tend to be habitual, practical purchases of consumables, such as bread or laundry detergent.

TYPES OF CONSUMER BUYER BEHAVIOUR

When the degree of consumer involvement is combined with knowledge of whether consumers perceive many or few differences between brands, it becomes possible to identify four distinctive types of consumer buyer behaviour. These are depicted in Figure 4.4 and may be summarized as:

- complex buyer behaviour
- dissonance-reducing buyer behaviour
- variety-seeking buyer behaviour
- habitual buyer behaviour

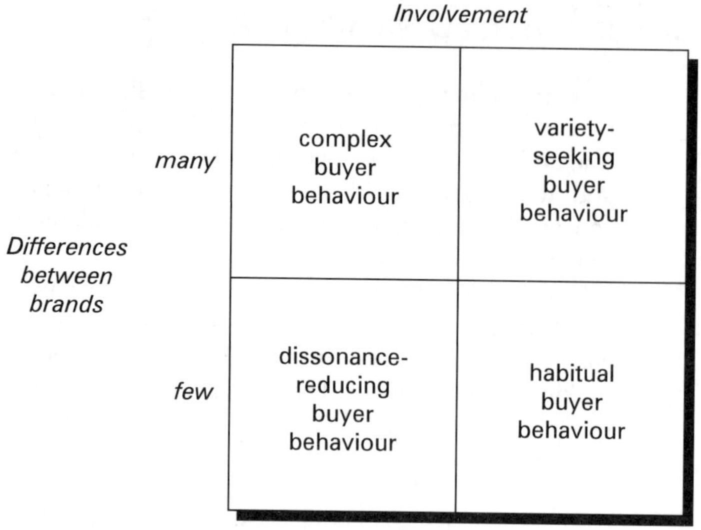

Involvement

		complex buyer behaviour	variety-seeking buyer behaviour
	many		
Differences between brands			
	few	dissonance-reducing buyer behaviour	habitual buyer behaviour

Figure 4.4   Types of consumer buyer behaviour

Complex buyer behaviour, often marked by consumer confusion, is demonstrated where consumers are highly involved in a purchase and perceive significant differences among brands. For many people, the purchase of a personal computer (PC) falls into this category. The rapid pace of technology is reflected in an overwhelming variety of features and applications, and to make an informed choice about which PC is best requires a personal investment of time and energy. Marketers are presented with an opportunity to influence the purchase decision at the stage where consumers seek information about a product's attributes and differential value. Well-trained sales staff can also proactively influence the purchase decision by providing consumers with guidance and advice. If the purchase is managed well by the selling organization, the chances are that the consumer will return to them for future purchases, thus increasing the customer's lifetime value to the organization. (This concept is explored further in Chapter 8.)

'Dissonance' describes the after-sales feelings of the consumer who believes that there has been some sort of shortfall between the purchase expectation and the purchase delivery. This post-purchase disappointment is often related to the product's actual performance. *Dissonance-reducing buyer behaviour* is demonstrated where consumers are highly involved with the purchase, perhaps because it is something expensive which they would seldom buy, and where they perceive there to be few differences between brands. Bed purchases are one good example. In order to address this type of behaviour, marketers need to concentrate their efforts on before- and after-sales communications to ensure that consumers feel confident about their choice of brand. This is essential to 'win over' consumers and to move them up the ladder of loyalty (see Chapter 8). Dissonance-reducing behaviour must be managed at all costs to prevent consumers from generating negative publicity by word of mouth.

Variety-seeking buyer behaviour is characterized by low consumer involvement and the perception of significant brand differences. This type of consumer will regularly switch brands within the same product category. Their behaviour is not driven by dissatisfaction with the brand, but rather a desire to sample other brands. In order to be successful in such markets, marketers need to encourage habitual buying by ensuring that target brands or products dominate the shelf space, that distribution strategies minimize stockouts and that communications and promotional activities constantly provide reminders and reinforcements. Once again, brand visibility and availability provide the key levers in building a relationship with variety seekers.

Habitual buyer behaviour occurs where there is low consumer involvement and few perceived differences between brands. This behaviour tends to be associated with low cost, frequently purchased products, such as flour. Consumers simply make their choice by reaching out for the same product time and again, and more out of habit than loyalty. Opportunities for relationship building may be perceived to be small but the shrewd marketer will focus on promotions which serve to build a sense of brand familiarity and which stimulate trial usage of the product. In these circumstances, it is important that the brand is always prominently displayed on the shop shelf and that out-of-stock situations are avoided. Visibility and availability are the vital elements in managing habitual buyers.

THE CONSUMER PURCHASE DECISION-MAKING PROCESS

While different types of buyer behaviour can be shown to exist, it is quite another matter to be unequivocal about why people buy what they buy. Decision-making is generally regarded as a linear process, starting with the recognition of a need. In the purchase decision-making process, as outlined in Figure 4.5, the first step is where buyers acknowledge that they have a need or a problem that requires a solution. This realization can be triggered through internal stimuli, such as hunger pangs, or external stimuli such as recalling a favourable review of a restaurant or noticing aromas emanating from a

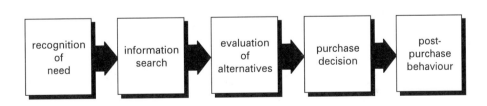

Figure 4.5   Model of consumer purchase decision-making process

restaurant kitchen. This initial acknowledgement is usually followed by an information search: the consumer reads the menu displayed outside the restaurant and evaluates the offerings. The consumer will then reach a conclusion and either enter the restaurant and order a meal, or move on down the road to a different dining establishment. After eating their meal, the consumer will demonstrate some form of post-purchase behaviour by making an assessment of his or her level of satisfaction with respect to expectation, and leaving a tip that reflects the outcome of that assessment.

Of course, most consumers pass through the decision-making process without giving it a second's notice. In instances where consumers are making a repeat purchase, they would enter the purchase decision-making process at one of the later stages.

APPROACHES TO CONSUMER BUYER BEHAVIOUR

A substantial amount of research has been conducted to try to explain consumer buyer behaviour. How a marketer should interpret and use the vast amount of consumer data available depends upon whether they believe it is more beneficial to direct marketing activities according to consumer psychology or according to consumer behaviour. This dilemma is related to perceptions of how consumers learn about products and services. The differences here are that a cognitivist approach focuses on what consumers think and feel, while a behaviourist approach is concerned with understanding overt consumer behaviour, or what consumers actually do.

These two approaches hold different implications for designing consumer research studies and subsequent RM strategies. The focus of research and promotional activity will depend on whether the marketer adopts a cognitivist or a behaviourist view of consumer buyer behaviour.

At a simplistic level, marketers of a cognitivist persuasion tend to favour image-based advertising and promotions, which appeal to consumers' values. They will offer brand benefits in ways that play on consumers' thoughts, feelings, attitudes and beliefs. Behaviourists, on the other hand, tend to use conditioning behaviour where the marketing message is reinforced through skilful advertising. For example, the association between the Marlboro man and the Marlboro cigarette is now so strong that in some cases the company no longer includes the brand name in its advertisements. This is because the brand has succeeded in transferring the meaning of an unconditioned stimulus to a conditioned stimulus.

So which marketing approach is right? Historically, advertisers have adopted the behaviourist philosophy. However, they are now shifting the emphasis towards creating a mood and eliciting an emotion, while still recognizing the importance of the association of products with symbols, colours and images. The debate is ongoing.

SUMMARY

An understanding of the buyer behaviour of individual consumers is necessary in order to make sense of markets and essential in planning a RM strategy. This requires that marketers work with the consumer's perception of reality.

Models of consumer buyer behaviour can, at best, help to promote this understanding and to demonstrate how consumers may be persuaded to buy one product, rather than another. The development of models involves delayering the social influences that have an impact on culture, subculture and social class. Forces which have a more immediate effect on consumer behaviour are close associates, namely reference groups and family. Of paramount importance to the purchase decision is the make-up of consumers themselves, encompassing their age, occupation, lifestyle, personality type and psychological motivation.

The interaction of two key dimensions – consumer 'involvement' and consumer perception of differences between brands – produces four distinct types of buyer behaviour: complex, dissonance-reducing, variety-seeking and habitual. Understanding how best to manage buyers of these persuasions enables marketers to develop long-term, profitable relationships with consumers.

Typical stages in the consumer purchase decision-making process can be identified, although these will not always represent conscious actions in the minds of consumers. It is the task of market research (see Chapter 7) to make these steps explicit in order that they may be better addressed and exploited by marketers.

Marketers must decide whether they favour a cognitivist or a behaviourist approach to understanding consumer buyer behaviour, if they are to give clear direction to the marketing activities which support consumer relationships, such as market research, market segmentation, branding and marketing communications.

Notes

1. P. Kotler, G. Armstrong, J. Saunders and V. Wong, *Principles of Marketing* (Englewood Cliffs, NJ: Prentice-Hall, 1991).
2. J. Paul Peter and Jerry C. Olson, *Consumer Behaviour and Marketing Strategy*, (Illinois: Irwin, 1987).
3. This section was sourced from articles appearing in the UK press during March 1999.

ORGANIZATIONAL BUYER BEHAVIOUR

Simon Knox

In this chapter:

- The changing business environment for organizational purchasing
- The typical composition of the decision-making unit for a new-task purchase
- The decision-making process
- The identification of buyer behaviours in mature markets
- The trend towards lean supply and longer-term relationships
- Case studies illustrating the benefits of central purchasing and customization

CHANGE DRIVERS IN THE BUSINESS ENVIRONMENT

A company involved in freight forwarding recently benchmarked how its customers perceived the added value that it contributed towards their business development. The evaluation revealed that some of its main customers, including global companies such as Compaq and Intel, are in the process of developing efficient end-to-end supply chains, from components-supply to end-customer delivery. Consequently, these customers will be seeking to work with suppliers who offer logistics capabilities across a wide range of products and services to serve them on a global basis. The company's research also confirmed suspicions that this fundamental shift in customer expectations and purchasing requirements was leading to a large-scale rationalization in the number of logistics companies their customers used. The world-wide logistics director of a US computer company said: 'Six years ago, we had 35 significant logistics suppliers (including freight forwarders), we are now reducing this to about five. International product flow should be within the capability of anyone, information flow and a willingness to provide customized services is where competitive advantage can be achieved.'

Faced with increasing customer demands, the challenge to suppliers today is to develop their businesses globally and to work closely with leading customers so as to align their logistics offer with customer requirements. Customers in other markets are pursuing similar purchasing strategies among their own suppliers. Table 5.1 shows the extent of supplier rationalization in a range of global companies and markets.

Table 5.1   **Supplier rationalization across companies**

| Company | Number of Suppliers | | % Change |
	Current	Previous	
Xerox	500	5 000	90
Motorola	3 000	10 000	70
General Motors	5 500	10 000	45
Ford	1 000	1 800	44
Texas Instruments	14 000	22 000	36

Source: Wall Street Journal.

The globalization of businesses is only one of many drivers that are changing the environment in which companies make purchasing decisions. Research at Cranfield shows that there are four other major forces that suppliers must take into consideration when dealing in business-to-business markets, comprising the following:

1. *Customer Expertise, Sophistication and Power* – as we have seen from the previous logistics example, customers are becoming more and more demanding in their expectations of quality, reliability and compatibility. The growing desire for customization stems partly from a better knowledge base, facilitated by developments in communications and IT, and partly from the concentration of buying into fewer hands.
2. *Lack of Market Growth* – in many mature markets, such as North America and Europe, market saturation has been reached. This state is characterized by overcapacity, increased competition and eroding margins. Under these conditions, customers are calling for greater operational efficiencies and 'value for money' from a smaller portfolio of preferred suppliers.
3. *Process Thinking* – a direct outgrowth of the technology explosion in information handling and electronic data interchange (EDI) has been the switch from a single-product approach to a systems orientation. The shift from marketing ready-made, tangible products to marketing by reputation, based on manufacturing capabilities and service delivery against exact client specifications, has fundamental implications for how companies organize to meet their customers' purchasing requirements.
4. *Time-Based Competition* – time horizons continue to become more compressed while the pace of change accelerates. The development of business systems, such as flexible manufacturing and just-in-time (JIT) deliveries, has encouraged companies to compete in terms of the speed with which they can deliver products and services to the market place.

In this rapidly changing climate of business-to-business marketing, how should companies go about managing customer relationships more effectively?

At a recent conference on RM held at Cranfield, Richard Hodapp of Managing Process Inc. reminded the audience of the need for business marketers to engage more fully in the customer's purchase decision-making

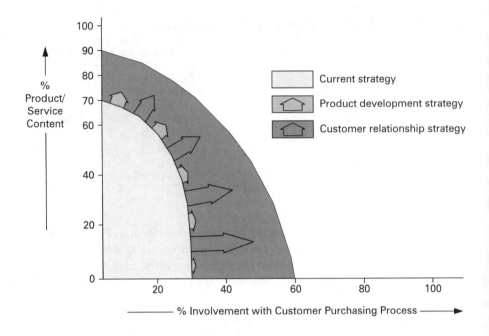

Figure 5.1 Product content versus involvement in the customer purchasing process

processes as well as to provide the customer with better products and services. While management endeavours to increase product and service content to inspire market share gains, this strategy is likely to produce only incremental gains for it relies solely on technologies, product development procedures and marketing know-how. In Figure 5.1, this is referred to as 'product development strategy'. However, enhanced knowledge of and involvement with customer purchasing processes (designated 'customer relationship strategy' in Figure 5.1) can lead to more significant market share gains. Comprehending *what* the scope of purchasing decision-making is and *where* the customer is at in the decision-making process can be hugely instrumental in influencing the purchase outcome. What is more, close relationships with a customer leading to a detailed knowledge of their operations are invisible to competitors and they can significantly promote product and service developments that fit more closely with customers' emerging requirements.

Meeting customer needs through a greater understanding of their requirements is similar to the approach which consumer marketers use when they develop their products for the supermarket shelves. Without an appreciation of consumers' changing attitudes, buyer behaviours and brand loyalty (see Chapter 4), the launch of a consumer product is likely to be unsuccessful. However, while the general approach to fulfilling customer needs may be similar, *how* the business purchase gets made and *who* influences the decision is fundamentally different from consumer marketing. A comparison of business-to-business and consumer marketing, as given in Table 5.2, serves to illustrate this point.

Table 5.2   **A comparison of business-to-business and consumer marketing**

	Business products	Consumer products
Customer base:	Few, with concentrated buying power.	Numerous, widely dispersed and limited buying power.
Buyer behaviours: (DMU)	Group decisions. Many buying influences.	Individual and family involvement.
(DMP)	Many purchasing procedures.	Impulse, planned or experiential.
Buyer/supplier relationships:	Very close relationships overtime. Pre-sale consultancy and problem-solving. After-sales services/support.	Short duration with very little close contact.
Product:	Technical complexity. Standard or customized.	Standard. Detailed specifications.
Price:	High unit price. Negotiating/bidding. Standard items from list.	Low unit price from list.
Promotion:	Emphasis on personal selling.	Mainly mass advertising and promotion.
Distribution/ Logistics:	Mainly direct for make-to-order customized items. Standard items often available from stock through distributors.	Stock items through a network of wholesalers and retail distributors.

In this chapter we will take a closer look at four key aspects of organizational buyer behaviour: the decision-making unit (DMU), the decision-making process (DMP), behavioural segmentation of customers, and managing buyer-supplier relationships (RM).

THE DECISION-MAKING UNIT

The size and composition of the DMU, being the management team involved in the purchasing process, varies according to the size of the company (as shown in Table 5.3) and the strategic nature of the purchasing decision.

In certain situations involving the first-time purchase of large-scale capital goods and services, as many as 40 people from across the company may

Table 5.3 **The DMU by company size**

Number of employees	Number of DMU members	Average number of contacts made by supplier's salespeople during purchase
0–200	3.40	1.72
201–400	4.85	1.75
401–1000	5.81	1.90
1000+	6.50	1.85

become involved at different stages of the DMP. The structure of the DMU can also be examined in terms of the different functions that are represented. These *roles* can be broadly placed into seven categories.

1. *Policy makers* are those individuals within the company that have the authority and responsibility for agreeing certain general policies that directly affect purchasing behaviour. The central purchasing of strategic items across a number of business units, such as media buying in Unilever, is one example of a company policy. The outsourcing of IT is often directed by similar policy decisions.
2. *Purchasers* are the actual buyers who are formally authorized to order products or services from suppliers. The purchaser's role can range from filling in purchase requisition forms to being the purchasing team leader who is responsible for making the final recommendation to senior management or the main board. Any assessment of the importance of the purchasing agent must consider the organization's attitude towards the purchase function, together with the level of risk associated with the purchase.
3. *Users* are the people who ultimately use the product or service. It is likely that they will be primarily concerned with product performance and ease of use. If installation or application is technically demanding for the customer, then the provision of post-sales consultancy and support will become crucial, to the point of overriding commercial considerations such as price and delivery times.
4. *Technologists* are the engineers and those with specialist knowledge who appraise the technical aspects of competitive offers and advise on key performance indicators (KPIs). It is the KPIs which enable the DMU to differentiate and judge suppliers against the company's own specifications – standards which the technologist is likely to have defined.
5. *Influencers* are the people who influence the DMP either directly or indirectly by providing information and criteria for the evaluation of alternative buying actions. Influencers can work inside the company or act as external advisers. For instance, companies will quite often employ a systems integrator as a consultant in a major IT purchase to guide the DMU from the earliest stages of the purchasing process. Sometimes the DMU may visit a company that has made a similar purchase to discuss their experiences of using the product and the supplier against KPIs.

6. *Gatekeepers* are people who control the flow of information to others within the company and the DMU. For example, buyers may have the authority to prevent salespeople from seeing users and deciders. Other gatekeepers include technical personnel and even personal secretaries.
7. *Deciders* are those with the authority to approve purchases. The decider is likely to be a senior manager where a complex purchase or company policy is involved. Otherwise, in more routine purchases, the buyer is usually the decider.

From a supplier's perspective, the make-up of the DMU is critical. The company's marketing efforts will reflect the individual priorities and interests of the constituent members as well as the overall group dynamics. In other words, in meeting the collective concerns of the DMU, trade-offs will be made during the purchasing process which will alter the perceptions of what are the key technical, problem-solving and relational benefits required from suppliers.

This need to deliver against key benefits is illustrated by the example given in Table 5.4 of marketing oil lubricants to a cement company. Even though the purchase is relatively straightforward, the DMU consists of six people who display six distinct roles.

Table 5.4   **Marketing oil lubricants to a cement company**

DMU role	DMU job title	Benefits sought
Specifier/user	Engineer	No technical problems
User/influencer	Storeman	JIT deliveries, palletted barrels
Decider	Buyer	Lowest price
Gatekeeper	Finance Manager	System uses a purchase order number and pays according to usage
Influencer	Cement Sales Manager	Quid pro quo for new cement business
Gatekeeper	General Manager	An innovative supplier that contributes to a lean supply chain

ORGANIZATIONAL AND PRODUCT INFLUENCES ON THE DMU

Various organizational 'demographics', such as a firm's size, purchasing policy or use of electronic data processing (EDP) and communications such as the intra- and extra-net, can change the composition of the DMU and *how* and *what* it buys.

Historically, much of the purchasing in companies consisting of many different business units has been carried out at the business unit level. Recently, however, some large companies have tried to centralize purchasing in order to obtain more purchasing clout as well as substantial savings. The following mini case study, featuring PepsiCo, provides an example of this move towards central purchasing.

Case Study 1: a move towards central purchasing

> PepsiCo aims to save $100 million a year out of a total cost of $2 billion by combining the buying power of their separate businesses.
>
> Paul Steele, European vice-president of sales and marketing, said: 'When we went through the list it was surprising. For example, Pizza Hut buys an enormous quantity of cardboard for the pizza boxes. Pepsi-Cola buys cardboard for soft drink trays. We're looking at whether we can leverage the scale.'
>
> They will now try the same with buying flour, salt, spices and cooking oil across their restaurant businesses which historically have developed separately. Now that they have the scale, central purchasing across preferred suppliers becomes a very exciting proposition.
>
> *Source*: Adapted from Diane Summers, *Financial Times*, 29 September 1994.

Product factors that influence buyers' decisions include frequency of purchase, the strategic nature of the product or service being considered, and loyalty to suppliers. Generally, there are three types of purchasing situation that impact the way that the DMU is organized and how products and suppliers are selected.

1. *Straight Rebuy* – the buyer reorders without requesting any product or service modifications. The buyer simply chooses a supplier from an approved list based upon past buying satisfaction. Because it is a routine reordering situation, the supplier may propose an automatic reordering system to both save purchasing time and reduce the risk of losing profitable, regular purchases.
2. *Modified Rebuy* – although the company has prior experience of the product, the particular purchasing situation demands some degree of customization, such as changes in the product specification, price, terms or supplier. Approved suppliers, including those currently under contract to the customer, may use the purchasing opportunity to make a better offer to the customer in order to win new business.
3. *New-Task Purchase* – a company buying a product or service for the first time may have no experience of supplier capabilities or performance evaluation. Consequently, the greater the cost or risk, the larger the DMU and its informational requirements. The new-task situation represents the marketer's greatest opportunity and challenge: the aim is to reach as many key purchasing influencers as possible and to provide help and information.

Case Study 2: a modified rebuy in systems cleaning

In the mid-1990s, the Canadian company, DiverseyLever, had a leading market share in the provision of systems cleaning services for plants of multinational food companies around the world. Many of its customers used different suppliers on a country-by-country or plant-by-plant basis as well as within each plant. Some of the plants required up to 14 different cleaning procedures to clean a range of areas, from surfaces of temperature-controlled, high-speed filling lines to washrooms and canteens.

In a strategic review of their key customers' needs, DiverseyLever marketing and sales management recognized the opportunity to develop a unified cleaning programme. Using the slogan 'one plant, one solution' and working with a leading customer who could also see the benefits of simplifying their cleaning procedures for health and safety purposes, DiverseyLever developed a specialist business unit which combined *elements* (products, services and equipment) and *systems* (applications) with *expertise* (multi-skilled cleaning teams) to deliver a customized cleaning *programme* for the customer's entire plant. As knowledge was accrued and trials were extended to other plants, the customer decided to outsource the cleaning of its entire North American business to DiverseyLever.

In time, as the appropriate key account management structure develops (see Chapter 17), DiverseyLever hopes to service the customer on a country-by-country basis. Meantime, other multinationals are inviting DiverseyLever to provide them with customized systems cleaning services, and demand will no doubt grow as health and safety legislation around the world becomes more complex.

THE DECISION-MAKING PROCESS

Buyers who face a new-task purchasing situation are likely to adopt a formal DMP which may involve up to eight separate stages. Purchases that are modified or straight rebuys may skip some of these stages. Referring to Table 5.5, let us now look at the DMP for the typical new-task purchase.

Although the DMP is shown to be a linear sequence of progressive stages, in practice the stages are rarely neatly sequential or discrete. Sometimes the stages may occur out of sequence or simultaneously, or not at all if it is a fairly straightforward rebuy. Nonetheless, the DMP does provide a helpful guide as to the distinguishing features of each of the typical buying stages.

Clearly, there is a relationship between the composition of the DMU and the DMP. Generally, as the *risk* associated with the organizational purchase *increases*:

- The DMU becomes more complex, with participants having more authority
- DMP members will have greater levels of experience and heightened motivations

- Suppliers with strong reputations and proven product solutions will be favoured
- Information searches and sources, particularly personal and non-commercial communications, will increasingly be used to guide and support decisions
- DMU role stress and conflict will increase, with bargaining negotiations taking place among members
- Buyer-supplier relationships and communication networks become critical to fostering an atmosphere of cooperation and reducing perceived risk

As business marketers become more involved with organizational buying procedures and customer practices in general, market segmentation can be improved, enabling the marketing mix to be tailored more specifically to the needs of distinctive customer groups. This requirement for customization is a characteristic of competitive, mature markets. The PLC (see Chapter 3) contends that prices drop with customer familiarity and an unwillingness to pay for consultation services from suppliers. In addition, heightened competi-

Table 5.5   The eight stages of the DMP

Buying stage	Characteristics
1. Problem Recognition	• Changing business needs • Supplier review • Current product/service dissatisfactions
2. General Need	• Innovation • Cost savings • Improved performance
3. Specification	• Buyer/supplier dialogue • 'Qualifying' criteria • 'Differentiating' criteria
4. Supplier Search	• Risk profile of purchase • Information gathering • Consideration set
5. Proposals Submission	• Qualification of suppliers • Choice set • Proposal solicitation
6. Supplier Selection	• Proposals reviewed • Buyer/supplier negotiations • Selection and ratification
7. Order Specification	• Blanket contract/order • Order fulfilment procedures • Relationship development
8. Performance Review	• Benchmark supplier performance • Evaluation performance • Endorse, modify or discontinue

tion results in the availability of equivalent products at similar or lower prices. Steadily, as the market becomes more of a commodity, customer differentiation is needed to target offers more effectively. In highly competitive markets, segmentation based on buyer behaviour characteristics can be used to help strengthen buyer-supplier relationships and reach the right levels of customization. Although we will be dealing with market segmentation in more detail in the next chapter, it is appropriate here to explore an organizational buyer behaviour approach.

SEGMENTING BUSINESS CUSTOMERS IN MATURE MARKETS

Given this market dynamic, customers in mature markets may be aligned along the two dimensions of price and cost-to-serve according to their purchasing characteristics, as portrayed in Figure 5.2. Customers who demand a low price can be offered a 'no frills' product with minimal service. Customers who value a customized offer will pay a higher price for tailor-made adaptations to products and services. Price differentials founded on product quality differences alone tend to be small because competitors are able to offer more or less equivalent products.

In keeping with this rationale, suppliers operating in mature markets may expect their customers' buyer behaviours to follow the path of the *value line* in Figure 5.2. Zone C of this line represents the unbundled offer or core product, while zone B denotes a customized offer based on a range of value-added services. In both cases, the value-for-money of the offer is equitable to the buyer and the seller.

From the buyer's perspective, an alternative strategy exists which is linked to the *market power line* in Figure 5.2. Customers see only the price dimension of

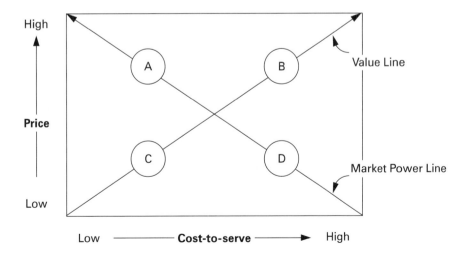

Figure 5.2 Buyer behaviour matrix

Source: Adapted from Rangan, Moriarty and Swartz, *Journal of Marketing* (1992).

the matrix, for they are price-driven and do not know or consider the supplier's cost-to-serve. Customers are likely to shop around for the best price given that products themselves are largely undifferentiated and to offer the bait of guaranteed purchase volume and large order sizes in order to drive prices down even further. Scrutinizing customers such as these choose to operate in zone D or C, depending upon their knowledge of competitive offerings and their own market power.

In terms of supplier performance, operating in zone A implies that suppliers retain market power. This may be due to their having a truly superior product offering which competitors are unable to match for reasons of technological excellence or patent protection. In such circumstances, suppliers are able to support a high price. Remember, customers in zones A and B seek value through the superiority of the products or services that the supplier provides.

All locations *above the value line* indicate that the supplier meets the value requirements of the customer segments it serves and generates superior profits. In the areas *below the value line*, customer segments will be less profitable for the supplier and possibly loss-making.

The buyer behaviour matrix serves to illustrate the possibilities of unearthing profitable customer segments using diagnostics closely associated with their patterns of buyer behaviour. Equally, as unprofitable customer segments are exposed, marketing and sales management will need to develop their marketing strategies, mindful of the costs of serving such price-conscious customers. Marketing planning may well involve the rationalization of customers who display blatant switching behaviours and who regard supplier relationships as purely transactional.

With increased turbulence in the market place, it is clear that firms are generally moving away from transaction-oriented marketing strategies and towards relationship-oriented marketing as a means of enhancing commercial performance and customer value. We believe that the next source of competitive advantage will stem from the type of relationships which firms develop with their suppliers.

RELATIONSHIP MARKETING AND ORGANIZATIONAL BUYER BEHAVIOUR

Earlier in the chapter, we noted the trend towards 'lean' supply in which companies have reduced their supplier base significantly (see Table 5.1). With a smaller number of suppliers to manage, it becomes possible for buyers and suppliers to develop closer, longer-term relationships to increase competitiveness. There are three underlying reasons why stronger customer relationships can help build competitive advantage.

1. *Systems cost reduction* – closer relationships achieved through multiple linkages between a preferred supplier and the customer enable better work practices, such as JIT deliveries, reduced inventories and order cycle times. As trust increases and sales volatility decreases, cost savings resulting from improved work practices can be shared by both parties.

2. *Increased effectiveness through innovation* – as supplier relationships solidify, the customer may ask key suppliers to invest in technology that will allow the supplier to provide a quality platform, offer direct deliveries and engage in information exchange. Suppliers are naturally more willing to innovate by investing in such assets and services when they enjoy a strong relationship with the customer.

3. *Enabling technologies* – electronic linkages, ranging from automatic reordering and invoicing to the use of the Internet for immediate inter-company communications, enable suppliers to become closer and more responsive to their major customers. IT also allows the cost of transactions to be tracked. Consequently, suppliers are better able to determine which customers are cost effective to serve (see Figure 5.2).

It is sometimes useful to picture supplier relationships as a continuum, with four levels of engagement defined according to the contribution the relationship makes to the buyer's competitiveness, as described in Figure 5.3.

At each relationship level, the supplier provides products and services as well as capabilities, such as R&D, risk management and training. However, as the relationship develops and there is increased interdependency, the offering becomes more weighted towards the supplier's capabilities. Let us consider each relationship level in turn.

Level 1

This basic level describes a traditional supplier who has a transactional relationship with the customer. The supplier sells specified products to the customer on the basis of price, service and quality. In most instances, the supplier adds limited value to the customer's overall competitiveness. This is a traditional buyer-seller relationship.

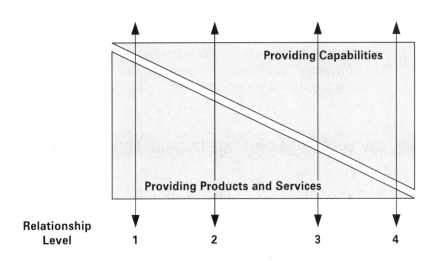

Figure 5.3   Supplier relationship continuum

Level 2

Here, the supplier works cooperatively with the customer to reduce total costs and to increase the customer's competitiveness. Procter & Gamble's work with US food retailers on achieving everyday low price (EDLP) across its product portfolio is an example of this level of engagement.

Level 3

Working in partnership with the customer, the supplier takes responsibility for a significant component of the customer's value-adding capabilities. The customer will also be dependent upon the supplier for innovation. Strategic sub-assembly deals in the automotive industry characterize this level of supplier relationship.

Level 4

At this level, a strategic supplier can enable the customer to move beyond its traditional competencies. For example, the Royal Bank of Scotland is a strategic supplier to Tesco Stores in that the bank helps the supermarket chain to extend its credibility into financial services. In the USA, Federal Express delivery has become part and parcel of the Internet-based shopping experience. FedEx's skills in dealing with the complex, logistical problems involved in home delivery serve to stretch the capabilities of home-shopping providers.

Buying companies are moving to higher levels of supplier relationships in order to increase their own ability to add value. Such firms are treating their preferred suppliers more like customers, investing in shared technology, resources and expertise so as to achieve mutual benefit. In short, buyer-supplier relationships with common business interests require shared RM and planning skills. The growing trend towards long-term business relationships both indicates and influences changes in organizational buyer behaviour. The tendency towards long-term partnerships represents one of a number of current trends in organizational buyer behaviour.

OTHER KEY TRENDS IN ORGANIZATIONAL BUYER BEHAVIOUR

Customers want what customers want

Increasing levels of customization mean more cooperation and co-engineering, with the transfer of people and know-how across both sides of the buyer-supplier relationship. The commitment, 'Our people are your people', becomes part of the supplier's offer.

Qualifiers and differentiators

The product- and service-related aspects of the supplier's offer have become hygiene factors, for they no longer serve to differentiate. Differentiation now flows from the problem-solving and relational capabilities that suppliers are able to demonstrate over a period of time.

Customer value, not risk reduction

As customers have grown more sophisticated in their purchasing processes, they have become less averse to risk. Unfettered by the need to manage downside risk, suppliers have come to be seen as a resource to enhance the end-customer's perceptions of value. In some markets, such as laptops and PCs, this has led to the co-branding of products and related services.

Conflict, what conflict?

The shift to flat structures and team-based working in organizations (see Chapter 16) is altering perceptions of the buyer's role and how the DMU functions in a purchasing decision. Conflict, role stress and trade-offs among DMU members become less evident as cooperative solutions replace traditional divides. The buyer's role is changing from one of managing conflict to one of facilitating a cross-functional team (see Figure 5.4).

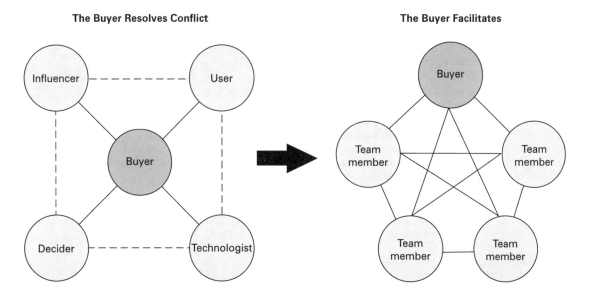

Figure 5.4 The buyer's changing role

SUMMARY

With the onslaught of ever more rapid and radical changes to the business environment, it has become imperative that business marketers fully understand their customers' needs. Knowing how people buy makes it easier to sell to them and, possibly, to anticipate future market demands. In mature markets, characterized by increasing levels of commoditization, customers are looking for positive added value from their suppliers in order to be able to discriminate between alternative products and services.

The move towards lean supply and RM is heralding an era of customization and open cooperation between buyers and suppliers. Whether the supplier is tendering for a new-task purchase or a modified rebuy, knowledge of the DMU and DMP will be critical in successfully influencing the purchase outcome. This trend towards customization requires a higher level of customer selectivity and skills in market segmentation practices among suppliers. A buyer behaviour approach to market segmentation can help suppliers to choose between customers as both parties seek to develop profitable, long-term relationships.

Looking to the future, as buying organizations move towards flat structures and team-based ways of working among DMU members, the nature of the DMP will simplify. There will be fewer suppliers considered in the search stage and more emphasis placed on the selection stage so that suppliers can demonstrate their capabilities in problem-solving and building relationships with the DMU.

References

Tim Denison and Malcolm McDonald, 'The Role of Marketing Past, Present and Future', *Journal of Marketing Practice: Applied Marketing Science*, vol. 1, no. 1, (1995) pp. 54–76.

Rangan Kasturi, 'Segmenting Customers in Mature Industrial Markets: An Application', HBS Case Note No. 9–594–089.

Simon Knox and Stan Maklan, *Competing on Value: Bridging the Gap between Brand and Customer Value* (London: Financial Times Pitman Publishing, 1998). [http://www.competingonvalue.com]

Philip Kotler, Gary Armstrong, John Saunders and Veronica Wong, *Principles of Marketing*, 2nd European edn, (London: Prentice-Hall, 1999).

Keith Thompson, Helen Mitchell and Simon Knox, 'Organizational Buying Behaviour in Changing Times', *European Management Journal*, vol. 16, no. 6, (1998) pp. 698–705.

MARKET SEGMENTATION

Malcolm McDonald

In this chapter:

- A discussion of to whom we sell
- The importance of correct market definition and market share
- The market segmentation process, including:
  market mapping
  identifying who buys and what they buy
  determining why they buy
  refining market segments by means of cluster analysis
- Case studies using market segmentation

This chapter contains some extracts from *Market Segmentation: how to do it; how to profit from it*. These are reproduced with the kind permission of the authors, Malcolm McDonald and Ian Dunbar (Macmillan, 1998).

THE DIFFERENCE BETWEEN CUSTOMERS AND CONSUMERS

Market segmentation is one of the key determinants of successful marketing and is fundamental to the matching process described in Chapter 1. In order to understand market segmentation, it is necessary to be clear about: the difference between customers and consumers; the meaning of 'market' and market share; and the sequential relationship between the various steps of the market segmentation process and its ultimate contribution to securing competitive advantage.

Let us start with the difference between customers and consumers. The term 'consumer' is generally interpreted to mean the final consumer, who is not necessarily the customer. For example, a parent who is buying breakfast cereals is probably the intermediate customer, acting as an agent on behalf of the eventual consumers (the family). In order to market cereals effectively, it is imperative that the marketer understands what the final consumers want as well as what the parent wants.

Given that we can appreciate the distinction between customers and consumers, and the need to be alert to any changes in the consumption patterns and requirements of final consumers, the next question becomes: 'Who are our customers?'

Direct customers are those individuals or organizations that actually buy direct from us, such as distributors, wholesalers, retailers, and so on. However, as intimated in the previous paragraph, there is a tendency for organizations to confine their interests, and hence their marketing, to those who actually place the orders. Adopting a 'tunnel vision' approach to marketing can be a major mistake, as can be seen from case study 1.

Case Study 1: a fertilizer company

A fertilizer company that had grown and prospered during the 1970s and 1980s because of the superior nature of its products, reached its farmer consumers via merchants (wholesalers). However, as other companies copied its leading technology, the merchants began to stock competitive products and were able to drive prices and margins down. Had the fertilizer company paid more attention to the needs of its different farmer groups and developed products especially for them based on farmer segmentation, it would have continued to create demand pull through differentiation. As it was, the fertilizer company's products became commodities and market power shifted almost entirely to the merchants. The company is no longer in business.

There are countless other examples of companies which have ceased trading because they did not pay sufficient attention to the needs of customers further down the supply chain and thus failed to provide any real value to their direct customers.

Case Study 2: Procter & Gamble

Procter & Gamble (P&G) in the USA, which supplies the giant food retailer, Wal-Mart, exemplifies good practice. As can be seen from the simple diagram below, it creates demand pull (hence high turnover and high margins) by focusing its operations on serving the needs of consumers. The company is also very attentive to the needs of its direct customer, Wal-Mart. Wal-Mart is able to operate on minimal margins because, as the bar code is swiped across the till, P&G produces an invoice, manufactures a replacement product and activates the distribution chain, all by means of integrated IT processes. This simultaneous and instantaneous system has reduced Wal-Mart's costs by hundreds of millions of dollars.

P&G $\Longrightarrow$ CUSTOMERS $\Longrightarrow$ CONSUMERS

Closely related to the question of what is the difference between customers and consumers is the question: 'What is our market share?'

MARKET DEFINITION AND MARKET SHARE

Most businesspeople understand that there is a direct relationship between having a relatively high market share and receiving a high return on investment (ROI). This relationship is shown in Figure 6.1.

Before attempting to evaluate market share, it is very important to define the term 'market': for instance, BMW are not in the same market as Ford, although both companies manufacture automobiles. Correct market definition is crucial for the purposes of measuring market share and market growth, specifying target customers, recognizing relevant competitors, and formulating marketing objectives and strategies.

The general rule for defining 'market' is that it should be described in terms of a customer need and in a way which covers the aggregation of all the alternative products or services which customers regard as being capable of satisfying that same need. For example, we would regard the company canteen as only one source of obtaining a meal at lunchtime; the alternatives include external restaurants, public houses, fast food outlets and sandwich bars. The market definition emphasis, therefore, is clearly on the word 'need'.

Aggregating currently available products/services, however, is simply an aid to arriving at the definition, one that will probably require revision as new products are developed which better satisfy users' needs. For example, the button manufacturer who believed its market to be the 'button market' was no doubt disappointed at the arrival of zips and Velcro! A needs-based definition would have enabled the company's management to recognize the fickleness of current products, to accept that one of their principal tasks was to seek out better ways of satisfying their market's need for fastenings, and to evolve their product offer accordingly. IBM would have saved itself a lot of trouble if it had realized earlier that mainframes were products, not markets.

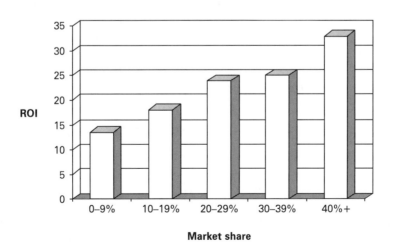

Figure 6.1 The relationship between market share and return on investment (ROI)

Source: Pims.

As well as highlighting the importance of getting the market definition right, these examples illustrate the necessity to arrive at a meaningful balance between a broad market definition and a manageable market definition. Too narrow a definition can restrict the range of new opportunities that could be exploited through segmentation, while too broad a definition could make marketing planning meaningless. For example, the television broadcasting companies are in the 'entertainment' market, which also consists of theatres, cinemas and theme parks. Because 'entertainment' is a fairly broad definition, television broadcasters may find it more manageable, when looking at segmenting their market, to define their market as 'home entertainment'. This definition could then be further refined into the pre-school, child, teenager, adult, or family home entertainment markets.

Having established what we mean by 'market', we can then proceed to measure, manage and maximize it.

To calculate market share, the following three criteria may be used:

- *Product class* – cigarettes; computers; fertilizers; carpets
- *Product subclass* – filter; PCs; nitrogen; carpet tiles
- *Product brand* – Silk Cut; IBM; Nitram; Heuga

Silk Cut as a brand, for the purpose of measuring market share, is only concerned with the aggregate of all other brands that satisfy the same group of customer wants. Nevertheless, the manufacturer of Silk Cut also needs to be aware of the sales trends of filter cigarettes and the cigarette market in total.

One of the most frequent mistakes that is made by people who do not understand what market share really means is to assume that their company has only a small share of some market, whereas, if the company is commercially successful, it probably has a much larger share of a smaller market.

We must never lose sight of the purpose of market segmentation, which is to enable us to create competitive advantage for ourselves by creating greater value for our customers. For instance, a London orchestra that defines its market as the aggregation of all London classical orchestras, rather than as all entertainment, has a relevant and realistic market definition that will potentially enable it to outperform its competitors and grow profitably. The company in case study 3 obviously did not understand the significance of market segmentation.

Case Study 3: a European airline

The chairman of a European airline, alas, now bankrupt, once told his assembled general managers that his ambition was for his airline to be the best in the world and to provide customer service to the point of obsession. The problem was that his airline did not compete in many markets and an unfocused customer obsession policy led to a provision of service the company could not afford. High-flown and ungrounded statements such as this chairman's can do more harm than good!

MARKET SEGMENTATION

Market segmentation is the means by which a company seeks to gain a differential advantage over its competitors. A methodology is required to achieve market segmentation.

Markets usually fall into natural groups or segments which contain customers who exhibit broadly similar needs. These segments form separate markets in themselves and can often be of considerable size. Taken to its extreme, each individual consumer is a unique market segment, for all people differ in their requirements. However, it is clearly uneconomical to make unique products for the needs of individuals, except in the most exceptional of circumstances. Consequently, products are made to appeal to groups of customers who share approximately the same needs.

The universally accepted criteria of what constitutes a viable market segment are as follows:

- Segments should be of an adequate size to provide the company with the desired ROI
- The members of each segment should share a high degree of similarity in their requirements, yet be distinct from the rest of the market
- The criteria for describing segments must be relevant to the purchase situation
- Segments must be reachable

While these criteria may seem obvious, market segmentation is one of the most difficult marketing concepts to put into practice. Yet, without effective segmentation, the company is susceptible to the 'me too' condition, where it offers the potential customer much the same product as any other company, which is likely to be the lowest priced article. This can be ruinous to profits, unless the company happens to have lower costs, and hence higher margins, than its competitors.

There are basically three stages to market segmentation, all of which have to be completed if any progress is to be made. In the first stage, the company takes a detailed look at the way its market operates and identifies how customer decisions are made about competing products or services. Successful segmentation is based on a detailed understanding of decision-makers and their requirements (see Chapter 11). The second stage is essentially a manifestation of the way customers actually behave in the market place and consists of answering the question, 'Who is buying what?' The third stage seeks to resolve the issue of 'Why do they buy what they buy?' and then to search for market segments based on this analysis of identified needs.

MARKET MAPPING

A useful way of tackling the complex issue of market segmentation is to start by drawing a 'market map' as a precursor to a more detailed examination of 'who buys what'. An example of a very basic market map is given in Figure 6.2.

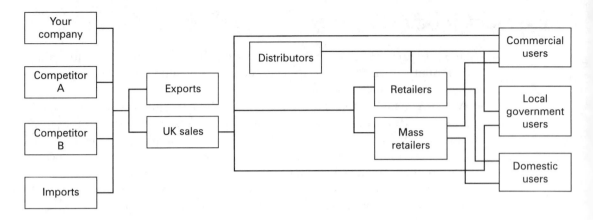

Note: This market map combines domestic and business-to-business end users, as some of the distribution channels are common to both of them.

Figure 6.2   A simple market map

A market map portrays the distribution, or supply and value chains that link the supplier and the ultimate consumer, or end user. It takes into account the various buying mechanisms found in the market, including the part played by 'influencers' (see Chapter 5).

In general, if an organization's products or services go through the same channels to similar end users then one composite market map can be drawn. If, however, some products or services go through totally different channels and/ or to totally different markets, then more than one market map must be produced.

It is probably sensible to treat different business units individually, as their respective business value or volume justifies a specific focus. For example, a farming cooperative that supplies seeds and fertilizer as well as crop protection, insurance and banking services will require a separate market map for each of these product groups, even though they all appear to go through similar channels to the same end users. In other words, it is advisable to start the mapping process (and subsequent segmentation process) at the lowest level of disaggregation within the organization's structure.

It is very important that the market map tracks the organization's products/ services, along with those of its competitors, all the way down the supply chain to the end user, even though the organization may not actually sell to the end user directly. A simple example of this is P&G, who do not sell to the consumer directly. Another example is a radiator company that does not sell directly to builders.

In some markets, the direct customer/purchaser will not be the end user. For example, the doctor we visit when seeking treatment is, in many respects, a contractor when it comes to prescribing medicine. The doctor is the designated bridge between the pill maker and the pill taker. The distinction is important because, to win the commission, in this case, the patient's custom, the doctor will have needed to understand the patient's requirements and, in treating the patient, would have addressed those requirements on the patient's behalf.

To omit the final user (the patient) from the market map would, therefore, have ignored an array of needs which the supplier (the pharmaceutical company) must be aware of (and must include in its offer) to ensure that its name appears on the contractor's (doctor's) list of preferred suppliers. The inclusion of a contractor on a market map is illustrated in Figure 6.3.

Making certain that the market map follows through to the end user is also important in situations where products/services are purchased for end users by their company's purchasing department. In such instances, the market map should track the products/services beyond Purchasing to the departments where the end users are found, listing each end user department separately as they have either utilized the product/service differently, or utilized it to achieve a different objective. (Where a single end user department, or individual, uses the products/services in multiple applications, they should appear only once on the market map.) The market map should include, where appropriate, the inherent purchasing procedures, such as committees, authorizations, sealed bids and so on, as shown in Figure 6.4.

The market map in Figure 6.4 also illustrates a particular purchase procedure that involves a purchase committee as well as the financial director, and they have therefore been combined into one box.

As these diagrams demonstrate, most market maps will have at least two principal components:

- The channel
- Consumers (final or end users)

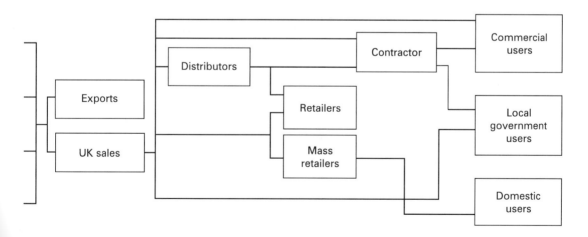

Note: In this particular market map the introduction of contractors has now reduced the similarity between the domestic and business-to-business end users. Mass retailers continue to be shared with a proportion of the commercial users, but this new contractor stage only operates in the business-to-business field.

Figure 6.3 Market map with contractor

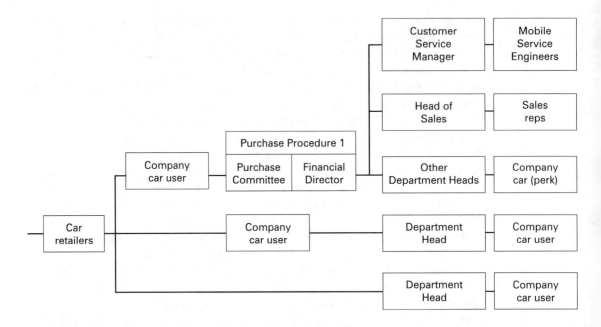

Note: In this market map, the physical delivery of the product to the final user (car retailer to car user) is insufficient in representing the sales route and purchasing routines encountered. The market map also assumes that all the final users who appear beyond 'Purchase Procedure 1' are subject to the same purchasing route. If this is not the case, ensure your market map reflects the reality. For example, all the departments in a company may use mail, but the advertising department may 'purchase' its mail through their direct mail agency and therefore bypass the normal purchase procedures.

Figure 6.4   Market map with business purchasing procedures

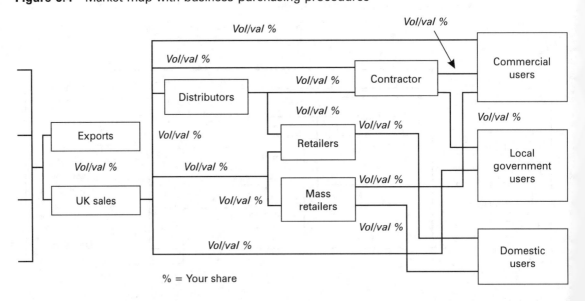

Note: This market map combines domestic and business-to-business end users, as some of the distribution channels are common to both of them.

Figure 6.5   Market map with volumes and/or values on each route

Be sure to draw a total market map, rather than just the part you currently deal with, to gain a comprehensive understanding of the market's dynamics. For example, beware of writing in only the word 'Distributor' if there are, in fact, different kinds of distributors that behave in different ways and that supply different customers. This point is explained further under the subsequent heading 'Leverage Points'.

With quantification playing an important role later on in the process, it is useful to mark along each 'route' the volumes and/or values (vol/val) which pass along that route (guesstimate if necessary). Also, note your market share, if known, as illustrated in Figure 6.5.

The market map should incorporate all of the transaction stages or 'junctions' *en route* that support the flow of products between suppliers and end users. These stages will, therefore, include points at which a transaction takes place and/or where influence or advice is given or where decisions occur. (The latter two may not constitute a transaction.) The involvement of influencers should appear on the market map just as if they were a transaction stage, as shown in Figure 6.6.

Each junction should be positioned hierarchically on the market map according to how close it is to the final user. The last junction along the market map would, therefore, be the final user. The junctions in the purchase procedure found in business-to-business markets are graded as a single junction (hence their enclosure in one box in Figure 6.4).

Note at each junction, if applicable, all the different types of companies/customers which occur there, along with the number of them that there are, as suggested in Figure 6.7.

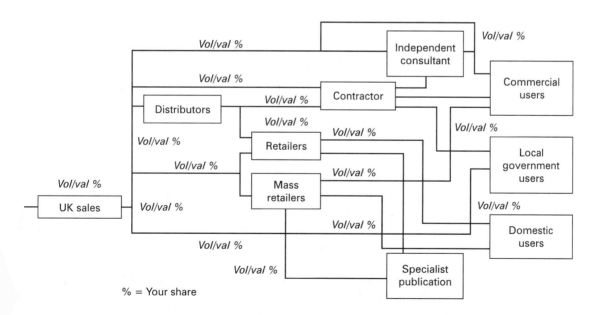

Figure 6.6 Market map with influencers

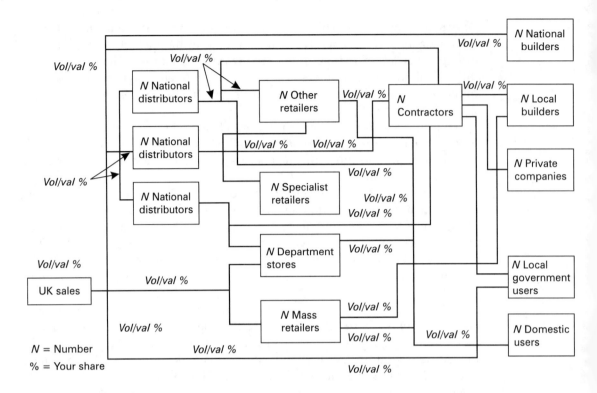

Note: It is now clear that within the 'commercial users' group, only a proportion of local builders go to mass retailers for their suppliers.

Figure 6.7 Market map with different company/customer types, their volumes and/or values, number of each type and your market share

Allocate to these different company/customer types the volumes and/or values they deal with (guesstimate if necessary), as shown in percentage terms in Figure 6.7. Also, note your market share, if known.

At this point, the market mapping routine may be challenging the traditional categories of company/customer types.

Leverage points

Leverage points are the fixed locations, or points, on the market map where power or influence may be exerted. To note those junctions where decisions are made about which of the competing products/services should be purchased, highlight them in bold print, as shown in Figure 6.8. Also, attach to each company/customer type the appropriate number of business units/individual purchasers it incorporates. In those instances where one company/customer type has been split into two boxes in order to distinguish between a leverage point and a non-leverage point (for example, CB1 and CB2), guesstimate the volume/value passing through each.

Mapping out the different transactions that take place throughout the company's supply chain has revealed how the individual transactions relate to

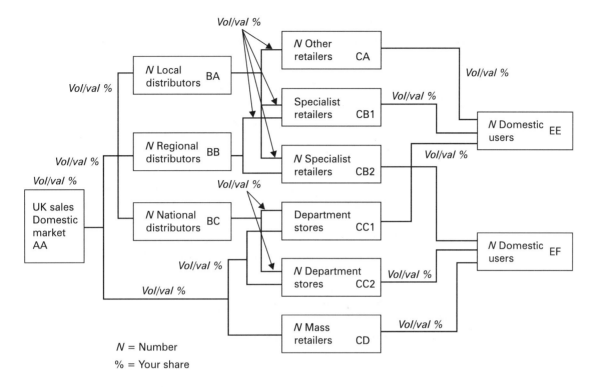

Figure 6.8 Leverage points at two junctions on a market map

one another. Quantifying these various 'routes' and determining the company's share along them has served to identify the most important supply routes and the progressive changes in the company's market position.

By pinpointing where in the supply chain decisions are taken which consider the products/services of competing suppliers, we can establish at which stages, or junctions, customers are expressing preferences and thus where segmentation could occur. For most companies, it is recommended that segmentation should first be implemented at the junction furthest away from the supplier/manufacturer where decisions are made.

Most importantly, however, market mapping provides a clearer understanding of the structure of our market and how it works.

WHO BUYS AND WHAT THEY BUY

Who buys

A useful method for dealing with this step in the market segmentation process is to refer to the market map and, at each point where leverage is exhibited, attempt to describe the characteristics of the customers who belong to that point. The analysis may consist of a single characteristic or a combination of features, depending on the market concerned.

Such customer analyses aim to identify the shared attributes within customer groups which can then be used to guide the development of effective communication strategies. No matter how clever we may be in isolating segments, unless we can find some common ground upon which to base our promotional activities and methods of information exchange, our marketing efforts will be to no avail.

The use of demographic descriptors can be helpful in identifying commonalities. For consumer markets, these include age, sex, education, stage in the family life cycle, and socio-economic group (A, B, C1, C2, D, E). A full list of the UK socio-economic groups is provided in Table 4.1.

Table 4.1 is based on the British census and, although this example is peculiar to the UK, similar socio-economic groupings and percentages exist for most advanced economies. This method describes people by their social status as represented by their occupations. Not surprisingly, A, B and C categories, which include most of the professions and senior managers, are light television viewers; consequently, if they are your target market, it does not make much sense to advertise your product or service on television. However, they can be reached effectively by means of certain newspapers and magazines where they comprise the principal readership. Thus the correlation between these socio-economic groupings and readership and viewing patterns can be useful in helping us to communicate cost-effectively and conveniently with our target market by means of advertising.

It is obvious that, at different stages in life, we have different needs and these distinctions provide another useful means of describing our market. Banks and insurance companies have been particularly adept at developing products for specific age groups. In this respect, because socio-economic groups are becoming less relevant as predictors of behaviour (for example, all classes now play golf and travel abroad), there is an emerging concept of 'contexts', including 'wellness', 'awareness', 'Euroness', 'traditionalism', 'expectism' and 'home-centredness', each one being related to a life stage such as 'single', 'nester', 'developer' and 'elder'. Thus Laura Ashley would clearly suit the 'traditionalism' context, while Body Shop would probably appeal to the 'wellness' context.

ACORN (A Classification of Regional Neighbourhood groups), which classifies all households according to 54 different neighbourhood types based on census data, is particularly useful to the retailing business because, when employed in conjunction with market research, it can be used to predict consumption patterns accurately in specific geographical locations.

SIC (Standard Industrial Classification) categories, which are defined by number of employees, turnover, and production processes, can be useful demographic descriptors for industrial markets.

What they buy

In respect of what is bought, the value of the market map should now become apparent. Market mapping is about representing, diagrammatically, the actual structure of markets in terms of volume, value, the physical characteristics of products, the place of purchase, the frequency of purchase, the price paid, and so on. Outlining the market's construction serves to indicate whether any groups of products (or outlets, or price categories, and so forth) are growing, static, or declining; in other words, where there may be opportunities or obstacles.

Case Study 4: a carpet company

A carpet company, whose sales were declining, discovered through analysis that although the overall market was buoyant and rising, the particular outlets to which it had traditionally sold were accounting for a declining proportion of total market sales. Furthermore, demand for high-priced products was falling, as was demand for the particular fibre types manufactured by the company. All this added up to a decline in sales and profitability, and prompted the company to refocus its marketing efforts towards some of the growth sectors of the market.

Case study 4 represents market segmentation at its most elementary level, yet it is surprising how many companies today run apparently sophisticated budgeting systems which are based on little more than crude extrapolations of past sales trends and which only hint at marketing strategies. Such unclear and inflexible systems usually cause serious commercial problems when market structures change, as in the case of the carpet company, which changed direction too late and went bankrupt. The same fate befell a shoe manufacturer who doggedly continued to manufacture the same products, in the same materials, for the same kind of outlets, irrespective of the rapid changes that were taking place in the footwear market.

Having determined the market's make-up, the next task is to list all relevant competitive products/services, whether or not you manufacture them. It is important to unbundle all the components of each purchase to ensure that the list of 'what is bought' is comprehensive.

The listing of purchases particular to a market should consider the following product/service features:

- Applications
- Physical characteristics
- Where they are bought
- How they are bought
- When they are bought

Consider the following examples:

Lawnmowers   Hover, cylinder, rotary, petrol driven, manual, electrically driven, 12 inch cut, 16 inch cut, any mower with a branded engine, extended warranty, with after-sales service, and so on

| Paints | Emulsion, gloss, non-drip coat, 5 litre cans, 2 litre cans, environmentally friendly, bulk, and so on |
| Petrol stations | Self-service, forecourt service, with loyalty programme, and so on. |

As part of this step of listing 'what they buy', and without attempting to link it with the earlier step of listing 'who buys', list all the channels through which the listed range of products/services are bought.

The list of supply channels (where bought) might include: direct/mail order, distributor, department store, national chain, regional chain, local independent retailer, tied retailer, supermarket, wholesaler, mass distributor, specialist supplier, street stall, via a buying group, through a buying club, door-to-door, local/high street/out-of-town shop, and so on.

It is also necessary to draw up a list of the different frequencies of purchase (when bought) which might include: daily, weekly, monthly, seasonally, every two years, at 50 000 miles, occasionally, as needed, only in emergencies, by degree of urgency, infrequently, rarely, at special events, only during sales, at the lowest price, and so on.

Then draw up a further separate list covering the different methods of purchase (how bought) and, if applicable, the different purchasing organizations and procedures observed in the market.

1. *Methods of purchase* – credit card, charge card, cash, direct debit, standing order, credit terms, Switch, outright purchase, lease-hire, lease-purchase, negotiated price, sealed bid, and so on.
2. *Purchasing organization* – centralized or decentralized; structure and distribution of power in the DMU, which could apply equally to a household or to a business. For instance, the decision to purchase is made at one level, the choice of suitable suppliers is made at a technical level, the negotiation of price is left to the purchasing department and the final decision is taken by senior management.

The next step in the market segmentation process is to build a representative model of the market by recording all the unique combinations of 'what is bought' and to identify for each of these 'micro-segments' the different customer characteristics associated with them, or 'who' buys. This step often produces a large number of micro-segments, each of which should have a volume or value figure attached. These micro-segments can be reduced in number by distinguishing the important features from the unimportant features, and then removing the latter. A full explanation of this procedure can be found in Chapters 4 and 5 of *Market Segmentation: How to do it; How to Profit from it.*[1] Some preliminary screening at this stage is vital in order to reduce this long list of micro-segments down to manageable proportions.

WHY THEY BUY

The third stage of analysing customer behaviour is to gain an understanding of why customers behave the way they do in order that we can better sell to them.

Benefit analysis

The most useful and practical way of explaining customer behaviour has been found to be that of *benefit analysis*, or the identification of the benefits that customers seek in buying a product/service. For example, customer choice may be based on utility (product), economy (price), convenience and availability (place), emotion (promotion), or a combination (trade-off) of all of these. For how else can the success of firms like Rolls-Royce, Harrods, and many others be explained? Understanding the benefits sought by different groups of customers helps us to organize our marketing mix in the way most likely to appeal to our target market.

Differential benefits

While it is important for an organization to go through this process of benefit analysis, it is vital that, in doing so, *differential benefits* are identified. Differential benefits are those benefits that are not provided by competitors and which offer the greatest prospect of a competitive edge over them. If a company cannot identify any differential benefits, then either it is offering a product/service that is identical to the offerings of competitors (which is unlikely) or it has not done the benefit analysis thoroughly enough. Differential benefits hold the key to success, which will only follow where the differential benefits are actually desired by target customers.

Having identified the relevant benefits, it is now appropriate to take each significant micro-segment selected in the second stage (who buys and what they buy) and to list 'why' they buy. In other words, what benefits is each customer group seeking by buying what they buy?

Cluster analysis

Our market segmentation is now almost complete. The final step of the third stage ('why they buy') is the culmination of all previous steps in the segmentation process: to look for clusters of segments that share the same, or similar, needs and to apply to them the organization's minimum volume/value criteria in order to determine their viability.[2]

While this concluding step can be difficult and time-consuming, any care lavished on this part of the market segmentation process will pay handsome dividends at later stages of the marketing planning process. Following is a useful summary of the issues surrounding market segmentation.

What is bought	Physical characteristics
	Applications
	Where bought
	When bought
	How bought

Who buys	Demographics
	Socio-economics
	Brand loyalty
	Heavy/light users
	Personality, traits, lifestyles
Why	Benefits
	Attitudes
	Perceptions
	Preferences

SEGMENTATION CASE STUDIES

Two case studies are provided to illustrate how superior profitability can result from successful market segmentation.

Case Study 5: a national off-licence chain

In the early 1990s, a national off-licence chain with retail units in major shopping centres and local shopping parades was experiencing both a decline in customer numbers and a decline in average spend. The original formula for success of design, product range and merchandising, meticulously copied in each outlet, no longer appeared to be working. The chain had become a classic example of a business attempting to be all things to all people, but managing to satisfy very few of them. Rather than waiting and hoping for the best, the company embarked on a project designed to provide a deeper understanding of both its actual and potential customer base.

In the first stage of this study, one of the more sophisticated geodemographic packages (CCN's MOSAIC) was employed to profile the residential regions within each shop's catchment area. Not unexpectedly, many geodemographic differences were found to exist and the business quickly accepted that the same retail formula was unlikely to appeal to all of the various target markets represented.

Instead of looking at each shop separately, the company subjected the catchment area profiles for each shop to a clustering procedure in order to group similar catchment areas together. The cluster analysis produced 21 different catchment area groupings, each of which was then profiled in terms of its potential to buy different off-licence products using purchasing data from national surveys. (The company's own in-house retailing data would, of course, only reflect the purchasing patterns of its existing customers, or, at worst, a proportion of their requirements if the data was limited to the company's current product range.)

However, stocking the requisite range of products in the relevant geographical locations would not necessarily serve to attract the respective target markets. The company was already associated with one type of offer which, in addition to including a particular range of drinks, also included the basic design of the shops and overall merchandising.

The project, therefore, moved into a second phase, in which the target customers' attitudes and motivations to drinking were explored and relative values were attached to their choice determinants. This was achieved through an independently commissioned piece of market research and resulted in the market being categorized into a number of psychographic groups. The categories included 'happy and impulsive' shoppers, 'anxious and muddled' shoppers, 'reluctant but organized shoppers', and 'disorganized, extravagant shoppers'.

Linking the findings on customers' attitudes and motivations to the demographic data enabled the original 21 clusters to be refined into a few distinct segments, each of which required a different offer.

The company then had to decide between two alternative strategies:

(a) to focus on one segment using one brand and to re-locate its retail outlets accordingly through a closure and opening programme; or
(b) to develop a manageable portfolio of retailing brands, leaving the shops relatively intact, and re-brand, re-fit and re-stock as necessary.

The company decided to pursue the second strategy.

Realizing that geodemographic profiles can alter over time and that customer needs and attitudes can also change, the company now carefully monitors its market and is prepared to modify its brand portfolio accordingly. For the time being, the company's five retail brands satisfactorily suit the five target market segments identified and sit comfortably together in the same shopping centre.[3]

Case Study 6: amber nectar

A privately owned brewery in the UK was enjoying exceptional profitability in its industrial sector. In terms of output, it was by no means the largest brewery in the UK, and in terms of geographic cover, it only operated within a particular metropolitan area.

At one of the regular meetings of the Board, it was agreed that the company had clearly developed a very successful range of beers and it was time to expand into new geographic areas.

The expansion programme met with aggressive opposition from other brewers, particularly the very large brewers. This came as no great surprise to the Board who, before embarking on expansion, had built up a large 'war chest' of mainly past profits in order to finance the plan.

As with all good marketing-focused organizations, the progress of the marketing plan was regularly monitored against pre-set targets by a specially appointed task force headed by the company's chief executive. In addition, the sales and marketing director, who was a key member of the task force, held regular meetings with his own senior staff to ensure the continuous evaluation of the sales and marketing strategies being pursued.

The marketing plan severely underperformed and was eventually abandoned.

In the post-mortem that followed, the brewery discovered the reason behind its traditional success and why that success could not be extended to other areas of the UK. To its loyal customers, the beers' 'local' flavour was a prime attraction. Historically, the brewer's market had been the metropolitan area in which it operated, where competitors comprised local brewers in other areas or owners of established local breweries.

Without the brewery realizing it, the UK beer drinking market had already segmented itself. The brewer's segment was known as the 'Regional Chauvinist'. Thus the company was able to secure considerable market share and hence its long-held profitability. Had the company appreciated earlier the significance of this segmentation structure, it would have spent its 'war chest' more effectively and achieved its growth objectives.

Conclusions from case studies

These last two case studies illustrate the importance of intelligent segmentation in guiding companies towards successful marketing strategies. However, without the benefit of hindsight, the problem for most of us is how to arrive at a definition of 'market segmentation' that will enable us to create differential advantage. This has been the purpose of this chapter.

SUMMARY

In today's highly competitive world, few companies can afford to compete only on price, for a product has not yet been sold that someone, somewhere, cannot sell more cheaply – and anyway, in many markets it is rarely the cheapest product that succeeds. What this means is that we have to find some way of differentiating ourselves from the competition, and the answer lies in market segmentation.

The truth is that very few companies can afford to be 'all things to all people'. The main aim of market segmentation as part of the marketing process is to enable a firm to focus its marketing efforts on the most promising opportunities. But what may be an opportunity for Company A is not necessarily an opportunity for Company B. Thus the firm needs to develop a typology of the customer or segment it prefers, based on a myriad of criteria, including:

- Size of the firm
- Its consumption level
- Nature of its products/production/processes
- Motivations of the decision-makers (for example, desire to deal with big firms)
- Geographical location

The purpose of segmentation is to enable a company to either:

(a) define its markets broadly enough to ensure that its costs for key activities are competitive; or
(b) define its markets in such a way that it can develop specialized skills in serving them to overcome a relative cost disadvantage.

Both strategies must relate to a firm's distinctive competence and to those of its competitors.
 Correct market definition is crucial for:

- Share measurement
- Growth measurement
- The specification of target customers
- The recognition of relevant competitors
- The formulation of marketing objectives and strategies

The objectives of market segmentation are:

(a) to help identify appropriate marketing strategies through the analysis of market trends and buyer behaviour;
(b) to help determine relevant and realistic marketing and sales objectives;
(c) to help improve marketing decision-making by enabling managers to fully consider future options.

Notes

1. Malcolm McDonald and Ian Dunbar, *Market Segmentation: How to do it; How to Profit from it* (London: Macmillan, 1998).
2. A PC-based package called *Market Segment Master*, the registered trademark for this process, has been developed to support the segmentation process summarized in this chapter. For further details, please contact Professor Malcolm McDonald at Cranfield University School of Management, Cranfield, Bedford, MK43 OAL, UK (fax: (0) 1234 752691), or Ian Dunbar at the Market Segmentation Company, Chandos House, 26 North Street, Brighton, BN1 1EB, UK (fax: (0) 1273 737981).
3. This section is based on John Thornton, Market Planning Manager, Threshers, 'Market Segmentation from Bottoms Up', *Research Plus*, December 1993.

7 MARKET RESEARCH

Susan Baker

In this chapter:

- The market research process
- Market research methods
- The difference between researching products and services
- A review of research across multiple markets
- Case studies demonstrating the market research process

INTRODUCTION

Market research and market segmentation are key elements in understanding markets. Market research is the process that links the marketer to the market by providing information and insights to aid RM decision-making. Market research both drives the market segmentation process and is influenced by it. While most managers never have to carry out market survey work themselves, they do need to know how the market research process functions in order to exploit its value fully.

In particular, marketers adopting a multiple markets approach will wish to understand how the research process can assist in building long-term, profitable relationships in principal markets. The output of the research process should be twofold: first, an analysis which identifies key customer groups; and second, an understanding of what constitutes customer value among each of these groups and how that value can be created, delivered and leveraged in a way that is perceived to be superior to competitive offerings. It is especially important that appropriate research methods are used in order that the data generated is relevant to the strategic decisions that are to be made.

So, what is market research? It is the systematic gathering, recording and analysis of data related to the marketing of goods and services. It is used to identify marketing opportunities and obstacles, to generate marketing actions, and to monitor marketing performance. As such, market research is crucial to understanding RM as a process. Market research, however, should not be viewed as simply an input into better decision-making. When used correctly, it can become a significant marketing asset, conferring competitive advantage. Many companies have demonstrated an awareness of the value of market research by extending the remit of their market research teams to cover marketing information systems or even knowledge management.

THE MARKET RESEARCH PROCESS

The four steps of the market research process are:

- Definition of the marketing problem
- Development of the research plan
- Implementation of the research plan
- Interpretation and reporting of the research findings

The market research process is directed and managed by the marketing manager and the research manager. Its success lies in a clear statement of purpose. Both parties need to work closely together to define the marketing problem and to set the research objectives. This initial step is usually the hardest part of the market research process and requires a degree of understanding on the part of the marketer of the researcher's job and vice versa.

Having established and agreed the research goals, the researcher is charged with drawing up the research plan. This outlines the sources of data (whether existing data will be used or new data will be required), research approaches, contact methods, sampling and research instruments, timetable, and costs. The written research plan can be discussed and further refined prior to its formal adoption.

The researcher then implements the plan, using external data collection agencies where necessary. (It is unusual for an organization to hold all the requisite information resources in-house.) Data collection is generally the most expensive part of the research process and also the part most subject to error.

Once collected, the data is processed and analysed. Finally, the researcher returns to the marketing manager with an interpretation and report of the research findings. This usually comprises a written report, although advances in software design, such as those offered by Memphis Survey Explorer or Pulsar, mean that results can now be presented in a user-friendly fashion on-screen. Interpretation is all about the researcher elucidating the findings to provide the marketer with a view on what the research results mean, rather than an outline of what the respondents actually said.

The research findings are then fed into the process of strategy formulation, as the resultant implications will have an impact on current activities and resource allocation.

INTERNAL VERSUS EXTERNAL RESEARCH

The marketer rarely begins the marketing planning process with a blank sheet, for internal market research based on sales figures or earlier market studies often provides a good deal of background data. As discussed in Chapter 2, there are frequently a number of intermediaries linking brand owners with consumers and they can be used to provide relevant data. Sales personnel and distributors can be particularly rich sources of up-to-date data.

The advances in database management that have been so instrumental in enabling organizations to pursue a RM strategy have had a significant impact on the breadth and depth of internal market research activities. Although many researchers view the development of database marketing with suspicion, believing it comes close to selling under the guise of market research, there is an inexorable trend towards using database marketing and market research techniques in combination. Technological advancements and the increasing demand for market information by both young and well-established companies have served to heighten the potential and profile of market research based on marketing databases.

This convergence of research provision and information demand has brought about the notion of the 'T-cube'. Imagine a cube: the top surface represents the whole population and the side axis indicates the depth of knowledge about individuals. Lifestyle databases, such as those run by Claritas, hold data on almost every household in the country, though the data is fairly basic. In contrast, consumer panels, such as AGB's Superpanel, hold information in enormous detail, but only on 10 000 individuals. The 'T' is formed where the same individuals appear in both a database and a consumer panel. This 'coincidence' makes it possible to identify patterns and to construct models of customer behaviour which can be used to target consumers who share relevant, similar characteristics.

There are, however, a number of issues that need to be clarified before the creation of such models of consumer buyer behaviour becomes acceptable, including that of ethics. Research respondents usually agree to take part in studies if a degree of anonymity is preserved. Because the modelling techniques described here can lead to the identification of individuals, care must be taken to respect and protect the rights of individuals whenever gathering or using information.

External market research, on the other hand, is conducted within the market and the wider competitive environment in which the company operates. Compared to internal market research, it generally accounts for the majority of total market research expenditure.

PRIMARY AND SECONDARY MARKET RESEARCH

Collecting information directly from individual respondents is known as primary research. This is in contrast to secondary, or desk, research, which involves scanning available information sources to see what has already been published. These might include: market reports, such as Mintel Marketing Intelligence, Keynote, and Financial Times Management Reports; company/competitor literature; press articles; and economic, social and demographic trend data. When an up-to-date piece of secondary data exists on a target subject and an analysis of a market is presented in a way that is relevant to the research, this is fortuitous. It is more usually the case that secondary data is out-of-date and markets are not analysed from the point of view of an individual organization's competencies. Trying to understand a market using only secondary data can provide key frameworks, but will probably give an insufficient amount of detail on buyer motivations and characteristics.

The remainder of the chapter deals with primary research, which may be qualitative, quantitative or quali-quant (a combination of both).

Qualitative market research

Qualitative market research is used largely to answer the 'why' question: 'Why do people buy what they buy?' It is exploratory or diagnostic in nature and usually involves only small numbers of respondents. Selections of people from key or different target markets are chosen by means of a sampling process. They are not meant to be representative of the larger population, but are intended to reflect the profile of known or desired customers. Non-customers may also be consulted for their independent input. In-depth interviews with these selected individuals are carried out and the data is then collated, analysed and interpreted. Hard and fast conclusions cannot be drawn from qualitative research because it is impressionistic, rather than definitive. Its value is in providing an idea of the characteristic traits of constituent members of target markets.

Qualitative market research techniques vary widely. One way of gathering information is through using 'focus groups', or group discussions led by experts on specific topics of interest. Focus groups are used in about 20 per cent of all market research projects and account for approximately £156 million per annum of market research expenditure in the UK. The role of focus groups has moved beyond the traditional applications (to better understand consumer brands or to improve the development of advertising and new products) to other arenas including politics, the media, the arts and even the monarchy. Here, they tend to be used to sample opinions and attitudes on particular subjects: for example, is the royal family 'modern' enough, or should a certain political party pursue a more populist policy?

Two key issues facing qualitative researchers concern validation and negative publicity. Validation is the act of ascertaining that respondents are who they say they are and that they do use or prefer the products and services that they claim to. Growth in the negative publicity surrounding this type of market research may be attributable to the poor quality of many research reports, which has given it a reputation for simply stating the obvious.

While focus groups and in-depth interviews form the core of qualitative market research, there are a number of alternative techniques, such as using friendship groups to understand peer pressures or studying couples to understand different attitudes and roles in certain domestic purchasing situations.

The advantages of qualitative research are that it: enables a thorough investigation of customers' views and market trends; offers a flexible approach; generates data which is based on respondents' own language and which can be used as an exploratory step in the research plan; can be carried out quickly; and provides easily accessible data for decision-making purposes. The disadvantages of this approach are that it: produces results that are not necessarily representative of the wider population; involves a relatively higher cost per respondent; and does not produce quantitative results.

Quantitative market research

Quantitative market research largely provides answers to questions concerning 'who, what, where, when, and how many'. It generally involves large numbers of people and offers the opportunity to measure responses. Respondents are usually chosen on a quota basis to create a representative selection of the larger population. Interviews are highly structured and seek to establish statistical evidence of market preferences and trends. Quantitative market research therefore enables more definitive conclusions to be drawn.

Omnibus surveys are a staple form of quantitative market research. These surveys are programmed to run regularly and client companies 'buy' questions in them. Thus omnibus surveys can contain questions on a number of different subjects, enabling clients to reach a representative cross-section of the population or a minority group within it. For example, clients can buy into surveys as diverse as Northern Ireland's youth omnibus surveys (1000 respondents aged 11 to 24) on a biennial basis or a telephone research programme that calls 1000 adults in the UK every weekend. For the latter, questions can be registered as late as Friday morning, with results returned on Monday morning. Other surveys work internationally. Capibus Europe, for instance, carries out personal in-home interviews among a controlled sample of 6000 adults in six European countries (France, Germany, Great Britain, Italy, Spain and the Netherlands). Clients have the facility to place customized questions in each weekly survey in any combination of countries.

Other techniques for collecting quantitative data include consumer panels (for tracking the effectiveness of television adverts), trade-offs (used in product testing), and continuous surveys (used to measure customer satisfaction levels).

Quali-quant market research

Over recent years, a hybrid type of research known as 'quali-quant' has emerged. This investigative approach involves mini-depth interviews, which are carried out at a central location with people recruited from the street. Around 60 respondents take part in 15–20 minute interviews conducted by qualitative moderators. Alternatively, they may be semi-structured interviews carried out face-to-face or over the telephone by a highly trained quantitative interviewer, using a sample of about 100 people. A large number of open-ended questions are usually included to provide richer data.

In the words of John Archer, director, BJM Research & Consultancy Ltd, these hybrid research approaches serve to 'put some bones into the jelly of qualitative research'. The quali-quant approach promotes hard numbers and normative yardsticks alongside the in-depth interpretation of spontaneous responses to open-ended questions.

CONTACT METHODS

Once the market research approach has been decided, it is then necessary to determine what means of communication will be used to survey the selected sample of respondents. The three standard contact methods are via mail, telephone and personal interviews. A fourth method, using the Internet, is fast gaining in popularity.

Postal questionnaires have many advantages. Large amounts of data can be collected at a low cost per respondent. Further, respondents may be inclined to give more open and honest answers as the process provides a degree of anonymity. However, this survey method suffers from a lack of flexibility, for it requires very clear and simply worded questions that are presented in a set order. Response rates to postal questionnaires tend to be low and it can take a long time for postal responses to be returned.

Telephone interviewing offers the best control of the research sample as interviewers can ask to speak directly to respondents who have the desired characteristics. Interviewers can also help respondents to clearly understand the questions being put to them and can ensure that only the most appropriate questions are presented. Response rates to telephone interviews tend to be high, although the cost per interview is greater than the cost of a mailed questionnaire. Computer aided telephone interviewing (CATI) is becoming a preferred technique as it enables data to be entered at the point of interview, thus saving time and minimizing errors. CATI systems essentially direct the interviewer at all stages of the interview by presenting interviewers with a script on-screen. This enables all inputs to be processed immediately and introduces an element of consistency.

Personal interviewing may involve the interviewer questioning an individual or a group. People may be interviewed in their homes or offices, in the street or in shopping malls. Personal interviews can last from a few minutes to several hours. Sometimes a small payment is made in return for the respondent's time. This 'in person' method of data collection offers excellent flexibility and the opportunity to collect large amounts of data. The accuracy rate of responses is enhanced by the fact that the interviewer is present to explain unclear questions or to pursue general responses to obtain more detailed information. Personal interviewing is, however, a very costly contact method and can be blighted by sampling problems. Interviewers have to be highly trained in techniques of recruiting respondents to overcome issues such as a bias towards certain types of respondent. The use of computer aided personal interviewing (CAPI) is increasingly prevalent. Again, as with CATI, it allows data to be entered at the point of interview.

Use of the Internet as a means of collecting data is still in its infancy, but is fast expanding. The Internet offers a facility to collect data of a reasonable quality rapidly, immediately and at a very low cost. However, as with a postal questionnaire, it is difficult to know exactly who is in the on-line sample. Also, as the Internet is a more indirect contact method, response rates may be low.

It is difficult to say which of these contact methods is best as the chosen method will depend to a large extent on the client's particular information needs and research budget as well as the speed of response required. Cultural factors can also influence the type of contact method preferred. In the majority of European countries, for example, researchers usually conduct face-to-face interviews to some extent. This is especially true in Greece and Ireland, but less so in Sweden and Finland where telephone interviewing takes precedence. Postal surveys are carried out almost as much as face-to-face interviews in the Netherlands, but scarcely at all in Ireland, Italy and Spain.

Whatever research method is adopted, it should be carried out with accuracy, thoroughness and professionalism. High research standards will ensure that the findings are valuable and usable. It is important to remember that the aim of market research is to help direct business strategy, which seeks to build and improve relationships with consumers by leveraging product and service quality to have maximum impact on consumer satisfaction levels. The following case study demonstrates the crucial role that research plays in developing business strategy.

Case Study 1: Abbey National – the role of research in developing strategy

Abbey National developed a research brief to investigate consumer perceptions of key brands in the financial and retail markets. The investigation was specifically aimed at finding out what differentiation existed and what consumers were looking for in brands so that Abbey National could successfully design new advertising and in-branch mer-chandising material. The company worked with an advertising agency as well as separate qualitative and quantitative agencies on the £200 000 research project. Over 200 product and service initiatives were evaluated and 20 were tested quantitatively. The study identified those initiatives which customers favoured most: staff not taking their lunch hour when customers take theirs; reducing queues through the introduction of 200 express service assistants; fair banking; flexible mortgages; and the consistent use of plain English in all communications.

The project served to detect the most popular and promising of Abbey National's brands, some of which were then further developed and promoted in a television campaign using the strapline, 'Because life's complicated enough'. Abbey National's advert sought to demonstrate the company's desire to make things easier for its customers and thus to differentiate its offerings from those of competitors. As a result of the study, an ongoing programme was put in place to monitor Abbey National's perceived image and advertising success so that other customer-focused initiatives could be developed. (*Research*, February 1998).

TESTING PRODUCTS AND SERVICES

Brand owners take the testing of products and services very seriously. Understanding how consumers react to products and services is critical to the future success of both existing and new brand offerings, and is key to the development of acquisition and retention strategies.

Products

Existing – as opposed to new – products are subjected to benchmarking and product formulation tests. Benchmarking involves assessing how the brand is performing against competing brands. This comparative knowledge is critical to maintaining product advantage. Formulation tests are carried out by brand owners to gain customer feedback on new recipe specifications. They can be carried out with in-home or hall tests. In-home tests are where respondents are given a product to trial at home. Hall tests are where large numbers of respondents are invited into a public building or hotel to try out the product then and there. Nescafé, for example, chooses to in-home test its coffee products in order that evaluations benefit from a realistic environment. Where a product is not normally consumed at home, hall testing is probably a better option. Hall testing is also appropriate where products are consumed 'as bought', as in the case of chocolates or chilled desserts. Further product testing considerations include whether the product under trial should be 'paired' with another product, be tested on its own (monadic testing), or be examined on a blind or a branded basis. A blind test (where the brand is unknown) has the advantage of determining how the product performs away from the influence of branding and packaging, while a branded test (where the brand is known) provides insight into the way that consumers perceive the brand.

Services

The testing of services requires a different approach from the testing of products. This is because services, unlike packaged goods, are more intangible and are experienced at the point of sale in a specific retail environment where they are delivered by trained staff. To test the quality of services, anonymous, contracted customers, known as 'mystery shoppers', are used. The UK mystery shopping market, in all its forms (whether mystery diners, drinkers or guests), is worth around £35 million per year, having grown from a very small turnover ten years ago. Mystery shopping is used to measure the service performance of the organization from the customer's perspective, thereby enabling the sources of satisfaction and dissatisfaction among the employees and customers of service providers to be better understood.

Researchers involved in the testing of services will be trained in techniques of observation, memory retention and memory recall where research interviews are not recorded on audio or video tape. For example, *Which? Magazine*, in its October 1998 edition, reported on a survey where briefed researchers visited 66 branches of different mortgage lenders to test the quality of their advisory services. Without disclosing their true intent, the researchers booked interviews at the selected branches, claiming that they had found a property, but wanted advice before committing to the purchase. The researchers were given one of two domestic situations to portray: first time buyers and existing owners. The report concluded that some lenders were not offering high quality advice and that the experiences of the mystery shoppers clearly demonstrated variability in the services offered.

MARKET RESEARCH ACROSS MULTIPLE MARKETS

The six markets that feature most prominently in RM are discussed in detail in Chapter 2, and are referred to here solely in respect to their significance to market research.

Customer markets

Market research has traditionally been deployed in consumer markets, particularly by aggressive consumer goods manufacturers who, in many respects, have shaped the research industry as it exists today. However, market research is increasingly being used by new industries. For example, the growth in the use of market research by major law firms mirrors the rise in demand for legal services to address issues of customer care.

Internal markets

Employee research is also taking a firm hold as the role of market research in human resource management is increasingly seen as critical to good management practice. For organizations embarking on employee research activities, it is important when 'selling in' the idea to establish the trust and cooperation of employees, as they may naturally be reluctant to divulge any information which might jeopardize their employment or relations with colleagues. Additionally, management may be unsure about how to react to any negative feedback and therefore company policy and procedure should anticipate the possible research outcomes. Employee research programmes that track results over time provide a useful tool for examining and improving management practices.

Influencer markets

Research in influencer markets involves interviewing key opinion-formers in order to gain their views on the organization concerned. Assessing corporate reputation in this way can help to identify where detrimental or incongruous messages and images are being communicated to different sectors. This external viewpoint can then be used to position the organization more effectively within the market. However, this type of market research does require gaining the trust of the respondents and handling all information discreetly.

Recruitment markets

Recruitment markets – made up of potential employees – can also be surveyed to assess external attitudes towards the organization. It may be, for example, that the organization wishes to raise its profile among new university graduates in order to attract more highly qualified and committed employees. Tracking the perceptions of potential or prospective employees enables the organization's performance to be measured over time.

Supplier markets

Supplier markets are a much overlooked source of information. Given the importance of supply chain management (see Chapter 6) and the value of buyer-seller collaboration, it is essential for the organization to acquire as much intelligence as it can on its relationships with suppliers.

Referral markets

Most referrals come from satisfied customers and therefore customer satisfaction research is usually placed high on the marketing agenda. This priority is driven by a growing appreciation of how improved customer satisfaction can have a dramatic effect on the profitability of a business (see Chapter 8).

It is estimated that customer satisfaction research represents around 8 per cent of all UK research expenditure. Customer Relationship Management, or CRM as it is known, utilizes a range of technologies from self-administered tent cards (mini questionnaires made available on restaurant tables or near shop tills) and surveys undertaken over the telephone or face-to-face in shopping malls, to interactive telephone response mechanisms and use of the Internet.

INTERNATIONAL ISSUES

Various macro-economic trends are leading to a convergence in consumer priorities and needs, but it is too simplistic to assume that the RM process therefore becomes easier. Shared aspirations among different consumer markets have developed due to increased personal wealth, opportunities for travel, enhanced communications and product availability. The emergence of niche markets, which transcend conventional market borders, has also provided further marketing challenges. It is every marketer's goal to build relationships with consumers across the largest market segments possible in today's increasingly unified global markets. However, as highlighted in Chapter 4, differences in consumer buyer behaviour within individual countries can trip up the most experienced brand owners.

The market research process is no less subject to the idiosyncrasies of national culture. For example, even by the mid-1990s, data collection on households and families in the European Union was by no means compatible across the different countries. Using the age of children living at home as a unit of analysis was fraught with difficulties: in Denmark, Finland and Sweden, children were considered members of the household up to the age of 18, while the age delineation was 25 in Luxembourg.

The main challenge facing global brand owners is how the marketing mix should be adapted to local market conditions, if at all. The answer requires a sound understanding of market conditions as well as a cultural sensitivity. The fundamental question for researchers, therefore, is how best to organize research investigations to assist global brand owners. When undertaking international market research, there is much to be gained from commissioning a specialist agency with a global perspective and, more importantly, direct local expertise.

The costs of undertaking local market research vary around the world, as highlighted by the 1997 ESOMAR (European Society for Opinion and Market Research) Prices Study. This study was based on quotes received from Society members for six hypothetical projects, involving different types of research. Three projects were quantitative (a usage and attitude study, a tracking survey, and a hall test), while two were qualitative (one involving groups, the other individual interviews), and one was a business-to-business telephone survey. The study concluded that research budgets cannot be allocated equitably across international markets.

The research findings showed that, overall, Japan is the most expensive country for local research, followed by Brazil and the USA. The lowest research prices were recorded in India, the majority of Asian countries, and Central and Eastern Europe. Research prices in Western Europe are, on average, half the level of those in Japan and, on balance, the northern countries of Western Europe are more expensive than the southern ones. In general, prices for quantitative research tend towards the extremes of being expensive or cheap, while prices for quantitative research and business-to-business research projects attract a more even spread.

ORGANIZATIONAL ISSUES

The way in which organizations organize their market research activities also varies. Many companies outsource most elements of their research processes, while others prefer to develop their own research expertise and outsource very little of their market research. Obviously, there are advantages and disadvantages with each approach. The former may well provide the organization with a constant flow of new ideas, whereas organizations that carry out the majority of their own research will, over time, accumulate an extensive in-house expertise which could serve as a source of competitive advantage.

While managing the market research process may be considered a complex issue, the dissemination of findings is usually even more so. The temptation to use market research findings selectively to support certain strategic decisions instead of using the analysis to lead marketing developments lies at the heart of much poor marketing. The following case study illustrates how P&G intends to further improve dissemination within the company by focusing research processes on product marketing centres in a management matrix.

Case Study 2: P&G – the sleeping giant wakes

In 1998, P&G initiated far-reaching changes within its market research operations. These changes formed part of a corporate-wide structural and cultural revolution, led by the Dutchman, Durk Jager, in the implementation of the corporate vision entitled 'Organization 2005'. The overall intention was to bring P&G products more quickly to the market place and to fast-track the company to achieve the promise it made in 1997 to double turnover to $70 billion by 2005. Consequently, P&G's old regional business structure was replaced with seven product-based global business units which were serviced by eight regionally-based market development organizations (see Table 7.1). The 75-year-old market research department was renamed Consumer & Market Knowledge (CMK) to signify the importance of the changes.

Table 7.1   P&G's new business structure

Structure	Location
Corporate Function	based in Cincinnati
Consumer & Market Knowledge	
Global Business Units	
Babycare	Cincinnati
Beautycare	Cincinnati
Fabric & Home care	Cincinnati
Fem Pro	Kobe
Food & Beverage	Cincinnati
Toilet Tissue	Cincinnati
Healthcare	Cincinnati
Market Development Organizations	
Latin America	Mexico
North America	Cincinnati
Asia Pacific	Kobe
Western Europe	Brussels
Central and Eastern Europe	Brussels
Middle East	Brussels
Africa	Brussels
General Export	Brussels

P&G boasts a number of longstanding relationships with suppliers of market research, including one dating back 51 years. The company has encouraged its roster of *ad hoc* agencies to form four consortia, made up of three access panel groups (Consumerscope, Target and IPSOS/NFO) and a collection of independent agencies (Nexus). In each case, P&G is the core client. The company applies methodological standardization across the world wherever possible, focusing not so much on the differences between consumers, but on their similarities. Says P&G's senior European head of research, Mahmoud Aboul-Fath: 'The Portuguese are not so different from Spanish consumers and the Swiss, Austrians and Germans have more in common than they actually have differences, so there is no need to repeat the research in every country.'

The emphasis on employing different research approaches is also forecast to change. In order to gain richer insights into consumer behaviour, P&G intends to use more qualitative research among smaller groups of consumers than hitherto. This faith in small-scale research is based on experience, which shows that research results can be validated in the same way as knowledge gained from research based on large, representative samples. This new approach will also involve a focus on key brands, the use of more continuous research (in terms of brand tracking and market measurement) and more efficient mining of existing data held in databases (adapted from 'The sleeping giant wakes', *Research*, March 1999).

SUMMARY

Market research is the process that links the marketer to the market, and its output – market intelligence – is the lifeblood of the marketing organization.

Market research is a structured process made up of four steps: defining the problem, developing the research plan, implementing the research plan, and interpreting and reporting the findings.

While a good deal of data can be generated from internal sources of information, the majority of the organization's market research budget will probably be spent on gathering information from external sources, involving both primary and secondary research activities. Primary research can either be qualitative (impressionistic, rather than definitive), quantitative (representational and statistical) or quali-quant (a combination of the two).

There are four contact methods for conducting research: via mail, telephone, personal interviews, and the Internet. Increasingly, computer technology is being used to support these methods.

The testing of products differs greatly from the testing of services. Products have traditionally been tested in classic in-home or hall tests, while methods for testing services have created a vast mystery shopper sector within the market research industry.

Market research is more commonly used within certain markets: namely, customer markets, internal markets, influencer markets, recruitment markets, supplier markets, and referral markets. When adopting a multiple markets approach, the type and extent of market research employed should reflect the nature of the market to be analysed and its importance within the wider business context. International market research activities must be culturally sensitive.

In terms of organization, the tendency to use market research agencies as data suppliers depends on the remit and expertise of the client company's in-house market research department.

Reference

Research, monthly magazine of the Market Research Society.

CUSTOMER RETENTION

Adrian Payne

In this chapter:

- A strategic approach to customer retention
- Why customer retention is so profitable
- The relationship marketing ladder of customer loyalty
- A framework for customer retention improvement
- A case study linking customer retention and profitability

CUSTOMER RETENTION AND PROFITABILITY

This chapter is concerned with developing a strategic approach to customer retention and achieving long-term customer profitability. First, we discuss the evidence supporting the need for improved customer retention. Second, we examine the RM ladder of customer loyalty and show how marketing effort needs to be balanced between customer acquisition and customer retention activities. Finally, we outline a process for improving customer retention, which has three steps: measuring customer retention, identifying causes of defection, and taking corrective action to improve customer retention. As part of this process, we consider why keeping some customers is more important than keeping others, and how market segmentation plays an important role in identifying those customers that are most likely to be of benefit to the company.

Many researchers have suggested that it costs around five times more to get a new customer than it does to keep an existing one. Despite this finding, many organizations have traditionally focused their marketing activity on acquiring new customers, rather than retaining existing customers. In part, this is due to cultural pressures, where customer acquisition has been rewarded to a greater extent than building long-term relationships with existing customers. Also, until fairly recently, there was little research that evaluated the relative financial benefits of customer acquisition versus customer retention. In 1990, Reichheld and Sasser published some revealing research findings,[1] which demonstrated the financial impact of customer retention. They found that there was a high correlation between customer retention and profitability across a range of industries. Even a small increase in customer retention produced a dramatic and positive effect on profitability. Their research indicated that a 5 percentage points increase in customer retention yielded a very high improvement in

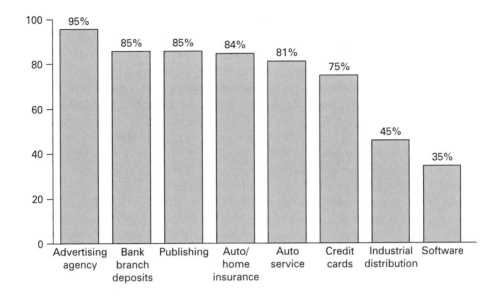

Figure 8.1   NPV profit impact of a 5 percentage points increase in customer retention for selected businesses

Source: Based on F. A. Reichheld (1994), 'Loyalty and the Renaissance of Marketing', *Marketing Management*, vol. 2, no. 2, pp. 10–21.

profitability in NPV terms. Figure 8.1 shows that this NPV profit impact varies from 35 per cent to 95 per cent among a selection of businesses.

Why should retention have such a great effect on profitability? Reichheld and Sasser suggested a number of reasons to explain their findings.

1.   Acquiring new customers involves costs that can be significant and it may take some years to turn a new customer into a profitable customer.
2.   As customers become more satisfied and confident in their relationship with a supplier, they are more likely to give the supplier a larger proportion of their business, or 'share of wallet'.
3.   As the relationship with a customer develops, there is greater mutual understanding and collaboration, which produces efficiencies that lower operating costs. Sometimes customers are willing to integrate their IT systems, including planning, ordering and scheduling, with those of their suppliers and this serves to further reduce costs.
4.   Satisfied customers are more likely to refer others, which promotes profit generation as the cost of acquisition of these new customers is dramatically reduced. In some industries, customer advocacy can play a very important role in acquiring new customers, particularly when there is a high risk involved in choosing a supplier.
5.   Loyal customers can be less price-sensitive and may be less likely to defect due to price increases. This is especially true in business-to-business markets where the relationship with the supplier becomes more valued and switching costs increase.

However, research by Payne and Frow[2] suggests that managers are slow to implement changes in marketing activities to emphasize customer retention. They surveyed the marketing practices of marketing directors and senior marketing managers in 225 UK organizations and examined how these organizations spent their marketing budgets. Their study found that the greatest percentage (41 per cent) of marketing budgets was spent on customer acquisition, while only 23 per cent was spent on customer retention. Given that the majority of firms surveyed were in mature industries, the research raises doubts about whether marketing budgets are being allocated in a balanced manner between customer acquisition and retention.

Payne and Frow also investigated which measures managers consider to be important and which they use to evaluate their RM activities. Their research findings suggest that, although many organizations say they understand the importance of customer retention and its links with profitability, very few measure the economic value of their customer retention strategies. Customer acquisition and customer satisfaction are much more frequently measured than are customer retention and profit per customer.

We are not suggesting that new customers are unimportant; indeed, they are essential for sustained success. However, a balance is needed between the marketing efforts directed towards existing and new customers. Also, customers vary in their attractiveness for retention. Some customers are likely to yield greater long-term profitability than others, and marketing strategies should reflect this fact.

THE RELATIONSHIP MARKETING LADDER OF CUSTOMER LOYALTY

The RM ladder of customer loyalty shown in Figure 8.2 emphasizes the two main marketing tasks of attracting new customers and retaining existing customers.

It is apparent that many organizations put their main marketing emphasis on the lower rungs of the ladder: identifying 'prospects' and attempting to turn them into 'customers'. Organizations often neglect the higher relationship rungs, where one-time customers are turned into regular 'clients', who are progressively converted into 'supporters' and then into active 'advocates' for the company. Finally, in a business-to-business context, the opportunity may exist to turn advocates into 'partners'.

However, moving customers up the loyalty ladder is not a simple process. Organizations need to have explicit and in-depth knowledge of the customer's requirements and how these may change over time. Also, organizations need to identify how to create the additional value that will successfully differentiate their offers from those of competitors.

Essentially, the only way to elevate someone from 'customer' to 'advocate' status is to replace customer satisfaction with customer delight, by offering a quality of service that exceeds expectations. Research by Jones and Sasser[3] on customer loyalty and customer satisfaction reached two major conclusions: only highly satisfied customers (for example, a '5' on a five-point scale) can be

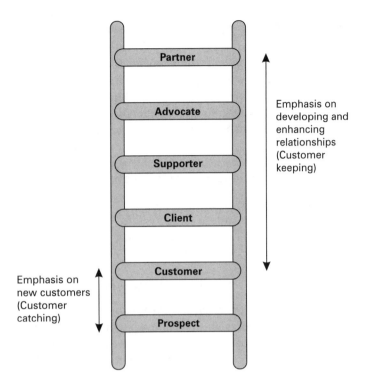

Figure 8.2   The RM ladder of customer loyalty

considered truly loyal; and customers who are just satisfied (for example, a '4' on a five-point scale) are only slightly more loyal than customers who are thoroughly dissatisfied (for example, a '1' on a five-point scale).

The RM ladder highlights the need to balance the allocation of limited marketing resources between retaining existing customers and acquiring new customers in order to achieve maximum long-term profitability. This balance is not often reached and usually too much of the marketing budget is devoted to attracting new customers.

In another piece of research (unpublished), the author explored the practices of managers in 120 services businesses to gain their views on how they were allocating their marketing budgets. The responses suggested that approximately 80 per cent of the managers considered they spent too much time and money on marketing efforts aimed at winning new customers and too little on keeping customers. About 10 per cent felt they concentrated too much on existing customers and too little on acquiring new customers. Only 10 per cent of respondents believed they had achieved the right balance between customer acquisition and customer retention.

Given the dramatic impact that improved customer retention can have on business profitability and the fact that many organizations continue to place too much emphasis on customer acquisition, there is a strong need for a structured approach which organizations can follow that leads to enhanced retention and profitability.

A FRAMEWORK FOR CUSTOMER RETENTION IMPROVEMENT

Figure 8.3 shows a framework for customer retention improvement, involving three major steps: the measurement of customer retention; the identification of root causes of defection and key service issues; and the development of corrective action to improve retention. Each of these steps consists of a number of critical tasks, which are now examined in turn.

Step 1: measurement of customer retention

The measurement of retention rates for existing customers is the first step in improving customer loyalty and profitability. It involves two major tasks – measurement of customer retention rates and profitability analysis by segment.

Customer retention measurement

The customer retention rate can be defined, at its simplest level, as the percentage of customers at the beginning of a period that still remain customers at the end of the period. This definition is appropriate for products such as motor insurance where the customer selects either a given company or one of its competitors. However, it should be recognized that other more complex definitions of customer retention rate might be appropriate (for instance, a customer may bank with more than one bank or shop at more than one supermarket).

Where customers buy products or services from many suppliers, it is necessary to weight customers by the amount they spend with a given organization (their 'share of wallet'). Also, it is important to track *changes* in customer spend, for apparently high customer retention rates can hide serious problems. For example, there are a number of banks that boast high levels of customer retention but which, in fact, have high levels of account dormancy. Customers may have defected to other banks with the majority of their business, but have not bothered to close their original accounts.

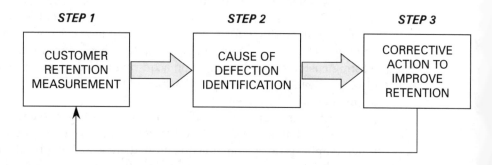

Figure 8.3   Customer retention improvement framework

To measure customer retention, a number of dimensions need to be analysed in detail. These include the measurement of customer retention rates over time, by market segment, and in terms of the product/service offered. If customers buy from a number of suppliers, share of wallet should also be identified.

Segment profitability analysis

The second task within this initial step is to ensure that relevant segmentation analysis is undertaken. It must not be assumed that companies will wish to retain *all* their customers. Some customers may actually cost too much money to service, and may never prove to be worthwhile and profitable. Clearly, it would be inadvisable to invest further in these customers. Market segmentation is examined in greater detail in Chapter 6.

Different customer segments need to be considered on the basis of both present and future profitability. Increasing customer retention of the most attractive segments should become a critical element of an organization's strategy. This will help identify the type and frequency of the marketing activity that should be directed towards the different segments. We term this activity 'developing a segmented service strategy'. To assist with this task, an index can be developed and used to grade the customer base according to profitability so that appropriate strategies can be devised to manage customer relationships most effectively.

Using such an approach may present some surprises. For example, a large insurance company discovered that it was not high net worth individuals that were providing the largest future profit streams, although this group had been the focus of much of the company's customer retention activity. Instead, segment profitability analysis showed that schoolteachers were actually the most profitable market segment. Previously, the company had never considered schoolteachers a worthwhile market segment and had directed little marketing activity towards them.

Measurement systems are needed which allow managers to analyse their customer base, to identify the profit potential within each segment and then to develop strategies to retain the most profitable prospects. An important part of this evaluation process is establishing both the existing and potential 'customer lifetime value'. Customer lifetime value is defined as the net present value of the future profit flow over a customer's lifetime.

The stage reached in the customer's life cycle can also impact profit potential. This will influence the pattern as well as the amount of customer profitability. For example, early in the customer's life cycle, profitability may be low. Marketing activity may be directed at relationship-building and gaining a greater share of wallet. However, later in the life cycle, when there is greater understanding and trust in the customer relationship, profitability may increase. During the advanced stages of the customer's life cycle marketing activity may decline, if the customer's needs change and other suppliers are able to provide greater value or a more appropriate offering.

Research by Bain & Company, highlighted the need for management to adopt a stronger focus on customer retention. However, this study did not allow managers to identify the value of retention in different businesses and for specific customer segments. Recently, Payne and Rickard[4] developed a model for calculating the profit impact of retention by customer segment within individual organizations. The model allows informed investment decisions to be made on how to balance retention and acquisition strategies, and which customer segments should be the focus of these strategies. This model has been used to review the profit potential of the customer segments of a large UK service company. Four key consumer segments were identified, each with very different profiles in terms of socio-economics, expected switching behaviour, and customer characteristics. Future profitability was modelled for each segment on the basis of both existing retention rates and improved retention rates, varying between 1 and 9 percentage points across the different segments according to the proposed segmented service strategy. This modelling revealed a significant increase in overall gross profit, before costs of improved service, of 48 per cent at Year 5 and 71 per cent at Year 10. The results within each of the four segments varied considerably because of differences in the improvement in retention rates and other inputs to the model.

The outcome of this first step should be a clear definition of customer retention, a measurement of present customer retention rates, and an understanding of the existing and future profit potential for each market segment.

Step 2: identification of causes of defection and key service issues

Once the customer retention and profit improvement potential has been measured, the second step in Figure 8.3 can be taken. This involves the identification of the underlying causes of customer defection. Four analytical approaches are useful in undertaking this task. These include root cause of defection analysis, trade-off analysis, competitive benchmarking, and customer complaint analysis.

Root cause of defection analysis

Traditional marketing research into customer satisfaction does not always provide accurate answers as to *why* customers abandon one supplier for another. All too often customer satisfaction questionnaires are poorly designed, superficial and fail to address the key issues, forcing respondents to tick pre-determined response choices. For example, a questionnaire for a major high street bank asked departing customers why they were closing their accounts. Among the available multiple-choice answers was 'the account is no longer required'. Not surprisingly, the vast majority of respondents ticked this box because it represented a safe and easy answer and none of the alternative answers addressed the real reasons for defection.

The root causes of customer defections should be clearly identified, for it is only by understanding them that the company can begin to implement a successful customer retention programme. It is imperative that root cause of defection analysis be undertaken by specially trained researchers. For example, customers may say that they no longer frequent a particular supermarket because the prices are too high, while in reality customers have been put off by unhelpful staff, long queues, difficulty in finding products on the shelves, and so on.

Trade-off analysis

It is also important to undertake research to identify the key customer service dimensions that result in customers being retained. This can be accomplished through trade-off analysis, which allows the different service features identified by the customer to be 'traded off' against each other in order to establish the customer's service priorities. The supplier can then use this information to develop service strategies that match customer needs and priorities. Trade-off analysis is described in more detail in Christopher, Payne and Ballantyne.[5]

Competitive benchmarking

Competitive benchmarking enables companies to compare their performance and that of their competitors on critical elements of customer service and retention performance. It is then possible to establish service standards that match or exceed those of competitors. The search for best practice may involve questions such as: what is the maximum length of time a customer should be left waiting in a queue? Should employees be expected to answer the telephone within three rings? What level of product knowledge should employees be expected to have about the products and services that they sell? Service standards are best set by examining how competitors perform and focusing on the service dimensions that are most important to customers.

Customer complaint analysis

Another useful way of identifying key service issues is to analyse customers' complaints. Customer complaint analysis not only highlights possible causes of customer defections, but also acts as an early warning system, enabling the company to resolve problems with customers early on and to implement preventive action to avoid the same problems recurring. Some companies are now developing 'customer recovery teams' which immediately move into action when a likely defector is identified. The recovery team is charged with finding out the real reasons for the customer's dissatisfaction. It can also be empowered to come up with solutions and to develop a rescue plan, which forms part of the final step.

Step 3: corrective action to improve retention

The third and final step in the process of enhancing customer retention involves taking remedial action. At this point, plans to improve retention become highly specific to the organization concerned and any actions taken will be particular to the given context. We can, however, identify some broad guidelines that should form part of any plan to improve retention. These include: marshalling top management commitment; ensuring employee satisfaction and dedication to building long-term customer relationships; utilizing best practice techniques to improve performance; and developing a plan to implement customer retention strategy.

Visible top management endorsement

Visible top management endorsement is vital to the success of any customer retention programme. Where senior management is seen to be genuinely enthusiastic and actively supportive of a new retention initiative, it is more likely that employees will be inspired to follow the example and to take the retention programme seriously. If, however, the initiative is seen to be just another management fad, employees will not firmly adopt the practices necessary to implement an effective retention programme. The level of commitment expressed by senior management to any programme is often regarded as indicative of the amount of support that employees should give.

Customer retention and employee satisfaction

A major driver of customer retention improvement is whether employees perceive that the organization gives priority to customer satisfaction and retention. There is increasing evidence to suggest that the internal customer service climate has a strong impact upon employee satisfaction and customer retention. Heskett and his colleagues[6] have developed a model – 'the service profit chain' – that links leadership and human resources practices with employee satisfaction, customer satisfaction and business performance.

The model proposes that the human resources practices of an organization are linked to the internal service quality perceived by employees and that this, in turn, impacts on employee satisfaction. Satisfied employees are likely to be more productive and to remain with an organization for a longer time, creating greater value for the customer. Generally, happy employees make for happy customers and vice versa. Improved employee retention is likely to deliver improved internal and external service quality. Customer satisfaction impacts on customer retention, and this affects business performance.

It is also important to select and recruit customer contact staff who have the appropriate interpersonal skills to build strong relationships with customers. These people should be willing to acquire the knowledge and skills necessary to identify customer needs and expectations, and to exceed the service standards specified. For example, South West Airlines in the USA recruits employees largely on the basis of their attitude and enthusiasm towards the job role. The selection panel includes customers who are asked to choose the applicants that they would like to have serve them. Employees are also invited to assist in the selection process by identifying candidates whom they feel will be good colleagues.

Utilizing best practice

Best practice is a useful technique for disseminating superior practices throughout a company and is concerned with utilizing information derived from benchmarking. In this context, it involves identifying those organizations within the industry (and within departments or regions of the organization) that exhibit excellent customer retention performance and examining their operations to see how they are successfully managed. Managers can then use this knowledge to develop new approaches to improve customer satisfaction and retention in their own businesses. Sometimes it is worth looking to other industries for ideas and advice on best practice as they may offer guidance that is more likely to effect competitive advantage.

Building switching barriers

In addition to the usual procedural steps that form the basis of any implementation plan, several additional opportunities to create customer loyalty should be considered. These relate to the building of barriers, which inhibit or dissuade customers from opting for alternative suppliers.

A good retention strategy should try to identify the causes of defection and to build barriers that stop customers from switching to the competition, no matter what inducements the competition is offering. *Strategic bundling* can be a means of building a barrier to customer defection. This is where groups of associated products or services are offered to the customer with the pronounced advantage of convenience and/or cost savings.

Banks with outstanding customer service, such as First Direct, illustrate the benefit of using strategic bundling to reinforce business patronage. For example, through the provision of superior service, customers are motivated to use the bank for mortgages and insurance policies as well as customary standing orders and direct debits. Bain & Company's research into financial services suggests that retention rates are significantly greater where customers use two or more of an organization's services than in instances where they use only one service. However, if customers feel that an organization is taking advantage of them, they may resent attempts to offer bundled products and cross-selling.

Team-based relationship management can provide an effective means of preventing customer defection in business-to-business marketing. This approach, known as Key Account Management, is described in more detail in Chapter 17. This is where a team, led by a key account manager, manages the customer relationship. The aim is to make the relationship more enduring by building as many links as possible between the customer and the supplier. For example, multiple linkages may be established between the supplier's production team and the customer's operations team, the supplier's marketing team and the customer's business development team, and so on. This is in contrast to the traditional buyer-seller relationship, which is dependent on a sometimes fragile and fairly limited connection between a supplier's key account executive and a retailer's buyer.

EDI can also be a 'tie that binds'. Getting customers to invest in sharing information about sales and inventories can provide a powerful disincentive to switch suppliers. The benefits of such collaboration are reduced system costs, enhanced efficiency, and increased customer and consumer satisfaction.

In many industries, barriers to switching behaviour should only be constructed if they serve the interests of both the customer and the supplier. This guiding principle is not based on business philanthropy but on common sense. Bad publicity generated by disgruntled customers who feel they have been locked into unsatisfactory supplier relationships can significantly reduce profits.

This is especially true in consumer markets where, if things go wrong, switching barriers can mean that customers may find they are in a situation from which they cannot easily extricate themselves. Customers may feel trapped, helpless and even cheated. For example, bank customers who feel dissatisfied with the service they receive often find the task of moving their account, with all its associated standing orders and direct debits, too onerous to carry out. This produces unhappy customers who will be reluctant to buy into any further services and who may go out of their way to tell others of their negative experiences with their bank.

On the positive side, customers who invest in understanding a supplier's business system and who are delighted with the supplier's service are often happily 'locked-in' to the relationship. Amazon.com, the bookseller, and Dell Computers exemplify such suppliers.

SUMMARY

Increasingly, organizations are recognizing that enhanced customer satisfaction leads to better customer retention and profitability. Many organizations are now reviewing their customer service strategies to find ways to boost retention rates as a means of improving their business performance. This often entails a fundamental shift in business emphasis from customer acquisition to customer retention. Achieving the benefits of long-term customer relationships requires a firm commitment – from senior management and all staff – to understanding and serving the needs of customers.

Even a small change in the rate of customer retention can have a major impact on business performance and so appropriate mechanisms for measuring and monitoring retention are critical. For organizations wishing to adopt 'best-in-class' practices, this involves not only monitoring customer retention and customer satisfaction levels, but also all the elements within the service profit chain. Collectively, this information can be used throughout the organization to improve profitability. The connection between customer retention and profitability is illustrated by the following case study.

Case Study 1: the connection between customer retention and profitability

Sears, Roebuck & Company, the leading US department store chain, provides a good example of the success of the service profit chain model. Sears Roebuck has undergone a radical transformation in recent years to reverse its business decline. Much of the company's success is due to rigorous measurement systems which track employee attitudes and their effect on customer satisfaction and profitability. Critically, management alignment has been organized around these metrics and there is a clear understanding throughout the company of how the service profit chain model works.

In 1992, the company reported massive losses of $3.9 billion on sales of $52.3 billion. Arthur Martinez was appointed to lead the merchandise group, and he undertook to streamline the business. He set up task forces to identify world-class status in key areas of the business. Gradually, it became apparent that what was needed was a model to show direct causation from employee attitudes, through customer satisfaction, to company profits. The company needed to know how management action, such as investment in sales training, would directly translate into improved customer satisfaction and retention, and higher revenues.

Using sophisticated modelling techniques, links were identified between employee measures, customer measures, revenues and profitability. The attitudes of employees towards their jobs and the company were found to be critical to employee loyalty and customer service quality, while customer satisfaction directly affected customer retention and the likelihood of customer referrals. After further refinement, the model was used as a predictor of revenue growth: a 5 unit increase in employee attitude would drive a 1.3 unit increase in customer satisfaction and a 0.5 unit increase in revenue growth.

The results at Sears Roebuck have been impressive. By 1993, the company reported a net income of $752 million: a dramatic improvement for a business in such a mature industry. Employee satisfaction at Sears had risen by 4 per cent and customer satisfaction had likewise increased by almost 4 per cent. These improvements created more than $200 million additional revenue, which was achieved through the value creation activities of both managers and employees.

While not every organization will be able to be as sophisticated as Sears Roebuck in implementing the service profit chain model, customer retention should always feature as a key business priority. Information systems should ensure that the profit impact of customer retention is appropriately and accurately measured so that retention strategies can be developed which successfully focus on those customer segments that are likely to yield the greatest benefit to the organization.

Notes

1. F. F. Reichheld and W. E. Sasser, Jr, 'Zero Defections: Quality Comes to Services', *Harvard Business Review*, September–October, 1990, pp. 105–11.
2. A. F. T. Payne and P. E. Frow, 'Developing a Segmented Service Strategy: Improving Measurement in Relationship Marketing', *Journal of Marketing Management*, forthcoming.
3. T. Jones and W. E. Sasser, 'Why Customers Defect', *Harvard Business Review*, November–December, (1995) pp. 88–99.
4. A. Payne and J. Rickard, 'Relationship Marketing, Customer Retention and Service Firm Profitability' draft working paper (revision), Cranfield School of Management, 1999.
5. M. G. Christopher, A. F. T. Payne, and D. Ballantyne, *Relationship Marketing; Bringing Quality, Customer Service and Marketing Together* (Oxford: Butterworth-Heinemann, 1991).
6. J. L. Heskett, T. O. Jones, G. W. Loveman, Sasser, E. W., Jr and L. A. Schlesinger, 'Putting the Service-Profit Chain to Work', *Harvard Business Review*, March–April 1994, pp. 164–74.

Further reading

M. K. Clark and A. F. T. Payne, 'Achieving Long Term Customer Loyalty: A Strategic Approach', in J. Bell *et al.* (eds), *Proceedings on Marketing: Unity in Diversity,* 1994 Annual Marketing Education Group Conference, Ulster. (Part of this chapter is based on this work, and is used with the permission of the authors.)
A. J. Rucci, S. P. Kirn and R. T. Quinn, 'The Employee-Company-Profit Chain', *Harvard Business Review*, January–February 1998, pp. 83–97.

PART III

CREATING CUSTOMER VALUE THROUGH THE EXPANDED MARKETING MIX

9 NEW PRODUCT DEVELOPMENT AND PRODUCT POLICY

Roger Palmer

In this chapter:

- The role of technology in product development
- New product development activities
- The stage-gate process
- Developing product policy
- Case studies illustrating the factors for successful innovation and the stage-gate process

INTRODUCTION

The new product development process allows us to take a longitudinal view of the product, from the earliest stage of development through to the introduction of the product into the market place. This chapter considers the key aspects of product policy that serve to detract from or deliver the product's success.

Let us first establish what we mean by a 'new product'. From the customer's perspective, it may be a product that delivers benefits not previously obtained, or one that delivers them in a more advantageous way. From a manufacturer's point of view, a new product could well be an established product with just an additional product line variant that requires separate storage, handling or management. Reaching agreement on a simple definition of a 'new product' becomes increasingly difficult as market demand and supply become more complex and customer-specific. Customers seek bespoke products while manufacturers want larger and more efficient plants with higher outputs. For instance, a manager in a large American plastics company was asked how many product lines the business offered. 'Around 8000', was the reply. And how many of them were customized to individual requirements? 'All of them!' came the exasperated response.

New products can also represent new technology, presenting further benefits and satisfying needs in a different way. The television set occupies a similar place in the home to the piano of 100 years ago, providing entertainment, amusement and relaxation in a domestic setting. However, the television manifests additional benefits in that it can offer a wide range of entertainment and requires no more expertise than the ability to switch it on.

THE ROLE OF TECHNOLOGY

While new technology is a precursor of new product features, it does not necessarily mean that there is a need for the benefits that are delivered by the new features. Technology-oriented companies are prone to deceiving themselves into thinking that the extreme novelty of their new inventions automatically presumes there is an untapped market for them. This misbelief is sometimes referred to as the 'myth of the big market'.

New technology can facilitate additional product features, but it may not provide the additional benefits that customers prefer and for which they are prepared to pay. For example, digital car instrument panels have so far been commercially unsuccessful. They are technologically advanced, but offer no extra customer benefits. Further, drivers accustomed to using analogue instruments find them intuitively more difficult to understand. It is now a cliché that most new products fail, however, the underlying reason for failure is that they do not deliver improved perceived value to the customer. From an RM perspective, understanding what constitutes customer value and being able to deliver it is integral to new product development.

While invention and new technology promote new product development, a technology is not marketable until an application has been found that enables the product's benefits to be delivered. Technology today is advancing at a faster rate than ever before and is increasing the potential for new products. However, it is also prompting higher costs of R&D prior to commercialization. Consequently, companies involved in invention and discovery have to manage the new product development process very carefully in order to ensure a commercially viable outcome.

NEW PRODUCT DEVELOPMENT ACTIVITIES

New Product Development (NPD) has conventionally been seen as a sequential process, where various functional departments get involved at appropriate intervals. Working within their area of expertise, each participant, including representatives from R&D, manufacturing, marketing and so on, contributes to the process at a designated point, enabling the new product to develop methodically as it passes from one expert set of hands to another. This kind of NPD process is typical of a functionally organized, manufacturing-oriented business.

NCR (National Cash Register) was originally dedicated to the business of making mechanical calculating machines, such as cash registers from which its name derives. Recognizing the competitive threat posed by electronic calculators in the early 1970s, the company then concentrated research efforts on devising smaller and better mechanical calculators. Not surprisingly, NCR was soon surpassed by market competitors who quickly realized and applied the new and developing technology that better fulfilled the needs of customers.

NPD activities, however they are managed within the organization, invariably contain some or all of the following elements.

Product development policy

This policy stipulates how the firm manages and directs its new product development process. Because so many new products fail, investment in R&D is crucial and requires the appreciation, management and minimization of risk. Managers will seek to reduce the costs of development and to improve the chances of success simultaneously. This style of management can be reflected in the culture of the organization. Leading companies, such as Hewlett Packard and 3M, understand the importance of encouraging an innovative and progressive organizational culture, and accept that occasional setbacks and failures are part of the growth process. Poolton and Barclay[1] have identified six key strategic factors of innovation which span managerial attitude and organizational style.

1. *Top management support for innovation*
   Supply resources, incentive and motivation

2. *Long-term strategy with an innovation focus*
   Adopt a long-term view; plan new products to fit with corporate strategy

3. *Long-term commitment to major projects*
   Understand target market potential; pursue a long-term approach; allocate funding

4. *Flexibility and responsiveness to change*
   Be able to add variety and speed to quality and reliability

5. *Top management acceptance of risk*
   Avoid low potential, low-risk 'me-too' products; apply tight screening criteria and conserve resources for more worthwhile projects

6. *Support for an entrepreneurial culture*
   Actively manage the culture and management style in response to the market.

Idea creation

Ideas for new products can come from a variety of sources, including customers, staff, competitors and other industry participants. However, just because the process is creative does not mean that it cannot be managed. Idea generation techniques, such as brainstorming, suggestion schemes, think-tanks and scenario-building, are all designed to stimulate a broad menu of ideas, providing a unfettered complement to those ideas generated by the more analytical processes of complaint and sales analysis, competitor monitoring and market research.

Idea reduction

In this phase of development, the ideas generated earlier are subjected to a series of filters to identify the few ideas which are likely to produce a commercially viable product. The choice of filters can vary, depending on the type of business concerned. A manufacturing company may concentrate on finding ideas to improve the return on capital investment related to equipment, using screening devices comprised of stringent criteria. The critical filter for a pharmaceutical product in development will be its effectiveness relative to competing products.

Concept test

The limited number of ideas that survive to this stage of product development will be refined in order to reduce the product to a form that is more meaningful to the customer. Qualitative and quantitative market research may be carried out to illuminate target markets and identify potential competitors. Land Rover, in the development of the Discovery model, used a mock-up of the interior and exterior of the vehicle as a focus for discussions with potential buyers. In this way, the company acquired valuable information on consumer expectations and competitor products as well as on general opinions of the new model.

Economic evaluation

To determine whether or not the investment in a new product is justified, some form of business assessment is normally undertaken. Companies with large potential investments and high opportunity costs, such as pharmaceutical companies, or those which incur major capital expenditure, such as aircraft manufacturers, will analyse projects in great detail within a wide context. Often such reviews are conducted using strict financial criteria to appraise investment return and profit achievement. The wisdom behind the economic evaluation is illustrated by the following example.

A major international manufacturing company neglected to conduct such an analysis and proceeded to develop a production facility for a novel product in a new market in Australasia. It subsequently became apparent that the product was too expensive to produce in comparison to other products offering the same benefits. To compound matters, the manufacturer had failed to assess the market potential properly. The plant is now running substantially under capacity and will not be profitable for the foreseeable future.

Product development

During this stage, the product is taken from the concept phase to a point of near commercialization. This transition may involve further testing to confirm product performance, refinement of design, development of tooling and production capability, packaging, distribution channels and so forth. Product development is a critical stage, for the organization is not only committed to the pursuit of a particular option, but also to significant expenditure and hence a higher level of risk.

Test marketing

Prior to full-scale commercialization, it may be advisable to pilot the new product under specific market conditions in order to gain feedback on actual market receptiveness to the product and the proposed marketing programme. Test marketing involves the limited launch of the product, usually in a restricted geographical area or through particular parts of the distribution network. The decision of whether or not to test market the new product will depend on the individual circumstances.

Is there a suitable opportunity and does the significance and scale of the product make the extra effort worthwhile? A manufacturer of animal health products first launched its new product in Australia in order to evaluate the performance of the product in comparison to that of a major competitor. To the company's unexpected delight, this served to demonstrate that a technical advancement in the product had enormous environmental benefit. The new-found benefit was then incorporated into the promotion mix for the European launch of the product, where the product was successfully introduced at a slightly higher price relative to the Australian market.

Product launch

By this stage, the organization should be confident that the new product is fully developed and will satisfactorily meet customer needs. This feeling of certainty should be supported by a practical business plan that outlines the product's market potential and objectives. The product launch will involve a series of activities to introduce the product to the market in such a way as to give the product an early boost into the PLC (see Chapter 3).

THE STAGE-GATE PROCESS

New product development has historically been of a haphazard nature. This randomness, combined with delays in bringing products to market, can represent a large waste of resources and a reduction of product value. McKinsey estimates that high technology products which arrive to market on time, but are 50 per cent over budget, earn only 4 per cent less profit over a 5-year period. Products that are on budget but are 6 months late earn 33 per cent less profit in the same time frame. A number of factors are critical to the success of NPD, including the following.

1. *Time to market* – in today's business climate where competition is increasingly global and intense, time to market has become a significant ingredient of competitive advantage. The McKinsey research suggests that time to market has a direct effect on profits, in that it provides a basis for product differentiation as well as cost reductions.
2. *Fragmented markets* – manufacturers face the constant challenge to drive down production costs while meeting higher and more demanding

requirements for customization. The phrase 'mass-customization' describes this paradox. Flexibility in manufacturing and change management throughout the supply chain is paramount to meeting these escalating expectations.

3. *Technological progress* – the rapid pace of technological change means that the competitive stakes increase as organizations develop more ways of satisfying customer needs. To remain competitive, firms must either increase investment or be more selective in the technologies in which they invest.

In response to these changing priorities, many organizations are now re-engineering their NPD activities and formalizing them into a structured process. Robert Cooper, an academic researcher in this field, developed the concept of the stage-gate process (see Figure 9.1).[2] This process involves formalizing and sub-dividing NPD activities into a series of stages so that managers 'own' specific groups of activities and are responsible for achieving the objectives within those activities. In order to progress to the next stage, the product is first assessed against the objectives set for that stage. Failure at any stage in the process will result in the conclusion of the development of the new product. The definition of development stages and evaluation criteria will be specific to the organization and industry concerned.

An international pharmaceutical company designed a sophisticated stage-gate process to manage its products as they were developed. Drug companies often spend up to 20 per cent of their turnover on R&D. New products are their lifeblood, and stringent technical and regulatory requirements mean that the product development process may take six or seven years. As pharmaceutical products may have a patent life of only 15 years, time to market is crucial in optimizing the window of opportunity in which the substantial R&D costs can be recouped.

Companies may have up to 50 products in various stages of development at any one time. A project team leader is usually appointed to manage each

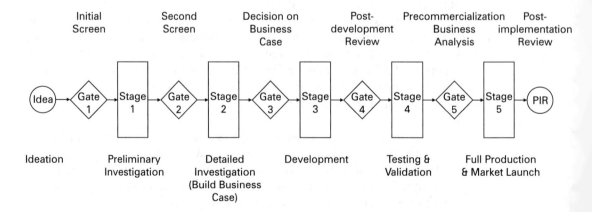

Figure 9.1 The stage-gate process

product development team, whose members may represent functional groups drawn from around the world. The team leader is responsible for managing the timescale and progress of the product through each stage of development. This project supervisor, in turn, is overseen by a committee of senior managers who report to the main board. It is their responsibility to ensure that sufficient and appropriate resources are made available and that any ensuing conflicts are resolved. Due to the huge costs incurred in the extensive testing of drugs for safety and efficacy purposes prior to product registration and launch, an early gate in the drug development process is an assessment of the product's medicinal worth and market potential. Products that do not pass this gate are not regarded as total failures, but are held pending subject to further relevant developments. Does this process work? It is said that Viagra was one such sidelined product!

The speed with which new products progress to the market can have a dramatic effect on profitability, as the pharmaceutical industry example demonstrates. Carefully analysing the stage-gate process into critical stages of development is one way in which efficiency can be improved, but to improve further still means not just working more quickly, but working differently. The product development lead time for complex projects such as developing a new model of car or designing an aircraft can be improved substantially by working cooperatively with suppliers and other alliance partners. The focus is on engineering out cost before it is incurred and saving valuable development time by employing processes such as simultaneous engineering, which enables development stages to be telescoped. The use of computer simulation techniques can mimic the production line on-screen; physiotherapists and psychologists can then design the work and production process to make it more pleasant and efficient. Advanced techniques such as these help to avoid mistakes, improve product quality and get products to market more quickly. The development time for a new model of car is now less than three years. This, combined with flexible manufacturing systems, makes smaller volumes profitable, so that the firm can serve more market sectors and gain greater competitive advantage.

PRODUCT POLICY

Once a new product is brought to market, it will almost certainly become part of a range of products marketed by the same firm. This raises a number of fundamental policy issues for the marketing manager, including:

- When should new products be introduced
- When should old products be deleted
- Which products should be offered in which markets
- How many products are needed
- How should products be differentiated within the range
- How can the range be managed for continuing profit

As mentioned earlier, new products include not just technological innovations, but current products that have been adapted or marketed to different audiences. The Ansoff Matrix (see Figure 3.3) is a helpful tool when considering NPD options. Using it in conjunction with the PLC provides an indication of how to balance the portfolio of products as well as the portfolio of opportunities and risks.

Business success is transient and to continue to satisfy and deliver increasing value to customers, businesses must never be complacent. Figure 3.3 describes, diagrammatically, the objectives of product strategies: to optimize the opportunities presented by the current range of products while anticipating possible future demands for product improvement, modification, or even deletion and replacement. By being both reactive and proactive in their operations, businesses can continually reinforce their relationships with customers and ensure that their products add real and superior value.

The concept of the product surround, as shown in Figure 9.2, demonstrates how the product range can be extended in order to develop product variants or appeal to new segments of the market. In highly competitive and mature markets, differentiation is most likely to be derived not from enhancement of product features but from the provision of better service or other intangible factors, such as an excellent reputation or an extended warranty. Indeed, it is said that in many cases the only advantage a supplier holds over a competitor is the nature of its customer relationship.

Careful tracking of the performance of the product against market movements can be accomplished by employing the PLC. This can be used to assist the coordination of product introductions and withdrawals. Having an excessive number of products runs the risk of 'cannibalization', where sales of one product replace those of another, thus affording no incremental growth in volume. Decisions about whether to delete a product from a range, or to remove a product from a market, will involve the results of sales monitoring mechanisms and evidence of the costs of maintaining the product, including

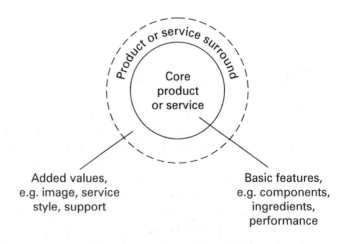

Added values,
e.g. image, service
style, support

Basic features,
e.g. components,
ingredients,
performance

Figure 9.2   The product surround: added values enhance basic features

manufacture, inventory, promotion and so on. However, other more subjective issues can arise when a product is removed from the market, particularly in relation to its role as part of a portfolio of products purchased in small quantities by large customers. In this case, a sound understanding of customer value, buying behaviour and customer needs is required.

If products successfully meet customer demands and remain within the capability of the company to supply, then they can be analysed and specified in terms of the features that deliver the appropriate benefits to customers. The needs of customers can be aggregated into segments, allowing for a sensible compromise between individually tailored and standard products. The insightful segmentation and careful specification of products can form the basis for building competitive advantage. The formulation of the product range also has to be taken into account, considering the ability of production to manufacture, sales to sell, distribution to deliver and the technical department to service.

The Boston Matrix, with its lucrative 'Cash Cows' (see Figure 3.4), suggests that product profitability lags behind product sales, as the costs of product development and introduction are progressively offset against an increasing volume of sales. The product profitability life cycle is shown in Figure 9.3. Product range profitability is obviously a factor of sales revenue over the product lifetime, as indicated by the PLC. The gap between profit and revenue represents costs, both development and introductory costs as well as the variable costs of the product post-launch. As the product range is extended, its profitability may vary due to lower incremental sales, meaning that there are lower volumes over which to allocate development and launch costs. With more products in the range, this will also mean additional costs of storage and handling.

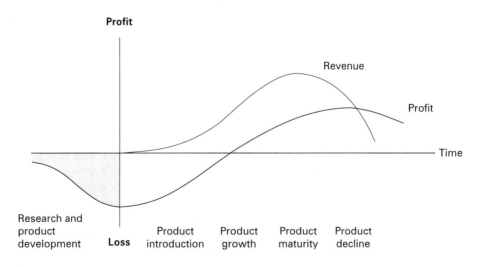

Figure 9.3   Product profitability life cycle

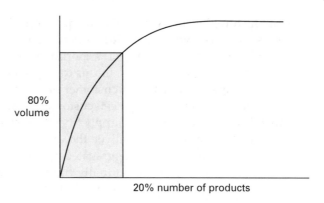

80%
volume

20% number of products

Figure 9.4   Pareto analysis

Pareto analysis, or the 80/20 rule, states that 20 per cent of products generate 80 per cent of volume/margin/profit, as described in Figure 9.4. When used together with a consideration of product costs, Pareto analysis provides a helpful aid in understanding the profitability of the product range. However, markets are not about products, they are about customers. The customer-buying portfolio, particularly that of the 20 per cent of customers who provide 80 per cent of the sales, is an important consideration in managing the profitability of the range.

It is relatively easy to improve short-term profitability: for example, by reducing the range and increasing prices. However, such measures fail to address customer needs and can make products less competitive. When customers desert to other suppliers, market share declines and customer relationships are severely curtailed or perhaps irretrievably damaged. Conflicts of interest can arise between short- and long-term profitability, and it becomes a critical matter of judgement to maintain a constructive balance.

The following two case studies illustrate the significance of product range management to profitability. A culture that generates an environment conducive to innovation, conscious of product value and sensitive to the market is more likely to generate profitable products and customers.

Case Study 1: the environment for successful innovation

3M is renowned for its approach to innovation. The company has an extensive range of products and a reputation that is second to none for its ability to develop new ones. Products that have been introduced within the past four years account for over 25 per cent of its sales. The company actively encourages its managers to work on 'blue sky' projects, by providing them with resources of time, expertise, materials and budgets. The company is committed to cross-functional collaboration, and to providing development funding and rewarding success. From such an approach has come the ubiquitous Post-It note, a small square of (originally) yellow paper with a semi-adhesive glue along one edge. The glue owes its development to 'failed' research into more conventional adhesives and has since evolved into a new product that offers unique and extremely popular benefits.

Compare the Post-It note example with the actions of the chairman of a large, listed company with businesses in various parts of the world, who was concerned by the generally poor level of performance across the group. Senior managers from the company would meet on a yearly basis to share business plans, discuss progress and developments, and agree objectives for the following year. The group had a hierarchical style of management and attendance at the annual conference was a mark of seniority in the organization.

Each conference programme adopted a theme and the chairman decided that, in this particular year, the theme would be innovation. He began his keynote speech by commenting on the company's poor performance and indicating that he expected to receive some full explanations and practical solutions by the conclusion of the conference. He went on to discuss the need to encourage managers to innovate and to develop new products as a way of improving business performance. To achieve this goal, he was in the process of setting up a committee that was to be chaired by the chief executive of one of the subsidiaries and staffed by other senior managers. A sum of money was to be allocated for speculative R&D projects, and the function of the committee was to review project proposals and grant awards to successful applicants.

A number of *ad hoc* groups of managers submitted proposals. Some of the groups were refused outright as their projects demonstrated little or no potential, while others were invited to resubmit their ideas with a strengthened business case outlining the cost/benefit ratio. A few awards were eventually made. One, in particular, was for a substantial sum to investigate an opportunity to diversify into a related market. After completing their project, the team members presented their recommendations to the company, one of which was not to enter the related market. The chairman expressed his concern that one of the few projects approved by the committee had ended in failure and asked to know why such a large sum of money had been wasted at a time when the group was already under financial pressure.

Although this company recognized the need for innovation, it failed to develop the appropriate culture and environment in which it could flourish. The committee system institutionalized what is essentially a creative process. Managers were demotivated when projects that they felt committed to were rejected by others who apparently knew better. The group whose application was accepted, felt that their work had saved the company from an inopportune investment, and had developed considerable insight into the market. Rather than seeing the project as a 'failure' and the money as 'wasted', they saw it as a sensible investment in a potential opportunity.

The company continued to decline and the chairman was replaced. The company was eventually sold off, with a substantial loss of shareholder value.

Case Study 2: the stage-gate process in action

Pilkington, one of the five major global manufacturers of glass for building and automotive applications, has developed a process known as the PIP (Pilkington Innovation Process), which is a stage-gate approach to new product development.

As inventors of the float glass technique, Pilkington had developed a manufacturing procedure that lowered the current cost of glass production by 40 per cent. By licensing the technology to competitors and continually improving and refining float glass technology, Pilkington grew from a family firm in the north-west of England into a world-class company. Pilkington now manufactures in 22 countries on four continents.

Technology and manufacturing excellence were critical to the development of Pilkington's prominent position within the glass-making industry and these strengths were no doubt nurtured by the company's highly innovative and entrepreneurial culture. Competitors eventually caught up with Pilkington's pioneering technology as the patents for both the float glass technique and subsequent enhancements expired.

Pilkington was wise to recognize that it needed to develop a more responsive organization in order to compete in the increasingly fierce markets of the highly competitive industry. A number of senior management changes were made, with the appointment of senior marketing staff to both its building products and automotive businesses. A major management development programme was also initiated to raise the profile of marketing and enhance the skills of managers.

Additionally, Pilkington saw the need to change the way it developed products in order to focus on markets, rather than technology. Although the company owned a number of research centres around the world, which were credited with technological superiority, the flow of new products remained slow, uncertain and uncoordinated. A few high-profile, technically excellent products had been launched, but these had failed to meet expectations. Senior managers naturally questioned the value of heavy investment in R&D.

Benefiting from past experience, Pilkington developed the PIP process to improve its product value and market responsiveness. The process involved not just technical staff, but managers from across the business. It adopted the principles of the stage-gate process and was designed to support NPD long into the future. R&D staff attended marketing programmes and a training package on the PIP process was developed for internal use. The process has now been installed across the business and is used not only as a tool for NPD, but also as a way of improving communication between the various centres of functional excellence, driving a permanent and positive cultural change within the company.

SUMMARY

The key to successful product strategy is a balanced portfolio of products that includes both established and new products. New products may result from pressures to customize or advancements in technological expertise. Technology-oriented companies should take care to maintain a market, rather than a product, focus.

Because new products run a high risk of failure, the use of formalized methods of appraisal is advocated, including market research and market testing as well as economic analysis. The Boston maxtrix can aid in analysing the options for product strategy, while the Ansoff matrix and the PLC can be helpful in balancing the product portfolio and the array opportunities and risks. The stage-gate process can be employed to minimize risk by improving NPD efficiency and assuring the timely input of suppliers and other alliance partners.

Notes

1. J. Poolton and I. Barclay, 'New Product Development from Past Research to Future Applications', *Industrial Marketing Management*, 27 (1998), pp. 197–212.
2. R. G. Cooper, *Winning at New Products: Accelerating the Process from Idea to Launch*, 2nd edn (Reading, MA: Addison-Wesley, 1993).

References

E. M. Rogers, *Diffusion of Innovation* (New York: Free Press, 1962).
H. Takeuchi and I. Nonaka, 'The New New Product Development Game', *Harvard Business Review*, Jan/Feb 1986, pp. 137–46.

MANAGING LOGISTICS AND CHANNELS

Martin Christopher

In this chapter:

- A definition of logistics and supply chain management
- The impact of logistics on customer value
- The importance of channel management
- The concept of the channel margin
- A case study highlighting the role of partnership in the distribution channel

INTRODUCTION

Of the many changes that have taken place in the marketing environment over the last two or three decades, one of the most significant has been the emergence of customer service as a critical issue. Customers in every type of market demand ever-higher levels of service. Thus original equipment manufacturers (OEMs) require their suppliers to make JIT deliveries of components with reduced order-to-delivery cycle times. Similarly, consumers' expectations of the quality of service they receive from their suppliers, such as retailers, hotels, banks and airlines, have increased dramatically.

The means by which value is delivered to customers and consumers has become a potential source of competitive advantage to those organizations that focus on the processes that create superior service. These processes underpin the related concepts of logistics and supply chain management.

LOGISTICS AND SUPPLY CHAIN MANAGEMENT

Logistics management is an integrative process that seeks to optimize the flow of materials and supplies through the organization and its operations to the customer. It is essentially a planning process and an information-based activity. Requirements from the market place are translated into production requirements and then into material requirements through this planning process.

It is now being recognized that, for the real benefits of the logistics concept to be realized, there is a need to extend the logic of logistics upstream to suppliers and downstream to final customers. This is the concept of *supply chain management*.

Supply chain management is a fundamentally different philosophy of business organization. It is based upon the idea of partnership in the marketing channel where a high degree of linkage exists between entities in that channel. Traditional models of business organization have been based upon the notion that the interests of individual firms are best served by maximizing their revenues and minimizing their costs. If these goals are achieved by disadvantaging another entity in the channel, then so be it. Under the supply chain management model, the goal is to maximize profit through enhanced competitiveness in the final market; this competitiveness is secured by a lower cost to serve, reached in the shortest time frame possible. Such goals are only attainable if the supply chain as a whole is closely coordinated in order that total channel inventory is minimized, bottlenecks are removed, time frames are compressed and quality problems are eliminated.

This new model of competition suggests that individual companies compete not as company against company, but rather as supply chain against supply chain. Thus the successful companies will be those whose supply chains are more cost-effective than their competitors' are.

What are the basic requirements for successful supply chain management? Figure 10.1 outlines the critical linkages that connect the market place to the supply chain. The key linkages are between the management of supply and manufacturing, and between manufacturing and distribution. Each of these three activities, while part of a continuous process, has a number of crucial elements.

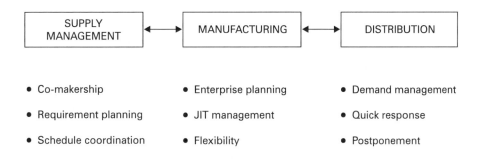

Figure 10.1 Critical linkages in the supply chain

Supply management

Historically, companies generally have paid scant attention to supply management. Even though the costs of purchases represent the largest single cost for most businesses, procurement has not been seen as a strategic task. That view is now changing as the realization grows that not only do procurement decisions and procedures dramatically impact costs, but also that innovation and response-to-market capability are profoundly affected by supplier relationships.

The philosophy of *co-makership* is founded upon the notion of a mutually beneficial relationship between supplier and buyer, rather than the more traditional adversarial encounter. With this partnership approach, companies will identify opportunities for taking costs out of the supply chain, instead of simply pushing them upstream or downstream. Paperwork can be eliminated, problems jointly solved, quality improved and information shared. By its very nature, co-makership will normally involve longer-term relationships based upon single-sourcing, rather than multiple supply points. Xerox in Europe has adopted the co-makership philosophy and this has had the effect of reducing the company's supplier base from 5000 to 300.

A major benefit of working more closely with suppliers can be gained through involving them in the new product development process. A great deal of innovation today is supplier-originated, and closer partnerships with suppliers can often lead to significant opportunities for new product breakthroughs.

Manufacturing

The key word in manufacturing today is *flexibility*. The ability to produce any variant in any quantity, without significant cost penalty, has to be the goal of all manufacturing strategies. In the past, and even now, much of the thinking in manufacturing has been dominated by the search for economies of scale. This type of reasoning has led to the formation of mega plants, capable of producing vast quantities of a standardized product at incredibly low unit costs. It also has led many companies to opt for so-called 'focused factories' which produce a limited range of products for global consumption.

The downside of adopting a flexible approach is that it can have the reverse affect of producing '*dis*economies of scale'. These diseconomies might take the form of a build-up of large inventories of finished product ahead of demand, an inability to respond rapidly to changed customer requirements or a reduction in the variety of product that can be offered to the customer. Instead of pursuing economies of scale, the search is now on to identify strategies that will reduce total supply chain costs, not just manufacturing costs, and that will offer maximum flexibility against changing customer requirements. The goal of manufacturing must be 'the economic batch quantity of 1', meaning that, in the ideal world, we would make things one at a time in response to known customer demands.

Time has become a major competitive issue in most industries and hence manufacturing and marketing strategies need to be closely coupled.

Distribution

The role of distribution in the supply chain management model has extended considerably from the conventional view that it is concerned solely with transport and warehousing. The critical task that underlies successful distribution today is *demand management*.

Demand management is the process of anticipating and fulfilling orders against defined customer service goals. Information is the key to demand management: information from the market place in the form of medium-term forecasts; information from customers, preferably based upon actual usage and consumption; information on production schedules and inventory status; and information on marketing activities, such as promotions that may cause demand to deviate from the norm.

Clearly, while forecasting accuracy should always be sought, it must be recognized that it will only rarely be achieved. Instead, therefore, the aim of distribution should be to reduce dependence upon the forecast by improving the quality and 'capture' of information about demand, and by creating systems that are capable of responding more rapidly to that known demand. The interlinking of logistics and information systems forms the underlying principle of *quick response* logistics.

Quick response logistics has become the aim of many organizations, enabling them to achieve the twin strategic goals of cost reduction and service enhancement. In essence, the idea of 'quick response' systems is based upon a replenishment-driven model of demand management: as items are consumed or purchased, information is transmitted directly to the supplier and this immediately triggers an appropriate response. Often, high-speed, smaller quantity deliveries will be made, the trade-off being that any increase in transport costs will be more than covered by reduced inventory in the pipeline and at either end of it, yet with improved service in terms of customer responsiveness. Certainly, information technology has been a major enabling factor in quick response logistics, linking the point of sale or consumption with the point of supply instantaneously.

In addition to quick response logistics, a further visible trend in distribution is the search for *postponement* opportunities. The principle of postponement dictates that the final configuration or form of the product should be delayed until the last possible moment. In this way, maximum flexibility is maintained, but inventory is minimized. The distribution function takes on a wider role as the provider of the final added value. For example, at Hewlett Packard, the objective is to minimize inventory held as finished product by instead carrying it as semi-finished, modular work-in-progress, awaiting final configuration once orders are received.

What is apparent is that distribution in the integrated supply chain has now become an information-based, value-added activity, providing a critical link between the market place and the factory.

THE IMPACT OF LOGISTICS ON CUSTOMER VALUE

The potential impact that logistics can have on customer value is considerable. Customer value can be defined as the benefits the customer perceives to flow from the supplier relationship compared to the perceived costs. The benefits will typically comprise both tangible and intangible aspects. Tangible elements of the benefit 'bundle' might include product features and 'hard' service elements, such as on-time delivery. The intangible components of the offer might include the corporate image as well as 'soft' service elements, such as the helpfulness of the customer service call centre.

The cost that the customer incurs will be more than just the price charged for the product or service. Sometimes there can be significant transaction costs involved in placing orders, actioning progress, checking and remedying quality defects, checking invoices and making payments. There may also be ongoing costs, termed life cycle costs, such as maintenance and running costs. It is the totality of these costs – often referred to as the total cost of ownership – which the customer evaluates against the perceived benefits.

Figure 10.2 draws these different ideas together and suggests that logistics, directly or indirectly, can have an impact on all of the component elements of customer value. For example, to a retailer, product packaging can have a significant effect on in-bound distribution costs and shelf space profitability. Suppliers who include logistics considerations in their product or pack design decisions can thus greatly improve customer value. A good example of this type of forward thinking is provided by P&G, who redesigned the pack of their global shampoo brand, Head & Shoulders, and as a result, enabled 25 per cent more product to be moved and stored on a pallet. This initiative benefited P&G's retail customers as well as the company itself, with a further significant benefit accruing to the retailer through better shelf space utilization.

Suppliers' logistics processes can also deliver enhanced customer value through ensuring more reliable delivery, thus reducing the customers' need to carry safety stocks. The supplier can provide further benefit to the customer by actively managing the customer's inventory, a concept known as Vendor Managed Inventory (VMI). Under VMI, the supplier monitors the customer's inventory levels and, using this information, decides when to replenish stocks

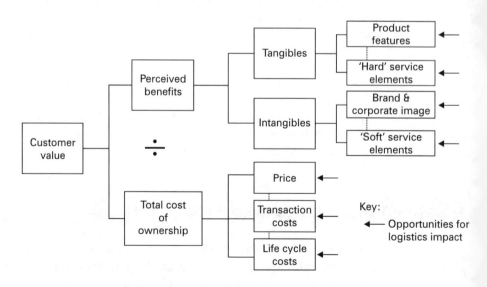

Figure 10.2 The impact of logistics on customer value

and in what quantities. The customer only pays when they use or sell the product. Large retail chains, for example, are increasingly forming partnerships with their suppliers to introduce these types of collaborative and mutually beneficial logistics arrangements.

From the standpoint of competitive advantage, this kind of value-adding logistics activity can be very positive. The more that the customer's processes become integrated with the supplier's processes, the greater is the barrier to entry that is erected against competitors.

The connection between logistics processes and superior customer service is self-evident. This transparency has engendered an acceptance that customer service is much more than simply a question of motivating employees or producing generalized mission statements and slogans. Instead, the dimensions of service need to be understood in detail and strategies need to be developed for effective service delivery.

THE CRITICAL ROLE OF LOGISTICS SERVICE

The importance of logistics in marketing strategy is that it is the *process* that delivers customer service. As markets increasingly take on the characteristics of 'commodity markets', where customers perceive little difference between products at a functional or technical level, customer service can provide a powerful means of differentiation. In markets as disparate as industrial chemicals or personal computers, the struggle is to find ways to avoid the commodity trap. For many companies, the solution to this problem has come through enhanced service performance. Today's customers are service-sensitive, requiring availability of supply at short notice, for they often operate on a JIT basis, whether they are a manufacturing business, a retailer or an end user. The era of 'time-based competition' has arrived.

Customer satisfaction at a profit is the goal of any business organization and the role of the logistics system is to achieve defined service goals in the most cost-effective manner. The establishment of these service goals is a prerequisite for the development of appropriate logistics strategies and structures. There is now widespread acceptance that customer service requirements can only be accurately determined through research and competitive benchmarking. Customer research may also reveal the presence of significant differences in service preferences among customers, thus indicating alternative bases for market segmentation in terms of service needs.

Tailoring customer service strategies to meet the precise needs of customers can be a powerful means of differentiation leading to enduring competitive advantage, and service segmentation is a key means to achieving this end.

Understanding customers' service preferences is the starting point for re-engineering logistics processes to ensure greater cost-effectiveness, and thus customers' service preferences should be the starting point for the development of logistics and supply chain strategies. The challenge to the organization then becomes one of how to re-engineer processes and re-structure conventional, functional systems to achieve these service goals at minimum cost.

Key to the achievement of these customer service goals is closer collaboration with downstream partners in the distribution channel. The way in which distribution channels are structured and the relationships within them are managed is crucial to competitive performance in any industry.

CHANNEL MANAGEMENT

The outlets at which our products are made available logically determine where our customers buy our products. Typically, many companies will not give much attention to the question of channel choice as it is not regarded as a variable in the marketing mix. More often than not, the distribution channel will have taken its current form as a result of unplanned and haphazard development.

Such disregard for this vital area of marketing discretion means that many opportunities for profitable market potential are passed over. For example, an international chemical company selling into Europe, using their own sales force to sell direct to customers, found that by using a chemical merchant, or middleman, they could reduce their own sales costs and take advantage of a ready-made sales organization with a host of local contacts.

A British manufacturer of high-quality shoes found it possible to open up a new and profitable market segment through the catalogue of a national mail-order firm. This facility provided the company with the opportunity to reach a wider audience without compromising its traditional channels (upmarket, specialty shoe shops).

Another British company, a carpet manufacturer, was perplexed by its falling sales as total carpet sales in the UK remained at a high level. It was felt that somehow the company had got its quality or pricing levels wrong. In fact, a deeper examination of the company's situation showed that the culprit was its continued policy of selling through small, traditional high-street carpet shops. The new growth outlets were clearly the edge-of-town carpet warehouses, which often offered discounted prices. These distributors now accounted for the lion's share of carpet sales. The manufacturer had missed a wonderful opportunity by failing to recognize the change in distribution patterns and to respond accordingly.

These three examples demonstrate the benefits of taking a fresh look at marketing channels. They each involved a reappraisal of the route by which the customer acquired the product, and a comparison of the costs and benefits of other distribution options.

Many companies do not rely on a single channel of distribution, but prefer instead to use multiple channels. They may choose different channels to reach different market segments or, alternatively, they may approach a single market via a dual distribution channel. In such cases it is important to ensure that no conflicts exist between channels, particularly in terms of price competition. For instance, an insurance company that is seeking to set up a direct telephone-based sales channel will have to be careful that its established business using insurance brokers is not adversely affected.

THE CHANNEL MARGIN

Ultimately, the choice of channel(s) must be based upon the long-term balance of the benefits and the costs of that choice. So what are the potential benefits and costs that should be considered? The potential benefits of using intermediaries include:

- Access to markets
- Economies of scale through consolidation
- Final product configuration
- Selling and promotion
- Provision of trade credit
- Holding inventory
- Installation and customer training

On the other hand, the costs of using intermediaries will comprise the margin forgone and a possible loss of opportunity, since the intermediary may not necessarily support or promote the product to the desired extent because of competing priorities. It is important to remember that any margin allowed to intermediaries should not be seen as a sharing of the supplier's profit. Rather, the margin should be regarded as a recompense for the transfer of cost from the supplier to the intermediary. Thus, for example, if a wholesaler carries inventory on behalf of a manufacturer, then the wholesaler will incur a holding cost on that inventory. Since, presumably, this relieves the manufacturer of the need to carry that inventory, the wholesaler can be recompensed to the extent of the cost saved by the supplier. The concept of the *channel margin* is important in this context.

The channel margin can be defined as the difference between the price in the final market (the 'street price') and price paid to the manufacturer (the 'factory gate price').

Channel Margin = Street Price – Factory Gate Price

One UK manufacturer of car batteries was surprised by what it learned when it commissioned a market research study on some of its Far East markets to see how high (and how variable) the street price was in comparison to the factory gate price. The question posed was: are the benefits we derive through our channel intermediaries, namely, market access, inventory carrying and so forth, greater than or equal to the cost we pay (the channel margin)? The company concluded that it should seek to establish a more direct channel to eliminate multiple steps in the chain from factory to consumer. A survey by McKinsey suggests that the channel margin can typically account for between 15 and 40 per cent of the retail price of goods.

For many years there has been little innovation in distribution channel structure. Organizations have assumed that distribution channels are, by their very nature, fixed and difficult to change. However, in recent years, a number of significant developments have taken place, which are now transforming the shape of many distribution channels. The rapid growth of the Internet is a classic example of how technology is rendering obsolete much of the conventional wisdom about how goods and services should reach the market place. One of the biggest effects of the Internet has been to accelerate the trend towards what some have termed 'disintermediation', or the removal of any intermediaries between the supplier and the ultimate consumer. This tendency has significant implications for business. For example, what will be the role of a travel agent now that the Internet enables customers themselves to thoroughly research and compare products, and to purchase tickets and holidays directly?

Other examples of disintermediation may be found in the banking and insurance industries where telephone-based companies such as First Direct and Direct Line have eroded the market share of their more traditional competitors.

Developments in logistics, such as worldwide express delivery through companies such as DHL and Federal Express, have also contributed to the emergence of new direct-to-customer distribution channels. Companies such as Dell Computer Corporation and Cisco have achieved leadership positions through the use of quick response logistics and supply chain strategies.

The implication of these developments is that channel strategy must be kept under constant review with the ongoing evaluation of the efficiency, effectiveness and sustainability of current channels. Figure 10.3 summarizes the key questions that need to be asked.

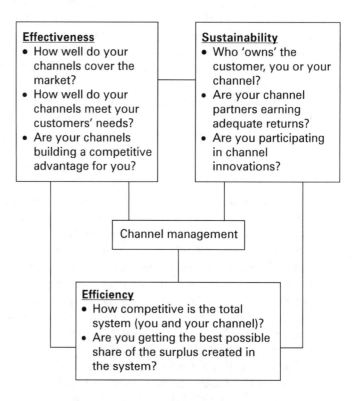

Figure 10.3 Key questions in channel management

PARTNERSHIP IN THE DISTRIBUTION CHANNEL

We are now entering the era of supply chain or network competition. What this means is that we no longer have individual firms competing against other firms; instead we have supply chain competing against supply chain. Thus, for example, Rover no longer competes against Ford, but Rover's supply chain competes against Ford's supply chain. In other words, it is the added value created by the network of suppliers, manufacturers and distributors that determines competitive advantage.

To liberate the greatest added value from this network at least cost requires a completely different approach from that used in the management of relationships in the distribution channel in the past; then it was more often the case that these relationships were, at best, distant, and at worst, adversarial. Now the key word is *partnership*.

While the word 'partnership' is often used loosely in business, the aim of a true partnership in the distribution channel is to secure 'win-win' relationships. Rarely will this mean that costs and benefits are shared equally; however, for partnerships to work, all parties must gain something from the relationship.

The intention is that, through cooperation and the joint determination of channel strategy, the 'cake' as a whole can be grown with bigger pieces available for all. In retailing, for example, the growth of the *category management* concept provides a good illustration of this philosophy. Category management is where the manufacturer and the retailer work together to enhance shelf space profitability. In essence, it focuses upon improving the profitability of a related family of products. A large retail store might well have over 200 categories of products, ranging from 'oral care' to 'oven-ready meals'. In the oral care category, for example, decisions will have to be taken on the breadth and depth of the merchandise stocked. This is likely to involve not only questions such as how many brands of toothpaste should be carried, but also questions of range, including toothbrushes, toothpicks, mouth washes, dental floss and so on. Furthermore, consideration must be given to how much space should be allocated to each item and brand within the category, and what position they should occupy on the shelf. Decisions such as these can have a significant effect on profitability across the category as a whole.

In this example, a partnership arrangement might involve the supplier conducting in-store research to observe how shoppers react to different layouts and post-purchase interviews to determine how choices are actually made. An analysis of electronic point-of-sale (EPOS) data can then be used to identify cross-purchasing patterns, or what products tend to be purchased together with other products.

The proactive supplier will seek to become the expert on the categories in which it competes, enabling the retailer (and the supplier) to increase profitability as a result. The point is that the supplier is often best placed to be the category expert as suppliers tend to compete in a limited number of categories while retailers will often be concerned with several hundred categories.

Companies in various industries are finding that developing closer relationships with channel partners can pay substantial dividends. The following case study, citing Allen-Bradley, shows how partnering with distributors can enable a supplier to build competitive advantage both for itself and its customers.

Case Study 1: the benefits of partnering with distributors

Allen-Bradley, the world leader in automation control solutions, is a good example of a company that manages its portfolio of partners to achieve its goals. Naturally, it has partnerships with suppliers, such as with Motorola for micro-processors, but even more interesting is its use of other partnerships. With its long-standing key distributors, for example, Allen-Bradley has steered away from traditional relationships towards *channel* partnerships.

Where once the company merely supplied its products to distributors of electrical/mechanical goods, it has now moved to strengthen the entire distribution chain. Today, it manufactures and ships more quickly to help reduce distributor inventory, works to build technical sophistication in distributor sales-forces and provides servicing for advanced software. In return, the distributors are not only selling more products, but they are also providing other value. For instance, the distributors are beginning to supply more detailed and timely point-of-sale data which will support Allen-Bradley in its drive for manufacturing productivity and excellence in customer service.

As many of its customers' needs are broader and more complex than the company alone can satisfy, Allen-Bradley also manages a portfolio of more than 80 partnerships with *peer* companies. To fulfil its objective of solving customer problems, it has sought out and carefully selected companies that complement its product and service offering, even though some of them are direct competitors in certain applications. Annually, Allen-Bradley convenes its peer partners at its own trade show for customers. Most importantly, through its relationships with these partners, the company is able to offer a complete portfolio of products to its distributors, negating the need for them to go to competing suppliers to fill our their product lines.

Through experience, Allen-Bradley has recognized the value of *customer* partnerships and has chosen a small number of global companies with which it can form close partnerships to develop new products, enter new markets, and build skill at creating customer value.

Source: S. F. Dull, *et al*. 'Partners', *McKinsey Quarterly*, No. 4 (1995).

SUMMARY

In the past, it was more often the case that organizations were structured and managed on the basis of optimizing their own operations, with little regard for the way in which they interfaced with suppliers and, indeed, customers. The business model was essentially 'transactional', meaning that products and services were bought and sold at 'arm's length' and that there was little enthusiasm for the concept of long-term, interactive relationships.

The new competitive paradigm that is now emerging is in stark contrast to the conventional model. It suggests that in today's challenging global markets, the route to sustainable advantage increasingly lies in managing the complex web of relationships that link together partners in a mutually profitable marketing channel.

Further reading

Martin Christopher, *Marketing Logistics* (Oxford: Butterworth-Heinemann, 1997).

Martin Christopher, *Logistics and Supply Chain Management* (London: Financial Times/Pitmans, 1998).

Douglas Lambert and James Stock, *Strategic Logistics Management* (Boston: Richard D. Irwin, 1993).

Jon Hughes, *et al.*, *Transform your Supply Chain* (London: International Thomson Business Press, 1998).

Gene Tyndall, *et al.*, *Supercharging Supply Chains* (New York: John Wiley, 1998).

PRICING
STRATEGY

Martin Christopher

In this chapter:

- Benefits, value and price
- The total cost of ownership
- Consumer and supplier surplus
- Trade-off analysis
- Competitive pricing strategy
- Price and the experience curve
- Relationship pricing
- International pricing management

INTRODUCTION

The pricing decision is one of the most important issues that the marketing executive has to face. Its impact will usually be reflected in the quantity of the product sold, the contribution to profits that the product will make and, even more crucially, the strategic position of the product in the market place. Additionally, in a multi-product company, it is frequently the case that a decision taken on the price of one product will have implications for other products in the same range. It is not surprising, therefore, that much has been written and discussed on the subject of pricing and that there is considerable controversy as to how the price decision should be made.

Frequently, this controversy has centred on the role that costs should play in determining price. Traditionally, the price of a product is based upon the identification of the costs associated with manufacturing, marketing and distributing the product, with the subsequent addition of a mark-up to reflect the desired profitability. Such an approach has been criticized on a number of counts. First, it can prove to be extremely difficult in practice to identify the true costs of a product. In many cases, the company will have joint costs and fixed costs that can only be allocated to a specific product on an arbitrary basis. Second, such a cost-plus approach to pricing ignores the demand sensitivity of the market place. It may be that a price determined on a cost-plus basis is higher than the market place will accept, or perhaps it may be even lower than the price that the market will tolerate. Attempts have been made to overcome these problems by using a *marginal cost* approach rather than a *full cost* approach. In this way, the pricing decision becomes one of attempting to maximize the contribution the product will make: that is, the difference between the *price* and the direct and attributable *costs*.

The basic problem with any cost-based approach to pricing is that it implicitly assumes that the customer is interested in *our* costs, whereas in reality the customer is only concerned with *their own* costs. This can be expressed another way: the customer seeks to acquire benefits and it is in order to acquire those benefits that they are prepared to pay a certain price. Seen from this perspective, the company making the price decision is faced with the need to identify the value – in the customer's eyes – of the benefits inherent in its product. The costs of that product thus become irrelevant to the pricing decision even though they are highly pertinent to the profitability of the decision. In other words, *costs* determine profits, not price.

BENEFITS AND PRICE

Throughout this book we have suggested that in any purchase decision the customer is seeking to acquire 'benefits'. A product must bring with it the promise of performing certain tasks, of solving identified problems, or even of providing specific gratifications. Thus the product is not bought for the particular components or materials that go into its manufacture *per se*, but rather it is bought for what, as an entity, it can do.

The implication of the benefit concept from a pricing point of view is that the company must first identify the benefits the customer perceives the product to offer and then attempt to ascertain the value that the customer places upon them. The key issue here is that it is the customer *perception* that is important. It may be, for example, that two competing companies offer products that are technically identical to all intents and purposes and yet one company can command a premium price. Why should this be? It may be that additional benefits offered by one company, in the way of technical advice or after-sales service, are perceived to be superior to those offered by another. Or it may just be that the 'image' of that company is seen as superior. Whatever the reason, there are many cases of this type of 'differential advantage' that cannot be explained simply in technical or quality terms.

Strong brands have always been able to command a price premium. 'Designer labels' on fashion garments or sportswear are obvious examples of the impact of brand image. Even in industrial markets the power of the brand can be significant.

Another way to look at this price advantage is to think of the maximum price at which the product could be sold as being the sum of two elements. First there is the 'commodity price' element, which is the base price for the generic product; this can be determined by supply and demand in the market place. On top of this should be added the 'premium price differential', which reflects the totality of the benefits that the customer perceives will be acquired through purchase of that product. Figure 11.1 shows this concept diagrammatically.

The existence of this 'premium price differential' can only be explained in terms of perceived benefits. The task of the pricing decision-maker, therefore,

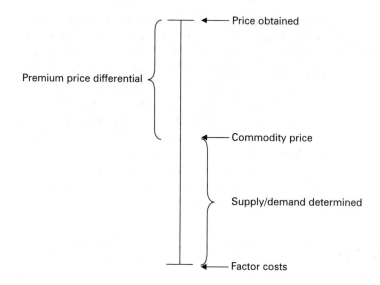

Figure 11.1 The components of price

becomes one of identifying these benefits and placing a customer value upon them. It is, in reality, a 'bundle' of benefits and so the first step in this suggested approach to pricing is to 'unbundle' the product and identify the individual benefit components that together constitute the totality.

The challenge to the pricing decision-maker is to shift the emphasis away from price towards a wider concept of the *total cost of ownership*. This idea is based upon the fact that with many products, the customer will incur many costs other than the initial price over the lifetime of the product. Thus in buying a motor car there are significant costs beyond the 'sticker price', such as running costs, insurance, service and depreciation. The Korean car manufacturer, Daewoo, has achieved considerable success in its European marketing campaign by highlighting the true cost of ownership of its model, as compared to competitors' models, for example.

PRICE AND VALUE

Every purchase by a customer is a 'trade-off'. The trade-off is between the value the customer places on the acquisition of the product versus the costs that are involved in that acquisition, plus any subsequent costs that might be involved, such as maintenance or upgrading costs.

There is nothing new in this idea. Economists have long talked about the concept of 'utility'. While some of their ideas on the relationship between price and demand may seem naïve, there is nevertheless an important message for the pricing decision-maker in the recognition that price must be seen in terms of *value*.

The Victorian economist, Alfred Marshall, was the first person to really articulate the idea of price as a reflection of the value placed on a product or

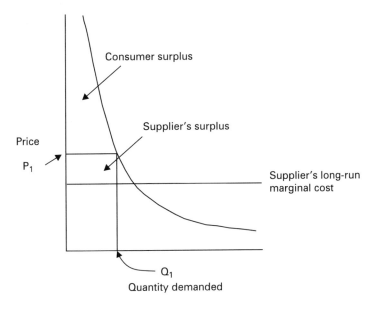

Figure 11.2 The demand curve

service by the consumer. He developed the concept of the *demand curve*, which simply stated that the higher the price charged for a product, the lower will be the demand for the product as potential consumers see the price exceed the product's perceived value to them. It is interesting to note that this concept suggests that the price charged for a product may be lower than the value placed upon it by some customers. This is the notion of a 'consumer surplus'. Figure 11.2 shows a demand curve for a particular product, with the price currently prevailing in the market place presented as P_1.

It can be seen from Figure 11.2 that there are some consumers, albeit few in number, who would be prepared to pay a higher price. The number of such consumers obviously declines as the price charged rises. The consumers who fall into this category are actually paying a price less than the value they perceive they are gaining through purchasing the product. They are enjoying a consumer surplus. At the same time, it can also be seen that the price P_1 is actually higher than the supplier's long-run marginal cost. In other words, in this case there is a 'surplus' accruing to the supplier as well. This analysis is an oversimplification of the real world, but it might be a useful focus for the price decision-maker to think of his or her problem along the lines suggested by Figure 11.3.

The pricing problem can be seen in this way as an attempt by the supplier to achieve the greatest possible 'surplus' over long-run marginal cost while still pricing no higher than the perceived value placed on the product by potential customers.

An alternative way of looking at this is to see the problem in terms of the need to identify what value the target market places upon the product and then to convert that value into a market price. The first step towards solving this

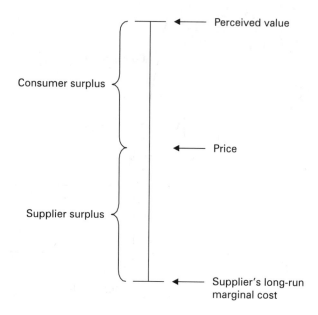

Figure 11.3 Consumer and supplier surplus

problem is to recognize that there will be different groupings of customers with different perceptions of a product's value. These groupings are, in effect, *market segments*. Thus we might identify a specific segment of the market that seeks certain benefits from a product and values them at a particular level.

However, it is not sufficient just to identify the customers' perceived value of a product and then set a price equal to that value. Frequently, there will be costs other than price that the customer will have to consider in acquiring the product. Supplemental costs over and above the purchase price could include freight, installation, training, maintenance, service, spares support and other 'life cycle costs', as they are sometimes termed. There may be additional perceived costs in terms of risk of product failure or, particularly in the case of consumer products, social and psychological risk.

From the customer's point of view, therefore, it can be argued that the decision to purchase is a trade-off between, on the one hand, all costs involved and on the other hand, the perceived benefits resulting from acquisition. This relationship may be expressed as follows:

Highest price the customer will pay = perceived benefits − costs other than price

Thus it can be seen that, in the pricing decision, it is as important to understand the cost structure of our potential customer as it is to know our own! It is essential to the pricing decision to recognize the total cost impact on the customer of the acquisition of our product. Even though the customers themselves may not have fully evaluated the implication of the acquisition, the supplier will be better positioned to sell to them if these costs are known. The appropriate concept here is that of 'life cycle costs', which refers to all the customer costs that will be incurred by the customer from the acquisition of the product through to the end of its useful life. For example, in pricing a piece of numerical control equipment, the manufacturer should identify the effects that the equipment will have on the customer's manufacturing economics, its likely life expectancy, any maintenance and upgrading costs, and its disposal value if any.

Given a full analysis of the life cycle cost implications of the product, the pricing decision-maker is then able to focus attention upon the identification and quantification of the product's perceived benefits.

BENEFIT EVALUATION

In recent years, a number of developments have taken place in the fields of mathematical psychology and psychometrics which have enhanced our ability to quantify the relative importance that potential customers place upon the various attributes of a product. These new techniques are based upon a type of trade-off analysis called 'conjoint measurement', which is a powerful device for quantifying the intangible as well as the physical benefits present in a product. The 'trade-off' approach to pricing follows a sequence of logical steps.

Step 1: identification of benefit components

It is important to recognize that potential customers for a product will have their own perceptions of the benefits contained within that product. To identify these perceived benefits, it is necessary to conduct a limited, small-scale survey of potential and/or actual customers. The purpose of this study is to elicit the key features or benefits that are expected to be acquired as a result of using the product. Direct questioning can be used, such as, 'What is it that makes Brand X different from Brand Y?' More sophisticated procedures for the elicitation of benefits exist, but they all have essentially the same purpose: to draw from consumers their own perceptions of product features, rather than the manufacturers'. So, in a study of customers for a new chemical compound, the following product attributes might emerge:

- Quality
- Availability
- Impact on customer's production yield
- Storage conditions necessary
- Technical assistance

The question then becomes: 'What relative value is placed upon each of these components?'

Step 2: quantifying benefit values

Since a product is, in effect, the totality of its component attributes, a way must be found of separating these and measuring their individual value to the

Table 11.1   **Product attribute levels**

Attribute	Product 1	Product 2
Quality	Impurities less than one part per million	Impurities less than ten parts per million
Availability	Make to order	Available from stock
Impact on customer's production yield	No impact	Improves usable output by 10 per cent
Storage conditions	Stable product, long shelf-life	Requires high-level storage environment
Technical assistance	Manufacturer provides high-level technical advice	Weak
Price	£5 a kilo	£5.50 a kilo

customer. It is here that conjoint analysis becomes particularly useful. Using the attributes identified in Step 1, the researcher presents to the sample of customers a variety of hypothetical products that contain different configurations of the previously identified attributes, with each configuration having a different price. Thus, for the example of the chemical compound, the hypothetical product configurations in Table 11.1 might be constructed.

Clearly, there are many different combinations of attribute levels. Only two examples are given here, but they will suffice to demonstrate the concept of trade-off. The question put to the survey respondents is: 'Given that the two alternative products above are available, which would you prefer?' Both products have their advantages and their disadvantages, and the final choice will be based upon the trade-off of these pluses and minuses. By extending the questioning to include other configurations of the same attributes, it is possible, using conjoint analysis, to produce a numerical 'weight' for each attribute which reflects the relative importance attached to each of the attributes in question. More specifically, it enables the researcher to identify for each attribute the weight given to different *levels* of that attribute. Thus for 'quality', it will be possible to determine the extent by which 'impurities less than one part per million' is preferred over 'impurities less than ten parts per million', or any level of impurity in the range under consideration.

However, the greatest advantage of using conjoint analysis in this context is that it also provides the researcher with *the relative utility of different price levels*. Thus we have a means of interpreting the price equivalence of differences in the perceived values of different combinations of product attributes. Step 3 describes this procedure.

Step 3: determining the price equivalence of value

The output of the conjoint analysis of the data collected in Step 2 might typically appear as in Figure 11.4. For each level of each attribute, a 'utility' is

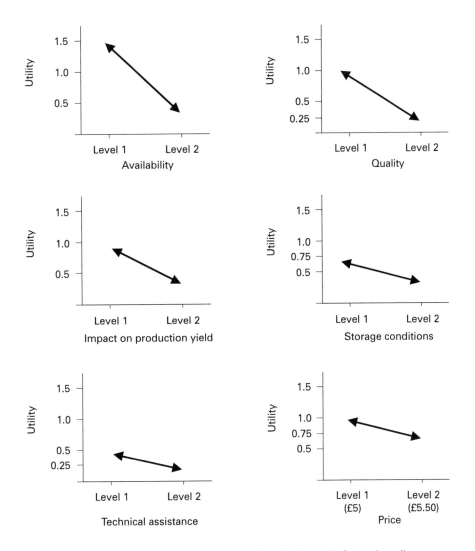

Note: Level 1 corresponds to the lowest level identified in the study for each attribute.

Figure 11.4 Graphical output of conjoint analysis

computed and this can be set out in a graph to give a visual indication of the importance of that attribute. More importantly, though, conjoint analysis enables the value of this arbitrary 'utility' measure to be given a price equivalence. It will be seen from Figure 11.4 that the difference in utility between a price of £5 and £5.50 is 0.25 (that is, 1.00 – 0.75); thus the price equivalence of one unit of 'utility' is (£5.50 – £5)/0.25, or £2.

Using this information, we can say, for example, that a 10 per cent improvement in yield is worth a price difference of £1 per kilo (£2[1.00 – 0.5]). Again, we can say that the benefit of a stable product with a long shelf-life is worth an additional £0.5 per kilo (£2[0.75 – 0.5]) over a product requiring a high-level storage environment.

Given this information, it is clear that the price decision-maker has a very powerful insight into the customer's perception of the components of value. The decision-maker can now also identify which product attributes have the biggest influence on value perception. In the case examined here, customers, say, see availability and quality as the two major components of value. A change from Level 2 to Level 1 in availability brings an increase in utility of 1.0, while a change from Level 2 to Level 1 in quality produces an increase in utility of 0.75 (worth £2 and £1.50 per kilo respectively).

This information on the 'price equivalence' of customer value can provide a basis for price determination that reflects the worth the market places upon our offer. Perhaps one of the most important features of the value-in-use approach advocated here is that it focuses our attention upon customer perceptions of product attributes and away from the more narrow-minded production orientation of suppliers' costs. In this sense, it is very much a market-oriented approach to pricing.

This approach to pricing also raises certain strategic issues, particularly with regard to marketing communications. It is well known that, in many product/market fields, there is a direct relationship between the price obtained and the customer's perception of quality. In other words, where there is a perception of 'added values', the demand/price relationship can be radically altered. Where added values are perceived to exist by the customer, the demand curve is, in effect, shifted to the right, as in Figure 11.5. In this particular case, the

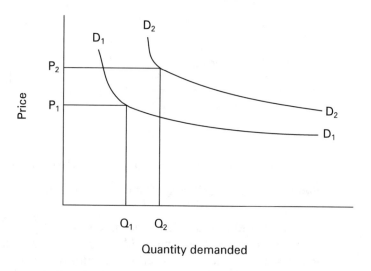

Key: D₁D₁ Original demand curve   Q₁ Original demand
D₂D₂ New demand curve   P₂ New price
P₁   Original price   Q₂ New demand

Figure 11.5 The effect of perceived added values on the demand curve

heightened perceptions of customer values have served to stimulate greater demand, but at a higher price.

To make use of this fundamental model for profit improvement, we must recognize two basic factors.

1. *Perception*: to what extent does the customer/potential customer perceive that our product embodies certain attributes?
2. *Value/utility*: to what extent does the customer/potential customer consider these attributes to be important in the purchase decision?

In the first case, if the perception of product performance falls below that of competitive products, what can be done? It may be that the problem is largely one of communication. Perhaps we have not been forceful enough in our attempts to inform the market about the strengths of our product or, if we have, the message still has not come across. Alternatively, it may be that our product is deficient in these attributes and it may thus be desirable to institute a programme of product improvement.

If, on the other hand, we identify that our product scores highly, but on attributes that are perhaps given less weight by the customer (that is, their value/utility is lower), then we could downgrade the product on these attributes to improve overall profitability or, indeed, reduce the price if it were deemed appropriate. Likewise, recognizing the value/utility placed upon the various product attributes should be of great help in designing and introducing new products or in reformulating old ones.

From the point of view of marketing strategy, value-in-use can become the basis of a more effective segmentation strategy. Since different customers will have different perceptions of a product's attributes and will also differ in the value/utility they place upon those attributes, it will often be possible to target products to specific groups, or segments, in the market. Price is one of the simplest ways of segmenting markets, but price segmentation can become far more effective when based upon value-in-use.

COMPETITIVE PRICING STRATEGY

Most marketing activity takes place within the context of some level of competitive activity. Thus pricing decisions must clearly reflect competitive positioning and the customer's perception of any differential values that are embodied in competitive offerings.

At one extreme is a market with a dominant supplier: say, 40 per cent market share as compared to the nearest rival with 15 per cent market share. Where that dominant supplier has an offer that is high in perceived added values, it is likely that a substantial price differential will be obtained. On the other hand, if there is no one dominant player in market share terms, and the market is effectively a 'commodity' market with no perceived product differences, then it is highly unlikely that any one supplier will be able to command a higher price.

In any competitive market place the following relationship will normally hold:

$$\frac{\text{Perceived benefits (market leader)}}{\text{Price (market leader)}} \geq \frac{\text{Perceived benefits (competitor)}}{\text{Price (competitor)}}$$

In other words, to maintain a position of market share leadership, the ratio of perceived benefits to price must exceed that of the competition. Using this relationship, it will be recognized that it is not sufficient to have a high level of perceived benefits if the competition has a substantially lower price. In some cases, a supplier may develop an offer with substantial added values and sell it at a high price, but in doing so, they will provide competitors with a price umbrella under which they can shelter while developing 'me too' products. The success of the so-called IBM-PC clones in the personal computer market provides a testament to this.

The position of the product in relation to the market life cycle will also be important in determining pricing strategy. Given the importance of maintaining or increasing market share in the early stages of the life cycle as a means of increasing the speed of movement down the experience curve – to ensure both higher profitability and cash flow as the market matures – careful attention must be paid to the benefit/price ratio.

In the past, marketing authors have distinguished between *skimming* strategies and *penetration* strategies, particularly in the context of pricing new products. It has been suggested that a penetration strategy (that is, a low relative price) is a route to early gains in market share if:

- Demand is price sensitive
- Economies of scale exist
- Competitive imitation is not difficult

An example of such a pricing strategy might be the low price established for the initial sale of domestic television satellite dishes and decoders.

Alternatively, it is argued, a skimming strategy (that is, a high relative price) may be appropriate where:

- Demand is not particularly price sensitive
- There is a relatively flat cost curve (that is, unit costs at low volumes are not so much higher than unit costs at higher volumes)
- There is limited danger of competitive imitation

The pricing policy adopted by Rolex watches is perhaps one example of this skimming approach.

Figure 11.6 suggests the possible pricing strategies that may be appropriate given the opportunities for value enhancement or cost reduction. Value enhancement is based upon building perceived benefits, while cost reduction can provide the basis for successful price competition.

The rationale behind each of these options can be demonstrated by using the experience curve concept. As we have seen, it is usually the case that

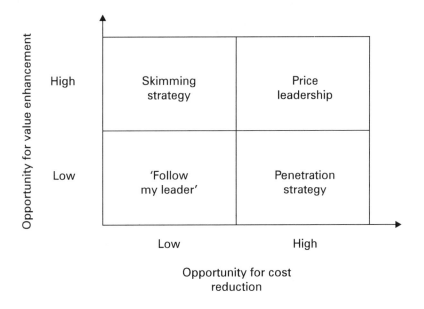

Figure 11.6 Appropriate pricing strategies

penetration strategies are more appropriate where the opportunity for cost reduction is greatest, (that is, rapid movement down a steeply sloping experience curve can be achieved).

On the other hand, a skimming strategy is more likely to be appropriate where rapid cost reductions are unlikely (that is, the experience curve is less steep). Figure 11.7 outlines the logic of each of the four pricing options.

Ultimately, however, neither a skimming nor a penetration policy will lead to a position of substantial market leadership unless the benefit/price ratio is maintained at a higher level than that of the competition. The achievement of a favourable ratio is obviously not down to pricing strategy alone; it can only come about through a total focus of the marketing mix upon differentiation while managing the operations of the business to provide a cost advantage.

RELATIONSHIP PRICING

It has sometimes been suggested that we have entered the era of the 'value driven' customer. This customer seeks even greater delivered benefits but at lower cost. Customers such as these can be found in every type of market, be it business-to-business or end-user. Price sensitivity seems to be as high as it has ever been and customers are often quite willing to move from one supplier to another if the price/value equation does not appeal to them.

To counteract this tendency, companies such as P&G have developed a philosophy of value-based pricing. Under value-based pricing the customer (and the consumer) is offered a guaranteed lower price through the elimination of non-value adding activities or strategies such as frequent promotions or

(1)

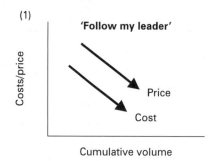

In this situation the industry price will follow costs and, in particular, the costs of the price leader

(2)

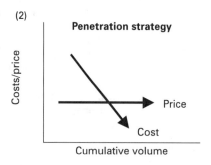

Here price is set low by the early entrant to gain advantage of the price-sensitive market and thus gain market share and hence lower costs

(3)

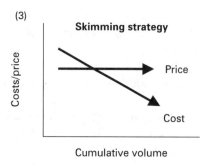

Under a skimming strategy it is assumed that the cost reduction opportunities are low, hence the less steep experience curve

(4)

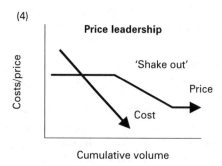

Through a combination of high added value plus low cost, these companies are able to bring down the price 'umbrella' and shake out the less innovative or higher-cost competitors

Note: All the above charts assume logarithmic scales; hence the experience 'curve' is shown as a straight line.

Figure 11.7 Price and the experience curve

brand extensions. The underpinning idea is that customers (or consumers) will not pay for non-value adding activities or elements of a marketing offer. Thus, in the USA, P&G used to offer over 20 variants of Crest toothpaste (different sizes, flavours, and so on). Research highlighted that such variety did not create additional value for customers or consumers. In fact, the customers (the retailers) were not prepared to find shelf space for such a range, and at the consumer level it only served to focus on the best-selling variants. This meant that significant complexity was taken out of the supply chain and hence costs came down without any loss of customer or consumer value.

In ways such as these, lower prices can be changed and yet margins are maintained. Customer relationships are built on many things, as we have observed throughout this book, but one of the strongest drivers of an enduring relationship is the perception by the customer that this supplier delivers 'more for less'.

Value-based pricing, or EDLP as it has been termed, is not just applicable in retail markets. In business-to-business markets the quest for value on the part of customers is just as great. Often this leads to 'deals' being offered by suppliers which are not based upon cost reduction and thus are not sustainable. The key to EDLP in this environment is for both parties to collaborate in the search for genuine cost reduction through process improvement to enable price to fall while margins are preserved. There is now a growing recognition in many industries that partnership between buyer and supplier is a better way to achieve enduring cost reduction than the previous strategy of the customer playing one supplier off against the other.

INTERNATIONAL PRICING MANAGEMENT

One of the most striking trends in recent years has been the rapid increase in the globalization of markets. Not only is this true in the case of well-established brands such as Coca-Cola, Marlboro and Gucci, but it is also apparent in markets as diverse as computing, motor cars and consumer electronics. Neither is the trend towards globalization confined only to products: we see similar transformations in services, whether it be banking, retailing or satellite television.

At the same time, the corporations that have created and developed these global brands are refocusing their operations so that they, too, are global in their scope. What this means is that an electronics company, for example, may source some of its components in one country and sub-assemble them in another country, while final assembly takes place in yet a third country. Managing these complex global networks becomes one of the prime challenges to the achievement of profitability.

This move towards the globalization of business has had a substantial impact on the pricing decision. First, there are implications for the cost of the product or service and second, it is quite likely that there will be significant differences from country to country in the price sensitivity of demand.

As we have noted, there is an increasing tendency for organizations to source materials and assemble and manufacture items offshore. The motivation for this is largely economic, based upon the search for cost reductions. These lower costs may be available through lower labour rates, lower costs of materials, lower taxes, and lower costs of capital or government assistance. At the same time, these organizations may also rationalize production so that individual country operations no longer produce a full range of products for their own national markets. Instead the company may now focus production on fewer factories making a limited range of items, but for a regional or even global market. The opportunities for enhanced economies of scale in production offered by such strategies may be considerable. Companies such as Unilever, for example, which previously manufactured soaps and detergents in local factories for local markets, have now rationalized their production on a regional basis with fewer factories producing for wider markets.

While the advantages of such strategies seem to be readily apparent, there are a number of implications for pricing.

Exchange-Rate Fluctuations

Given the volatility of exchange rates between currencies, there is significant inherent risk in companies committing themselves to long-term offshore supply arrangements. Companies with the ability to switch production from one location to another at short notice clearly have an advantage. For example, Heinz can increase or decrease the production of tomato ketchup in its regional plants with a high degree of flexibility in order to take advantage of exchange-rate fluctuations. Companies that lack this flexibility can often find themselves faced with substantial cost increases as a result of changes in exchange rates.

Changes in Factor Costs

Closely allied to the risk of exchange rate fluctuation is the problem of changes in factor costs such as labour, land or capital. Many companies decided to locate production in what were then perceived to be low-labour-cost countries, often in South-East Asia, only to find that with rapid economic development that advantage proved to be transitory. Also to be taken into account is the way in which the costs of transport from the source of supply to the end market can change, in some instances eliminating any production cost advantage.

Transfer Pricing

In complex, multi-level production and distribution systems within a single company, the issue of internal transfer pricing arises. In other words, at what internal price should products or supplies be 'sold' to the next stage in the chain? Sometimes these decisions will be determined by tax considerations, but often other factors will influence the transfer price, such as internal accounting practices that allocate overhead costs on an arbitrary basis, hence distorting the cost that is passed on down the chain. There are countless examples of companies that have been forced to charge higher prices in end markets because of an accumulated cost that reflects the real costs of supply.

Parallel Imports

Often the same product may be sold in different markets at different prices. This practice, known to economists as 'price discrimination', is made possible by the different demand and supply characteristics of these different markets. However, once the price difference between markets exceeds the cost of acquiring and transporting those products from one market to another then arbitrage or 'parallel imports' can become a serious problem for the company. This is a phenomenon that is frequently encountered in both consumer and industrial markets. One partial solution to this problem is to develop a unique brand for individual markets, accepting that it may not allow economies of scale in sourcing, production and distribution to be achieved.

Global/Regional Purchasing

In the same way that suppliers are tending to operate on a global, or at least regional, basis, so too are their customers. If a major European retailer, for example, sees that a product is being sold by a manufacturer at a lower price in one market (because of supply/demand considerations) then that retailer may insist on buying that product at that low price for all the markets in which it operates. This will become more of a problem for suppliers as customers increasingly band together into regional or global buying groups. Across Europe, a number of such groups already exist, particularly in grocery retailing. Furthermore, the introduction of the single currency in the European Union will enhance price 'transparency' and make price discrimination across those markets more difficult to maintain.

A further challenge to international pricing management arises where the same brand may be positioned quite differently in different national markets. Stella Artois, for example, is a premium-priced lager in the UK, whereas in its home country of Belgium it is seen as a 'regular' beer sold at standard prices.

Given these potential problems, what are the options for a company seeking to develop an international pricing strategy?

The overriding consideration, as with pricing decisions generally, is that the price must reflect the value proposition that is presented to the customer in each market in which the product is offered. Based upon this principle, the 'target cost' for that market can be identified: that is, the achievable price less the desired profit margin. Decisions on sourcing must be made in the context of that target cost, taking into account total supply chain costs (preferably undistorted by transfer pricing manipulations). No pricing strategy will eliminate the risks we have identified above, but careful and continuous management of the pricing decision on a global basis will help to minimize them.

SUMMARY

The pricing decision is one of the most important issues to be faced by the marketing manager. Almost every market is influenced to some extent or another by the relative price of the products that compete in that market.

When customers buy products they are making choices based upon their perception of the relative value of competing offers. The maximum price at which a product or service can be sold can be no greater than its perceived value.

In this chapter we have proposed that price should be related to the value of benefits that our product or service delivers. Techniques such as trade-off analysis can be utilized to assist in reaching pricing decisions, particularly in the valuation of benefits.

Further reading

André Gabor, *Pricing : Principles and Practices* (London: Heinemann, 1977).
Kent Monroe, *Pricing: Making Profitable Decisions* (New York: McGraw-Hill, 1979).
Thomas Nagle, *The Strategy and Tactics of Pricing* (Englewood Cliffs, NJ: Prentice-Hall, 1987).
Hermann Simon, *Price Management* (Amsterdam: North-Holland, 1987).

BRANDING AND POSITIONING

Simon Knox

In this chapter:

- Brands as assets
- How successful brands are developed
- How brands work in building relationships across multiple markets
- Developments in corporate and global branding
- Cases demonstrating brand augmentation and brand positioning

BRANDS ARE THE BUSINESS

Oscar Wilde once said that a cynic is someone who knows the price of everything, but the value of nothing. He might have been talking about people's attitude towards their company's brands. It is only relatively recently that managers have started talking about brands as assets. If anyone is in doubt about the value of brands, they need do only two things: see what companies are prepared to pay for top brands and look at the extent to which the market capitalization of branded-goods companies exceeds their tangible asset value.

In the last decade, there has been a spate of acquisitions by brand-led businesses in an effort to accelerate product ranges and geographic expansion strategies. In many instances, large premiums were paid for the companies. When the Swiss food giant, Nestlé, bought Rowntree in the UK, it paid £2.5 billion for the company, which had a balance sheet value of £0.4 billion. While this premium does reflect the potential value of Rowntree's distribution, customer relationships and branding know-how, the largest share of the premium was, without doubt, for the confectionery brands which the company had carefully nurtured for decades: Kit-Kat, After Eight and Polo mints.

Coca-Cola, the global soft drinks company, calculates that only about 4 per cent of the company's value can be attributed to its plants, machinery and sites. The real value of the company lies in its intangible assets and first among these is its brand. Likewise, the computer chip manufacturing company, Intel, famous for its 'Intel-Inside' advertising, believes that about 85 per cent of its worth rests with the company's brand equity and intellectual capital: its brand name, patents, expertise and people.

It is a misconception to think that brands are all about soft drinks and soap powder. Speakers from an impressive range of world-class organizations, including Hilton Hotels, ICI, Whirlpool, and BP, recently addressed an *Economist* conference on brands. They all spoke about how their businesses had prospered by embracing the most modern thinking on branding.

In business-to-business markets, where customers are buying on behalf of their organizations (see Chapter 5), brand preferences can also be quite marked. Many of the mega business brands have emerged from the IT industry, such as Microsoft with its Windows software products and Dell computers which now sells more desktop PCs directly to corporate clients than does IBM through its dealer network. Equipped with a clear understanding of how customer value is created, the offer can be branded and positioned so as to create customer preferences and enhance the value of the brand.

THE VALUE OF BRANDS

Why is it that, in terms of 'tangible' measures, BMW cars and Levi jeans are not significantly better than their rivals, but customers will pay significantly more for them? Why is it that Marks & Spencer's customers are prepared to pay twice the price a greengrocer would charge for a kilo of tomatoes because they are branded St Michael's? The difference between a brand and a 'named' product or commodity can be summed up in the phrase 'added values'. To illustrate the power of these added values, consider the findings of a *blind test* (where the brand identity is concealed) in which Diet Pepsi was compared against Diet Coke by a panel of consumers:

Prefer Pepsi	51%
Prefer Coke	44%
Equal/Can't say	5%

When the same two drinks were given to a matched sample of consumers in an *open test* (where the true identity of the brands is revealed), the following results were produced:

Prefer Pepsi	23%
Prefer Coke	65%
Equal/Can't say	12%

How can this outcome be explained, if not in terms of the added values that are aroused in the minds of consumers when they see the familiar Coke logo and packaging? Here, the customer value is emotional and it has been consciously fostered over the years by successful Coca-Cola advertising. Similarly, telecommunications companies, such as British Telecom (BT), have shifted the thematic thrust of their advertising from generic telephone calls to calls to friends and relatives overseas. BT employs the slogan, 'It's good to talk', emphasizing the importance of relationships between people, and the significant role that communications play in connecting people and thus in adding value to society.

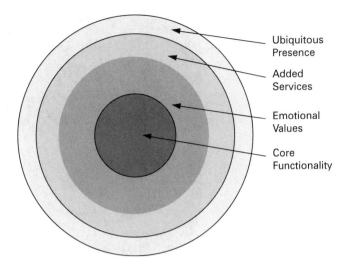

Ubiquitous Presence

Added Services

Emotional Values

Core Functionality

Figure 12.1   The augmented brand

It is not only in the area of emotional and psychological benefit that companies create new forms of added value and differentiation for their brands. The notion of 'the augmented brand', as shown in Figure 12.1, illustrates this fact.

Many companies now view added services as a major component of their brand offer. For instance, some airlines provide their valued customers with transport to and from the airport, offering them an end-to-end service. Freight forwarders provide logistics support so that their services can compete on a basic offer that is at lowest cost. Industrial component manufacturers offer engineering services in order that their companies are seen to supply more than merely parts.

Another way of adding value is by making it easier to buy the product or to use the service. A home delivery pizza company in Toronto grew by uniquely advertising its telephone number in the form of a memorable tune and not by talking about its products or Italian heritage. Telephone and on-line banking companies also add ease of access to their core product benefits via the provision of 24-hour services.

Successful brands are constructed through this augmentation process. Müller Yogurts, for example, represented in Figure 12.2, started from scratch in 1987 and became a market leader by 1992. From its launch, the Müller range was very different from other yogurts on the market in that it was positioned as 'luxury, not low-fat; indulgence, not health'. The company successfully differentiated and augmented its brand by meeting the following standards:

Core functionality	– luxury (creamy, tasty, unique packaging and design)
Emotional values	– indulgence (spoil yourself, special moments)

Figure 12.2 Müller Yogurts: 'The greatest thing to happen to yogurts since milk curdled'
(Reproduced with kind permission of Müller Dairy [UK] Ltd)

Added services   – superior margins for distributors and retailers with an auxiliary sales force to undertake merchandising

Ubiquitous presence – distribution and category saturation (ranges in each of the seven major market segments).

Having developed a superior product and this unique positioning, the Müller brand has now become the eighth largest brand in the UK, with sales of over £240 million per year.

By creating superior customer value, the size and value of a brand will increase over time. But how is the value of a company's brands measured by the company's management? The management consultants at Interbrand specialize in determining the financial value of company brands. They currently consider the world's top twenty brands to be as follows:

1.	Coca-Cola	11.	Nokia
2.	Microsoft	12.	Mercedes
3.	IBM	13.	Nescafé
4.	General Electric	14.	Hewlett Packard
5.	Ford	15.	Gillette
6.	Disney	16.	Kodak
7.	Intel	17.	Ericsson
8.	McDonald's	18.	Sony
9.	AT&T	19.	Amex
10.	Marlboro	20.	Toyota

Source: Interbrand, 1999.

Interbrand estimated the financial value of these leading brands using the following four criteria:

Brand weight – The influence that the brand has over its category or market
Brand length – The stretch or extension that the brand has achieved
Brand breadth – The level of franchise that the brand has achieved in terms of age spread, consumer type and international appeal
Brand depth – The degree of commitment and loyalty that the brand has achieved among its customers

This type of assessment enables managers to put a financial value on their brand assets for the purposes of both balance sheet and off-balance sheet activities. In this chapter, we shall concentrate on the latter, since we want to look more closely at how brands work in customer and supplier markets as well as in internal markets.

HOW DO BRANDS WORK?

A brand is an entity that offers customers (and other relevant parties) added value based on factors over and above its functional performance. These added values, or brand values, differentiate products and provide the basis for determining customer preference and loyalty. Traditionally, the marketing mix has focused on building the customer relationship by branding the offer in such a way as to generate greater profits. However, it is now being recognized that company brands can also work across multiple markets as a means of improving customer retention rates and long-term profits (see Figure 12.3).

A successful brand is one that customers prefer to buy and that channel intermediaries, such as retailers, choose to stock. It attracts a high market share and a premium price. Typically, the brand leader obtains twice the market share of the number two brand, and the number two brand obtains twice the market share of the number three brand. The brand with the highest market share is always much more profitable, as the well-known PIMS study found: brands with a 40 per cent market share generate three times the ROI of those with a market share of only 10 per cent. Figure 12.4 depicts this relationship between market share and profitability.

Superior profitability is created by customer purchasing preferences and loyalty as well as by word of mouth endorsement of the brand, which can readily generate new customers for the company. First Direct, the world's first telephone bank, boasts a 97 per cent customer retention rate and generates about one-third of its new customers through referrals by loyal customers. The converse of this referral process is also true: negative word of mouth can cause customers to switch brands and produce a loss of sales. Studies have shown that when a bad brand experience is encountered, approximately 30 per cent of people will tell their friends about it, and sales can suffer as a direct result.

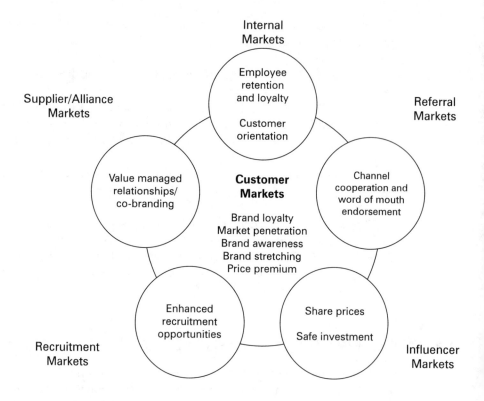

Figure 12.3   Successful branding and the potential rewards

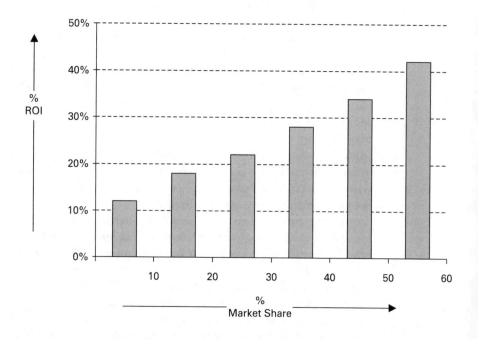

Figure 12.4   Profit improvement through market share

Suppliers and their alliance partners are quick to recognize the power of successful brands, since being a preferred supplier can yield new business opportunities, less volatile sales and higher revenues. In the process of helping Tesco Stores to develop their financial services, The Royal Bank of Scotland has been able to win new business for itself from among the grocery chain's English customers. Some of the best brand-led companies to have mastered value-managed supplier relationships are from Japan. Japanese automobile suppliers, on average, fulfil orders worth 24 times more per vehicle than their US counterparts. This is because Japanese automobile manufacturers use one-tenth the number of suppliers, which means that the suppliers benefit from more business and longer-term contracts with each customer. These closer relationships between manufacturers and suppliers also enable closer relationships between suppliers and customers, where suppliers work together with their customers to develop systems, reduce costs, innovate products and processes, and achieve a greater overall ability to supply.

Generally speaking, a company that is successful at branding has a customer-orientation approach and a culture that puts customers first. This commitment to customer satisfaction is usually reflected in enhanced employee satisfaction, which leads to improved employee retention. Higher levels of employee retention mean reduced operating costs, consistency in operations and a 'feel-good' factor across the company. The feel-good factor associated with many brand-led businesses also makes recruitment easier, by attracting local employees, graduate trainees and senior managers from other companies. When staff enjoy their place of work, they are often prepared to work for less money, a reality which some strongly branded companies, such as Microsoft and Manchester United in the UK, have fully exploited to leverage profitability!

To reap the lucrative benefits of branding and premium pricing, a company has to carefully manage the reputation of its brands so that customers will uniquely associate them with superior value. Otherwise, the process of decay

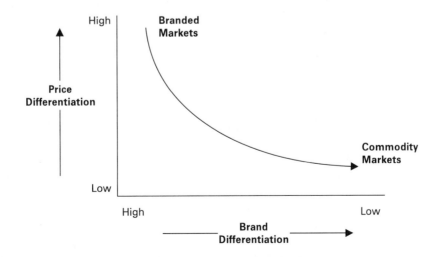

Figure 12.5 Process of decay from brand to commodity

from brand to commodity will set in as the distinctive values of the brand become less clear to the customer. The process of decay from brand to commodity is illustrated in Figure 12.5.

To prevent this potential downturn, the company's brands are often managed as mini-businesses with brand managers acting like mini-Chief Executive Officers (CEOs) who compete for the company's resources in order to uphold the brand's distinctive advantage and grow market share. In the next section, we will look at how brands have been traditionally managed and how the emphasis in marketing is now shifting towards customer management and company branding.

HOW ARE BRANDS MANAGED?

P&G, the detergents company, is widely credited with inventing the concept of 'one-man-one-brand' in the 1930s, some 50 years after it launched Ivory Soap in the USA. P&G found that as its brand portfolio increased, traditional functional management could no longer handle the complexity of the product portfolio. In order to maintain and further develop superior customer value, P&G decided to break the company into mini-companies centred around brands. Each major brand was handled by a brand office, which was run by a brand manager who was responsible for marketing, advertising, pricing, promotion, packaging and innovation. The brand management system represented a highly effective organizational design for managing change, product innovation and customer requirements. Central management controlled those functions that presented clear economies of scale, including manufacturing, warehousing, sales, finance and personnel. Brand managers were encouraged to compete with their colleagues and no brand was allowed to escape the discipline of full competition. On the supermarket shelves across Europe, Ariel competed with other P&G products, such as Bold and Daz, just as fiercely as it did with its arch-rival, Persil, and the other Unilever brands. In order to compete effectively in this intense environment, brands were skilfully positioned by brand managers to provide customers with distinctive choices according to their expressed needs.

BRAND POSITIONING AND MARKET MAPS

While it is often necessary to augment a brand to create a powerful brand, augmentation alone does not secure success. Competitors are quick to copy successful brand innovations, imitating their core functionality, added value services or emotional appeal. Branding expertise only becomes a significant corporate asset through effective differentiation between one brand and another. Critical differentiation has traditionally been achieved through the development of the unique selling proposition (USP), arguably the single most important component of modern branding practice. The USP is a succinct statement about the brand's most important customer benefit, supported by psychological or functional evidence. In practice, the USP is usually a one-sentence distillation of why the customer will buy one brand as opposed to another. At its best, the USP is translatable into a mnemonic device or slogan that permanently differentiates the brand from its competitors and that embeds it in the minds of customers. Examples of successful USPs include:

> 'A Mars a day helps you work, rest and play'
> 'Timex watches – takes a lickin' and keeps on tickin''
> 'All because the lady loves Milk Tray'
> 'Always Coca-Cola ...'

Competition in the soft drinks market is fierce, particularly between the brands Coca-Cola and Pepsi. This means that positioning the products is crucial as, indeed, is gaining an understanding of the criteria which customers use to discriminate between the two brands. Marketers can accomplish both these tasks by using a marketing research technique called *market mapping*, whereby customers are asked to identify the main purchasing motivators or attributes and to rate each brand on this basis. As customers often identify many choice determinants, it can be necessary to analyse their responses by computer in order to develop the market map. The soft drinks market map is shown in Figure 12.6.

Although Coca-Cola and Pepsi are closely positioned on the market map, the brands appeal to slightly different target markets: young professionals prefer Pepsi (and Pepsi Max) while family buyers prefer Coca-Cola.

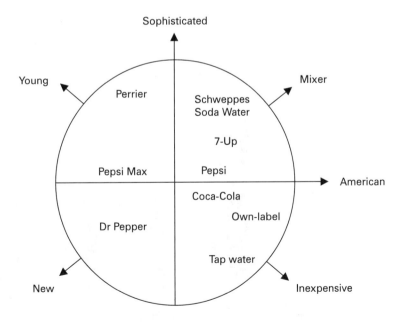

Figure 12.6   The soft drinks market map

Perrier has been notably successful in positioning itself as a young people's drink with a degree of sophistication. It has also distanced itself from tap water and hence its premium price.

In many markets, including soft drinks, own-labels or the retailer's own brand are becoming a significant market force. Across Europe, sales of own-labels are on the increase and in the UK, own-labels account for nearly 38 per cent of all grocery sales, as indicated in Figure 12.7.

The popularity of retailer-branded products among consumers, and the level of consumer trust that is now accorded to retailers in general, has become a major challenge for branded goods manufacturers and service providers. Over the years, retailers have successfully repositioned their brand image from being the manufacturer's selling agent to being the consumer's purchasing agent. In the UK, the top five grocery retailers now control 70 per cent of the grocery market. They exert considerable power and influence through extending consumer choice and pursuing a value-for-money strategy on behalf of their customers.

A good case in point is Tesco Stores, which has become the number one retailer in the UK by investing in better retail environments, value-added services, employee training, supply chain efficiencies and customer relationship management. The company has an enviable reputation for being innovative by offering good value across an extensive range of products while providing a convenient, quality shopping experience. Tesco is blatantly aware of the fact that customers regularly appraise the Tesco brand according to these criteria, and it uses this knowledge to employ a coordinated and proactive marketing approach successfully.

In positioning a brand, marketing management can apply the market mapping technique at the product or service level, or to a portfolio of products or services within a strategic business unit. The technique can also be used to brand the company itself.

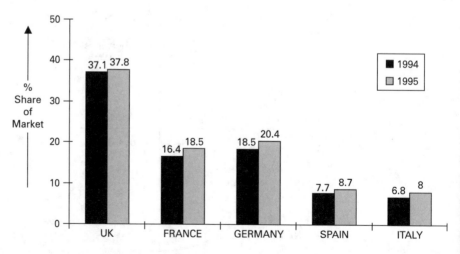

Figure 12.7 Own-label grocery share

Source: AC Nielsen (and estimate for Aldi in Germany).

THE PRODUCT PORTFOLIO AND COMPANY BRANDING

Many large and sophisticated brand owners are currently seeking to associate their corporate name and values with their product name. For instance, Nestlé now puts its brand name on all its product portfolios – from breakfast cereals through to confectionery and pasta – in order to build synergies. By promoting familiarity and confidence in the *corporate* name, a company can encourage consumers to sample its new or existing products, even where they would normally buy a competitive offering.

When McVitie's launched the Go Ahead!® brand in 1995, the company's management adopted the McVitie's house name, which stands for quality and reliability, to help penetrate the cakes, snacks and desserts markets as well as to build market share within the biscuit market where it is the brand leader. Figure 12.8 outlines the market spread of the McVitie's Go Ahead!® brand at launch.

Within each market sector, a portfolio of products was launched under the Go Ahead!® name, which has become synonymous with a low-fat market positioning, but with the added McVitie's endorsement. In the three years since its launch, the product range has more than trebled, and projected annual sales for biscuits alone are expected to reach £45 million.

From a review of the world's top 20 brands given earlier in the chapter, you will notice that about three-quarters of them are actually company brands. As the trend towards the globalization of markets, product portfolios and competition continues, it is likely that branding will increasingly be regarded as a company-wide activity, for senior management will seek out higher levels

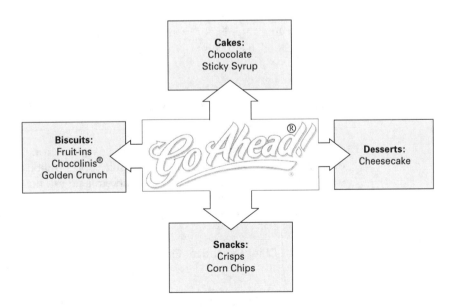

Note: ® Registered Trademark of United Biscuits (UK) Limited

Figure 12.8   McVitie's Go Ahead!® brand at launch

of consistency in developing, communicating and delivering customer value across national borders.

Branding a company or a strategic business unit (like the McVitie's Go Ahead! product portfolio) requires a different approach from that used by the one-man-one-brand convention previously discussed. There are a number of very good reasons for this. First, it is the organization's good name and reputation that is at stake, rather than the name associated with a product or service in a particular market. The risk of a service or product failure becomes greater as the portfolio increases and the market diversifies. Second, corporate reputation is more complex and thus difficult to manage, since it is founded on the cumulative effect of a diversity of customer perceptions and behaviours. The nature of a company's reputation reflects its values, ethics, policies and practices. Neither individual brand managers nor the products they manage have the necessary authority or scope to commit the entire organization in these areas, or to manage the full range of stakeholder relationships necessary to achieve the desired reputation. Third, by implication, customer value may also be created through a company's people and processes. Each of these three value-adding activities lies outside the traditional domain of marketing, which tends to think in terms of products and services and to manage value by applying the 4Ps marketing mix.

Although there is clearly more risk associated with developing a company brand, as opposed to a product brand, there is also more potential reward. As the context of the brand expands to embrace employees, know-how and organizational systems (as well as products), senior management can consider a broader set of capabilities in developing and delivering superior customer value.

The four components of company branding that can be used by senior management to strategically position the organization in the supply chain can be best explained using First Direct Telephone Bank as a mini case study.

Case Study 1: the one-to-one future – First Direct Bank

'First Direct has spent the last decade building our brand, so that we have now reached a point of huge brand equity and credibility, something not seen before in the financial services marketplace. We now need to take this forward, by continuing to build individual relationships with our customers and making sure they trust us to get the job done for them, again and again'.

Alan Hughes,
Chief Executive, First Direct (a member of HSBC ◀▓▶ Group)
December 1999

Since opening for business in October 1989, First Direct representatives have signed up over 950 000 customers for their telephone banking services. Without a branch network to support, the company's staffing costs are about half that of a typical retail bank. Its efficient information system has been instrumental in keeping costs down, and the use of information technology enables efficient access to its on-line customer database which forms the hub of all business operations. Employing an automatic call distribution system, customers' calls are routed to unoccupied operators across the company's four call centres. Each banking representative has instant access to every customer's accounts and banking history. Day-to-day transactions, such as balance enquiries, the electronic payment of bills and the transfer of funds between accounts, can all be completed by the same representative. For more specialized information on items such as loans and mortgages, customers are transferred to trained advisers. The full range of traditional banking services is offered in a friendly and efficient manner – 24 hours a day, 365 days a year – for the cost of a local telephone call.

The First Direct brand tries to communicate and deliver a no-frills, hassle-free approach to banking that is more in tune with customers' life styles. Customer feedback from the bank's surveys suggests that these objectives are being achieved with customer satisfaction levels running at over 85 per cent, in comparison to a typical retail bank's success rate of less than 60 per cent. Commercially, the world's first telephone bank is very successful with a return on equity of over 25 per cent and an ROI that is equally attractive.

So, how has First Direct managed to create these brand values and to position itself as the bank-of-choice in the eyes of its customers? This fundamental question may be answered by analysing the four components of the First Direct brand using the Brand Monitor©, as shown in Figure 12.9.

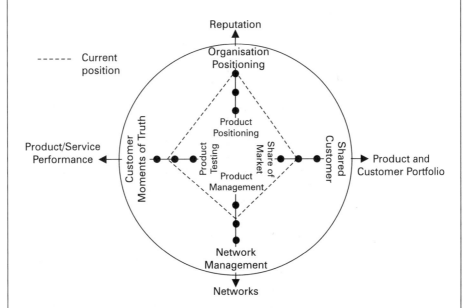

Figure 12.9 The First Direct Brand Monitor©

Source: S. Knox and S. Maklan, *Competing on Value* (London: F. T. Pitman, 1998).

Reputation

The First Direct brand is not seen as product-specific: its reputation is built upon the complete portfolio of the organization's activities and values. Consumer trust and commitment are engendered by the company's ability to be flexible, responsive, accessible and highly competitive. All aspects of the company's operations contribute to this positioning and it is not a by-product of the marketing efforts behind individual brands.

Product/Service Performance

This component refers to how the bank's products and service delivery are perceived by customers. These comprise the 'moments of truth' experienced by customers in their day-to-day dealings with the bank. Even though the customer does not formulate an ongoing working relationship with one or more particular bank representatives, the customer is left with the impression that the company's culture is very customer-oriented. This belief is the result of thorough staff training and an immediate knowledge of the customer's usual needs gained through the use of IT at the workstation. The bank endeavours to build the customer relationship through 'listening and serving', rather than 'selling financial services'.

Product and Customer Portfolio

In developing its customer portfolio, the 'new customer' team rejects about 40 per cent of all applicants. The bank's existing customers are predominantly professionals, aged between 25 and 44, who work in metropolitan areas. These busy people are attracted to the bank's offer of speed, convenience and a full range of financial, travel and information services. With the accurate matching of customer and product portfolios, customers make extensive use of the bank's services and this generates higher profitability. A *New York Times* journalist estimates that the average balance of a First Direct customer is *ten times higher* than a that of typical high street bank customer, while overall transaction costs are 60 per cent lower. The bank makes money on 60 per cent of its customers, as compared to 40 per cent at the average British bank.

The bank's strategic focus is to balance market share growth (primarily from customer referrals) with share of customer spend targets, which are aimed at encouraging existing customers to spend more with the bank across its product portfolio.

Networks

In service delivery, the bank uses a number of IT providers for transaction clearing, card service processing, and credit scoring. Likewise, in developing its product portfolio, the management team has established networks both within the HSBC group and among external insurance and assurance companies. However, these professional relationships are not overtly branded. It is possible to imagine that the network could become part of the company brand proposition: 'When you "buy" First Direct, you get many value-added partners.'

Overall, the First Direct brand offers outstanding customer service through the skilful management of each customer interface and the adoption of an individualistic style that is both respectful and open. Thus, the strength of the brand lies in the company's customer relationship management capabilities and in the service values inspired by the senior management team.

'First Direct is all about how customers feel when they have finished talking to us, whether by telephone, PC or any other channel. Yes, we supply financial services, but it's all about *how* we do this, rather than the products themselves.'

Peter Simpson, Commercial Director

DEVELOPING GLOBAL BRANDS

While we have witnessed some exemplary global branding successes, such as Coke, Sony Walkman, Marlboro cigarettes, and the Big Mac from McDonald's, not all attempts at global branding give cause for celebration. Perhaps sales never matched expectations, economies of scale failed to appear, or higher shares and greater margins never materialized. No doubt frustrated local managers have been heard to mutter 'I told you so' in 50 different languages.

According to McKinsey, there is a three-step process for getting it right with global brands.

Step 1: Challenge the benefits of going global

To move beyond a generalized notion of 'global is good', marketing managers need to analyse the key contributors to success and to consider the costs as well as the benefits of going global. What has created competitive advantage in country X or Y? What has made the market leader unique? Superior brand benefits may be attributable to core functionality, engineered through hard-to-copy innovation, such as that enjoyed by Polaroid instant cameras or Pampers nappies. Alternatively, as in the case of Dunhill or Cartier, brands may be cleverly positioned to deliver clear emotional benefits that are of significant interest to current and potential customer segments in major cities around the world.

Step 2: Standardize only the core elements

Creating an effective global brand does not mean rote standardization. The task, instead, is to review, separately each element of the offer and to determine the *degree* of standardization that is appropriate. Successful global marketers tend to standardize only the core elements (those elements described in Step 1 which create the brand's competitive edge). For instance, Bacardi, the best-selling spirit brand in the world, only standardizes its product formulation, packaging and brand name. Its brand positioning, advertising and pricing reflect significant local adaptation, as does its sales approach. American Express does not compromise its brand name, positioning or service offer, while other elements of the company's offer, such as advertising, pricing, sales and sales channels are adapted to national conditions.

Step 3: Central versus local control of business development

The challenge of brand globalization is to find a solution that avoids the extremes of a totally 'hands-off' approach or one of destructive intervention. P&G has tackled this problem within its European operations by creating 'category managers' in major national subsidiaries who supervise manufacturing, sales and marketing. Category management teams are responsible for developing and optimizing the product portfolios of retail customers in the national and international markets where they compete. Such a role requires business process skills in supply chain management (see Chapter 10), new product development (see Chapter 9) and customer relationship management. Heinz, on the other hand, follows a decentralized approach in its core food business: CEOs hold a countrywide remit and there are no centralized functions for business development.

Global branding does not specify a single strategy, and neither does it guarantee business success. However, it is undoubtedly true that the growing trend in branding and positioning is moving steadfastly from national to multinational marketing and brand development.

OTHER KEY TRENDS IN BRANDING AND POSITIONING

The focus of brand trust is shifting from products to people and processes

It is becoming increasingly difficult to sustain superior product performance due to cloning, reverse engineering and by-passing. Customers are developing preferences and investing trust based upon their experiences of dealing with the company's people and processes as well as using its products. To encourage and exploit custom better, the context of branding and positioning needs to have a broader meaning than that implied by the traditional, product-centred approach.

Brands no longer close the sale

Nowadays, marketers want to extend their contact with customers over lengthier periods of time in order to exchange views and information, to cross-sell, and to encourage loyalty through repeat purchasing. The brand promise is increasingly defined by the quality of the supplier-customer relationship and is no longer confined to the product's features, attributes and benefits.

Brands are strategic management tools

As the brand comes to represent the company and to embody its reputation and values, branding is being regarded as a fundamental marketing activity and is moving to an earlier place in the decision-making process. The way in which a company is positioned to enter new markets and committed to existing markets has been shown to be critical to business success, and branding has proved to be the common denominator.

The price of a brand is not what customers pay for it

The price of a brand includes everything the customer has to do to realize its value. This means the time and money spent searching for the right product and sales outlet, as well as related travel, purchasing, consumption and disposal costs. This broader view of value is transforming the marketing agenda.

Branding moves beyond marketing

Managers are increasingly realizing that their companies touch customers in a myriad of ways, which extend far beyond marketing messages about product and service benefits. Marketing communications now take a supportive, rather than a leading, role in brand communications as organizations attempt to express brand values to customers via every possible link: personal, financial, operational and relational. Responsibility for the brand has moved beyond the scope of the marketing department.

Brands are spanning corporate boundaries

Thirty years ago, most brands represented individual products. Marketers have since discovered the power of brand extensions, corporate endorsement and the company as brand. However, the company as brand is only a halfway house: increasingly, brands represent not just the activities of one company, but the combined activities of many companies through a prevalence of alliances and networks.

SUMMARY

A brand is not simply the name on a product or service. Brands can be valuable company assets, for they can create customer preferences among target markets and can deliver superior profit and market performance. Branding know-how within a company becomes a significant capability when customer preferences are sustained through effective brand differentiation and positioning. Branding and positioning techniques can be applied not only to products, but also to strategic business units as well as to companies themselves.

There is no one solution to growing global brands from local brands. Indeed, the process can be very challenging for senior marketers of multinational companies. The pursuit of global brands does, however, remain a key feature of most markets as competition and customer bases increasingly develop on an international scale. Successful branding and positioning relies, to a large extent, on a clear recognition of and concerted responsiveness to the multiplicity of trends that distinguish today's business dynamics.

References

Simon Knox and Stan Maklan, *Competing on Value: Bridging the Gap between Brand and Customer Value*, (London: F.T. Pitman, 1998). [http://www.competingonvalue.com].

The World's Greatest Brands, edited by Nicholas Kochan for Interbrand (London: Macmillan Business, 1996).

Daphne Parmenter, Jean-Claude Larréché and Christopher Lovelock, 'First Direct: Branchless Banking', Insead Case No. 597-028-1, 1997.

Hajo Riesenbeck and Anthony Freeling, 'How Global are Global Brands?', *McKinsey Quarterly*, no. 3 (1992), pp. 3–9.

13 THE COMMUNICATIONS MIX

Helen Mitchell

In this chapter:

- The changing nature of marketing communications
- Developing a marketing communications programme
- Marketing communication tools
- Integrated marketing communications (IMC)
  Case studies demonstrating IMC
  Barriers to IMC
  The future of IMC

MARKETING COMMUNICATIONS: A TIME FOR CHANGE

The role of marketing communications is to inform the market clearly and persuasively about the company, and its products and services. The *communications mix* is made up of all the methods available to marketers to achieve this objective, and is becoming ever more complex.

Over the last decade, the field of marketing communications has seen many dramatic changes, not least of which are the advancements in marketing technologies. The Internet, smart cards, customer databases, easily accessible data warehousing and cost-effective direct mail have all contributed to a huge increase in the amount of information exchanged between companies and their customers: not only information that is communicated *to* the individual customer, but information that is accessed *about* the customer. For example, when Tesco's loyalty card was launched in 1995, it was estimated that the data generated by the company in one week about its customers' behaviour was equivalent to the total amount of information available on the Internet at that time.

As the variety and scope of opportunities for information exchange continues to increase, marketing communications is in danger of being sidelined as a peripheral business function. Sir Dominic Cadbury, Chairman of the Chartered Institute of Marketing (CIM) in the UK, was quoted as saying 'A fixation with advertising and agencies makes it unsurprising that marketing has a struggle to be taken seriously in the boardroom' (*Marketing Week*, 29 May 1997). His remark reflects the view of many other senior business leaders that marketing communications has only a trivial role to play in the strategies behind today's more successful companies. However, this view is only valid if one adheres to traditional models of marketing communications.

Earlier concepts of the role of marketing communications have been based on the mass production era of the 1950s and 1960s, in which marketing communications was predominantly concerned with stimulating and persuading customers to react to short-term, persuasive 'buy me' messages. These messages were delivered via mass media channels and evolved from a need to sell products quickly during a period of high consumer demand. Indeed, many companies *could* be accused of having a fixation with advertising and agencies, as this mass media approach was usually the only method used to sell products and services directly to customers.

Historically, marketing communications programmes have been founded on the classic brand marketing communications formulae used by the great mass producers, Unilever, Shell and P&G. Put simply, 'If you were the first organization to develop laundry detergent, had a reasonably good understanding of consumer needs and wants, and had sufficient funds to dominate the channels and the media, you usually dominated the consumer as well'.[1]

Communicating brand values was primarily a one-way process and was epitomized by the language of the advertising industry that used the imagery of aggressive warfare: the consumer was 'targeted' and advertising results were measured in the number of 'hits' or 'impacts'.[2] The use of 'dogmatic' communications was seen in many commercial monologues of the time, both in television advertising to consumers and in 'hard-sell' personal selling techniques in business-to-business markets. Unfortunately, they missed the fundamental point of marketing: listening and responding to customers.

In contrast, the marketing communications task of the 1990s and beyond is the pursuit of *dialogue* with customers. The growing interest in relationship marketing means that companies now seek to build mutually beneficial, long-term relationships with a number of audiences, including customers, consumers, suppliers, shareholders, legislators and employees. There is a recognition that many traditional communication tools are less appropriate for this task, and that the development of new technology and interactive media provide an opportunity to communicate with consumers as never before.

One-to-one marketing communications, driven by behavioural data and enabled by powerful databases, are becoming the norm. Since interactive media provides the potential for enhancing customer involvement with particular goods and services providers, marketers are now seeking to use a much wider range of communication tools to facilitate dialogue with customers. Figure 13.1 shows the extent of both the rapid growth in the use of what were historically called 'below the line' media, including direct mail, sales promotion and sponsorship, and the decline in the use of traditional mass market advertising, or 'above the line' media. ('Below the line' refers to campaigns paid for directly, whereas 'above the line' campaigns were paid for via commissions of 15 per cent on media purchasing.) Note that some elements of the communications mix, such as internal communications, are not included in these figures as it is difficult to measure true expenditure.

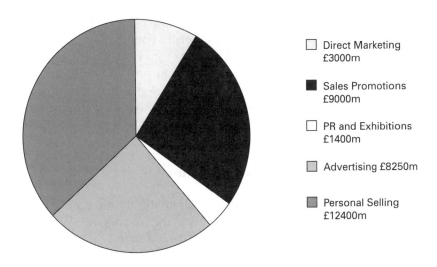

Figure 13.1 Estimated UK communications mix expenditure (1995)

Source: Advertising Association (1995).

This shift from mass advertising to more direct methods of selling reflects a number of changes that have consequently served to elevate the role and status of marketing communications. Recent research shows that the drivers of change in marketing communications practices represent three main areas: the consumer, the business environment, and the media.

The consumer

Consumers are shaping the market place of the future, forcing communication and distribution channels to develop to suit *their* needs. Consumers are becoming more sophisticated, sceptical and marketing literate, presenting the marketer with formidable challenges. Increasingly, consumers will decide when and how they wish to communicate with supplying organizations, as well as how much information they wish to impart about themselves, and all at a time that is convenient *for them*.

The growth in consumer power and the rise of the 'cynical individual' response to advertising means that companies also have to consider the transparency and integrity of their marketing messages. Ethical issues are assuming greater importance on the marketing agenda, for consumers are no longer passive receivers of messages, but generators of their own messages. The power of the consumer 'voice' was vividly illustrated by the recent Monsanto fiasco. Early in 1999, adverse consumer reactions to media stories about genetically modified (GM) foods caused retailers such as Marks & Spencer and J. Sainsbury's to backtrack on their original support and promotion of GM foods and to de-stock all such products. The companies also launched marketing campaigns reassuring customers that they had listened to them and acted on their concerns.

As well as being individually and collectively empowered, consumers are also no longer regionally or nationally bound; they are members of a global society. Advancements in media technologies and coverage have opened up the world, giving consumers a global consciousness and conscience. Increasingly, consumers are apt to distrust the corporate world and marketers can no longer assume anything about them. It is only through winning their trust that companies can hope to build relationships with them and gain a competitive edge.

The business environment

Businesses have changed dramatically in the last decade, and the most significant catalyst has been the impact of computer technology on the everyday lives of organizations and individuals. Information and communications technology, or ICT, has facilitated a revolution in the sheer amount, lightning speed and plummeting cost of information processing. For businesses, one of the biggest impacts has been the access to information about customers and consumers. While this obvious advantage is available to many, the most successful companies are those that use this information to deliver superior customer value.

In the UK, retailers have developed loyalty schemes which allow them to do just this, and customers have responded by becoming increasingly committed to a relationship with their supermarket, rather than any individual brand of product. However, many organizations have seen their influence over the consumer deteriorate rapidly. This is because the 'relationship' that existed between supplier and buyer was based on a promise of superior value, which was proved hollow with the advent of good quality, low-priced, own-label products. This was especially the case for FMCG (fast-moving consumer goods) manufacturers who, as stated earlier, relied on mass communications.

Developments in computer technology have also allowed companies with large customer bases to provide a superior level of individualized service and to customize their product or service offering to suit the customer. First Direct (see Chapter 12) revolutionized personal banking by offering greater customer access and convenience through the introduction of a 24-hour banking service. This customer-focused initiative has won the company many profitable customer relationships, as well as regular recognition for having the most satisfied customers in the sector.

Interestingly, many high street icons are suffering in the UK business environment of the late 1990s, Marks & Spencer being the most famous of them. It seems that the most successful companies today are those that change the rules, such as Amazon.com, the Internet book retailer and Dell, the computer company. These companies are engaging with customers in a new and innovative way, which involves facilitating a longer-term relationship with the customers they win. Rather than regarding the changing business environment as unwelcome, they eagerly exploit it, to the ultimate advantage of the consumer.

The media

In the last ten years, the world's media map has been redrawn as a result of media proliferation and fragmentation. In the past, it was easy for companies to reach a large number of consumers with relatively few advertisements. For example, in the USA in 1960, an advertisement on prime time network television reached over 90 per cent of all households. However, by 1994, the same three networks could deliver only 50 per cent of all households. The increase in network and satellite television channels, information and entertainment provision via the Internet, magazines, and radio and teletext services, and a switch to alternative leisure habits have meant that consumers take part in a much wider range of activities than ever before. With so many competing forces, their attention is more difficult to capture and their patience with marketing messages is waning. It is estimated that consumers are bombarded with up to 3000 communications and messages every day, and as a result they have become much more discerning as to which ones they listen to, never mind respond to. This reduction in access to large groups of potential customers through television has made it much harder and more expensive for advertisers and their agencies to communicate via mass messages.

Research by Howell, Henry, Chaldecott, Lury (HHCL) found that people who watch television regularly also practise various activities in front of their television sets, using them like a radio as background entertainment. Additionally, the escalation in the use of remote control devices and videos means that many viewers channel-hop or fast-forward the moment any advertisements are broadcast, diminishing the delivery and impact of the advertising messages. This growing habit among viewers has major implications for any marketer considering spending £150 000 to show their latest advertisement on a 30-second slot during a popular television soap opera such as 'Coronation Street'.

In the UK, consumption of 'relatively' mass market commercial stations is now much higher among older viewers and lower socio-economic groups. Henley Centre research confirms this, showing that the more 'up-market' a shop is, the less likely it is that branded goods are purchased from there. This finding is attributed to the light television viewing of higher level socio-economic groups who are not influenced by the branding messages transmitted on the major broadcasting channels. Many marketers acknowledge that it has become very difficult to communicate to high earners and younger males, as their media habits are increasingly individualistic and diverse.

As well as changes in the types of audience that can be reached via more traditional media channels, the tremendous growth in the supply of media has made the implementation of a communications programme a much more complex task. The choice of communication tools and media is extensive and, as Figure 13.2 demonstrates, prospective and existing customers can now be reached in a far larger number of ways than was possible only a decade ago.

Consumer enthusiasm for new media is defining communications of the future. The development of interactive devices in advertising, direct mail and the Internet have helped to increase the diversity of methods for communicat-

THE COMMUNICATIONS MIX

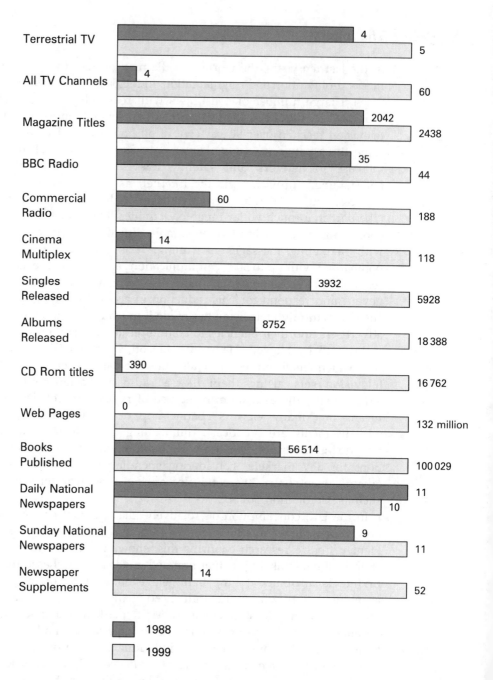

Figure 13.2 Growth in media supply 1988–99

Source: The Henley Centre, COMET Model.

ing and exchanging information. In particular, e-mail, discussion groups, data interchange and downloading, on-line advertisements and linked web sites all provide new ways of developing, strengthening or influencing relationships with customers, employees, media, suppliers, and even competitors. It is certain that the escalation in the access to and usage of Internet technology will mean that communicating directly with customers will become a much cheaper and faster option for marketers.

In summary, consumer empowerment, technological advancement, media fragmentation and the pressure on marketers to justify the returns on marketing communications expenditure are intensifying the need to re-examine exactly how marketers plan and implement their communication strategies. Only recently has there been widespread recognition of a requirement to *integrate* the variety of messages, information and images that are used to influence the company's range of stakeholders.

In the next sections of this chapter, we will consider how to develop successful marketing communications programmes that work to build relationships with stakeholders, and will examine some of the changes in the choice of communication tools available and the individual benefits of these tools. Finally, we will explore how integrated marketing communications (IMC) can help to address the problem of effectively managing marketing communications in today's highly competitive and rapidly changing business environment.

THE ROLE OF COMMUNICATION IN BUILDING RELATIONSHIPS

As Chris Fill points out in his excellent book, *Marketing Communications, Contexts, Contents and Strategies*,[3] much of relationship and network theory focuses on how connections between people and organizations develop and evolve. In looking at this phenomenon, Taylor and Altman[4] identified a number of progressive layers in the construction of relationships. They saw that relationships move forward by the gradual revealing and exchange of information between parties. Mutual trust and confidence grow as a greater amount of information is disclosed, assimilated and stored. The behaviour of the participants is then based on this knowledge, which deepens and develops as the relationship matures. In time, other participants may enter the relationship, and what was originally a dyadic coupling soon becomes a network. As supplier and customer contacts multiply, communication becomes vital to information flow and functions as the coordinating mechanism for all members of the network. When considering marketing communications in the light of the multiple markets model, it is clear, as Figure 13.3 suggests, that the carefully selected and relevant use of communication tools for each individual stakeholder is essential. Inadequate attention to this point can lead to discord and misunderstanding in the relationship, which can potentially damage the relationship and perhaps destabilize the entire network.

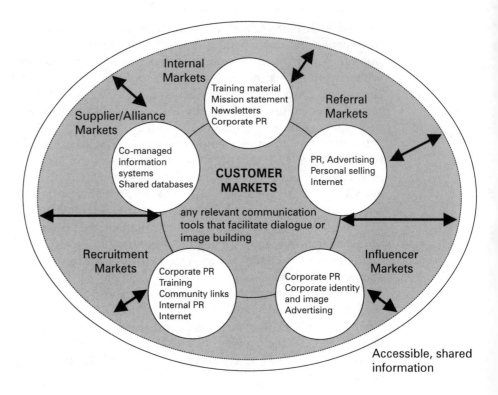

Figure 13.3 The role of communication in building relationships

DEVELOPING A MARKETING COMMUNICATIONS PROGRAMME

A major theme in this book is the need to plan and integrate the marketing mix elements against clearly defined and agreed objectives. Therefore, the chosen communications mix must reflect and reinforce both marketing and corporate strategies. Figure 13.4 shows the logical link between communication strategy and overall business objectives.

Figure 13.4 places communication strategy in its proper place, following the establishment of business objectives and marketing strategy. From this position, it will be clear exactly what the communication strategy must be designed to achieve. Is the objective to increase market share? Is it to improve the company's overall reputation in certain markets? Giving proper consideration to the consequences, as well as the aims, of initiating marketing communications programmes will help guide strategic decision-making processes and the tactical planning of promotional campaigns to deliver clearer, sharper and more consistent messages. Marketers setting a communication strategy within a relationship marketing approach will especially need to consider the wider impact that their messages may have on existing relationships with stakeholders.

Promotional plans will vary depending on the communication task in hand: customers may need information about specific products, while stakeholders may need messages that communicate company values. Questions that are useful to ask when formulating a plan include:

- What do we want to say?
- To whom do we want to say it?
- Why do we want to say it?
- How do we choose to say it?
- Where shall we communicate the message?
- When shall we say it?
- What do we want them to do?
- How should we respond?
- What processes have we set up for dialogue?
- What is our budget?
- What is the planned schedule, and who does what?
- Does everyone in our network understand the communication objectives?
- What are our measures of success?

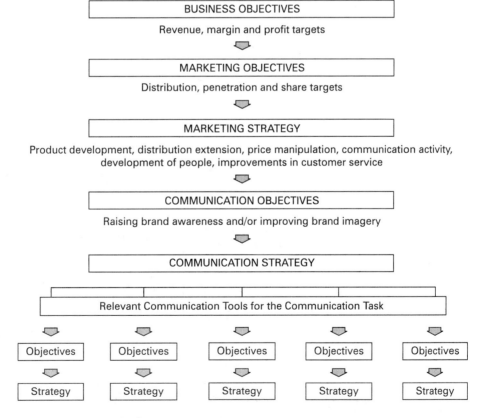

Figure 13.4 Communication strategy in the planning process

From the 1960s onwards, it has become accepted protocol that the proper way to set objectives for the creative content of marketing communications is to think in terms of desired consumer responses. It is not an issue of what an advertiser should put into an advertisement, but what the receiver should get out of it. Stephen King, at JWT, developed a theory of communicating that focuses on how different advertising messages have varying desired outcomes.[5] His framework for the influence of marketing messages, as depicted in Figure 13.5, was based on the idea that marketing communications affect consumer reactions, and most often in an indirect way.

This model emphasizes the significant influence that marketing messages have on the consumer and provides an indication as to their ultimate effectiveness. To gain a fuller understanding of the influential role of advertising, as one example of marketing communications, let us apply a familiar campaign to the framework.

The UK campaign to modify attitudes to drinking and driving has been run over many years by successive governments. A generation ago, when there were fewer road users and driving regulations, the temptation to risk driving while over the alcohol limit was less of an issue. Gradually, however, through a combination of informative advertising and stringent law enforcement measures, consumer attitudes have changed. Now, very few people would

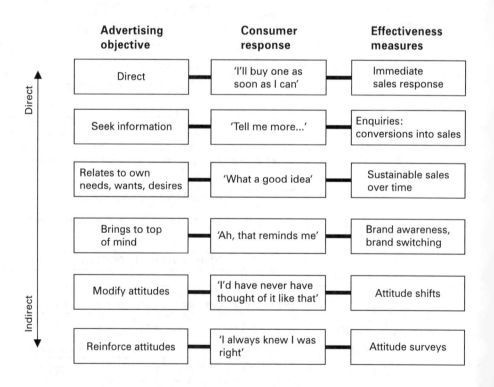

Figure 13.5 Influences on consumer behaviour

Source: Adapted from Stephen King, 'Practical Progress from a Theory of Advertisements', *Admap* (1975).

consider driving while under the influence of alcohol. In this case, advertising is aiming to modify consumer attitudes to an existing product in order to guide the way that the product is used. However, modifying consumer behaviour is a very slow process and measuring its success can only be achieved by evaluating consumer attitudes and behaviour over an extended period of time.

In a contrasting example, rather than attempting to alter consumer attitudes, BMW advertisements have been built around a strategy of reinforcing consumer beliefs, helping to attract new customers and, most importantly, reassuring existing customers that they have made the right choice of supplier. Fundamental to successful advertising is obtaining the desired response from consumers, as summarized in the remark, 'I always knew I was right'. For brands that enjoy high brand loyalty, this type of advertising works by strengthening the depth of customer loyalty. As King points out, in reality many advertisements work at several points on the framework simultaneously, thus prompting discussion about key advertising issues and helping to set advertising priorities.

While this model was developed some time ago, it still provides valuable indicators for understanding how marketing communications generally work. The difference today is that marketing communication methods, or tools, have grown in number and evolved in nature. In the new media environment, the consumer not only has an opportunity to act in response to a message, but also to communicate back to the sender of the message. This 'interactive' and 'bilateral' quality can be managed to enhance the effectiveness of marketing communications and thus the strength of supplier/buyer relationships. Additionally, marketers are exploiting more traditional avenues of communication in other ways to augment their products' value and to reinforce their relationships with customers. In BMW's case, its advertising will have the effect of creating reassurance and reducing dissonance among its customers (see Chapter 4 on consumer buyer behaviour). BMW has further encouraged strong customer relationships through the regular issue of a quality owners' magazine that features exclusive offers, customer-relevant articles, and special invitations to events at dealer showrooms for pre-launch test drives.

Today's marketers have a far more complex range of communication opportunities (not to mention obstacles) to consider than did their predecessors. The next section assesses the newer developments in marketing communication tools and examines their contributions to the task of building long-term, profitable relationships with customers.

MARKETING COMMUNICATION TOOLS

There are many excellent textbooks that detail the varying attributes and advantages of each marketing communication tool. For the purposes of assisting readers who are considering adopting a relationship marketing approach, we will focus here on the recent changes to some of these tools that have important implications for relationship marketing.

Sales promotion

Originally defined as an activity which adds value to a product or service for a limited time period by offering an incentive to purchase, sales promotion has always been about offering extra benefit, in terms of price, volume, prizes, gift packs or associated charitable donations. Like most traditional forms of marketing communication, sales promotion has generally been about a mass offer. However, the character of sales promotion is changing rapidly as a result of improved supplier relationships.

Tesco have recently worked closely with St Ivel, their yogurt 'category champion', to develop best practice approaches to the planning, implementation and evaluation of sales promotions. St Ivel's promotions in Tesco's are now planned strategically so that they can be assessed by suppliers, via the Tesco Information Exchange IT system, within one hour of their launch. Category managers at both Tesco and St Ivel can also analyse the information from each yogurt product category to increase the promotional impact of the chosen promotion. The ultimate benefit to consumers is improved stock availability of the promotional offer. The benefit to Tesco and participant suppliers is a reduction in stock levels and supply chain costs. This innovative and analytical approach is being further developed by Tesco to make their sales promotions more relevant for different types of customers.

Database marketing

With each year that passes, it becomes less expensive to store and manipulate massive stores of data. As market segments have fragmented, it is more necessary than ever to treat customers as individuals. Marketing information held on the company's customers and competitor's customers is now a vital part of the marketer's toolbox. In the past, such information constituted mere mailing lists. Today, customers' names and addresses can be assimilated with other data, such as geodemographics, credit data, lifestyle data, smart card data, and transactional data to give marketers an in-depth insight into customers' behavioural patterns. Customer profiling (see Chapter 4) is now emerging as an important new approach in developing dialogue with individual customers.

Interactive media

The Internet is growing at a phenomenal pace. Current estimates reveal some 50 million individual Internet users, of which 70 per cent are in the USA and 20 per cent are in Western Europe. Of these, 60 per cent are students or academics, 30 per cent are business users, and 10 per cent account for home connections. In the UK, there are two million Internet users connected via 500 000 computers, and this figure is growing by 50 000 users a month. Total annual net advertising spend on the Internet is estimated to be $350 million, and rising. The opportunities for communicating to customers and markets via the Internet are profound.

As a marketing medium, the Internet provides an ideal platform for one-to-one communication, offering instantaneous and interactive exchange across the globe. Additionally, the facilities of e-mail and discussion groups mean that self-nominated alliances and networks (of suppliers or customers) can grow rapidly. One example of a company that has used this medium successfully is Amazon.com, the book retailer. Visitors who regularly visit its web site to place orders find that, after a few visits, the web page becomes personalized for them. On-screen prompts appear advertising books that are similar in type or subject matter to those previously purchased, making the customer's search for further books easier, as well as conveying a sense of personalized service. These computer prompts are based on data gained from the company's earlier experiences of the customer. Customers can also register to receive e-mail providing book reviews and recommendations for latest publications on topics related to their expressed interests.

The Internet can be used to display and sell products/services, and to offer information, as well as to augment offerings through links to other web sites. Some business-to-business companies have also used it to build close relationships with customers in technological markets. For instance, one manufacturer of highly complex controls for energy plants has created a virtual building site on its web page, which gives information on installation and safety regulations for recent purchasers. Only time will tell how great an impact the Internet will have on business activities, but it is already evident that the Internet is a unique and effective tool for personalizing marketing communications.

Personal selling

As was shown in Figure 13.1 earlier, personal selling is by far the most expensive communication method. Yet, in some markets, it is easily the most effective. This is particularly true in business-to-business markets or where the purchaser requires a large amount of complex information (see Chapters 5 and 17). The rise of cooperative buyer/seller relationships has meant that the salesperson is now expected to be the link between the customer and the company. Their role is to act as the coordinator and manager of customers, and to facilitate long-term customer relationships. George S. Hall, a maintenance facilities provider, no longer sees its staff as salespeople, but as customer managers. These 'customer managers' are located at the customers' sites and are linked via a co-managed network system to ensure the optimum energy efficiency for the customers. The level of trust in these customer relationships has reached the point where George S. Hall now also purchases energy for its customers.

Internal communications

Many companies underestimate the power of their employees in augmenting marketing communications programmes. In the case of service companies, staff members are often the only communication interface that a customer might have with the company. One example of this is recounted by Stuart Bull, then Director of KHBB, a division of Saatchi's. KHBB had developed for the Automobile Association the highly successful 'I know a man who can' advertising campaign, which highlighted the reliability of the AA serviceman. However, no internal campaign was delivered to the patrolmen and they were introduced to it on television at the same time as consumers. At the next sales conference, Bull was amazed to see hundreds of home-made badges and stickers declaring 'I'm a man who can'. The enthusiastic reception of the sales force to the campaign was acknowledged, and subsequently the company included the patrolmen in future 'personal service' oriented advertising campaigns.

Internal marketing is fast becoming a priority, and internal communications are playing an increasingly critical role in changing, reinforcing or questioning the prevailing corporate culture. In their business interactions, stakeholders form a perception of the company that can influence the future of the business relationship. It is, therefore, exceedingly important that all members of a company's network are aware of a company's intentions and actions: not only employees, but influencers, suppliers, and so on.

Having outlined some of the changing tools found within the marketing communications toolbox, the next section looks at the development of IMC as a means of utilizing and managing these tools effectively.

INTEGRATED MARKETING COMMUNICATIONS

Ultimately, IMC is the strategic coordination of all marketing messages and the alignment of all methods of communicating to customers, be they consumers or other targeted, relevant (external and internal) audiences. IMC has evolved as marketers have moved away from traditional mass media based communications strategies, towards those that are more personalized, customer-oriented and technology-driven.

Perhaps the most useful way to define integrated marketing communications is to illustrate what happens when a marketing campaign is not integrated. The marketing communications activities of the personal computer and software markets provide such an example. Companies such as Apple, Tiny, and Microsoft spend millions of pounds on advertising and direct mail in order to increase consumer awareness of their brands. The point of sale, usually with a dealer, is full of sales promotion activities designed to persuade the customer to upgrade their equipment or purchase more powerful programs, and to benefit from improved software support and other ancillary services.

However, once the purchase transaction has been completed, the consumer soon realizes that the marketing messages they received prior to the purchase concerning customer service provision do not ring true. There have been many instances where customers have had to hold on a telephone helpline for over two or three hours to speak with a service operator, only to learn there is no opportunity for dialogue or redress, despite advertising campaigns to the contrary. In this case, dialogue has been encouraged through promotion, but the company has failed to integrate its services and provide an effective feedback loop to deal with customer concerns and requests for help. The result is a seriously frustrated customer and a relationship heading for breakdown.

One of the main aims of IMC is to harmonize the promotional tools so that audiences receive a consistent and substantiated message. Integration within marketing communications works on two main levels: the creative and the strategic.

Creative integration

The shift from a transaction to a customer focus acknowledges that *all* marketing is about communication, for people form their images of brands and companies from information provided by a variety of sources. One of the most important aspects of IMC is that it encourages a view of marketing communications from the customer's perspective, or as a flow of information from indistinguishable sources.

The IMC approach has been successfully used by Tango, the soft drinks company. Tango initiated a direct response campaign that invited television viewers to write in with comments about Tango products and promotions. The company received an overwhelming public response, which it then used to invent different media opportunities that had not previously existed. For instance, consumers had written to Tango saying they wanted to communicate with the orange Tango can character, and consequently they received handwritten postcards from all over the world from the 'travelling Tango can'. Characters from Tango advertisements also appeared in unlikely places, underlining the idiosyncrasy and anarchic image of the brand message: for example, one character was seen standing behind a senior UK politician as he was being interviewed by 'News at Ten' in Parliament Square. Actions like these have provoked thousands of letters from viewers, confirming brand awareness, and have encouraged consumers to be vigilant of further quirky Tango messages.

It is important to remember, however, that the 'message', as opposed to the delivery, has to be the central focus of IMC. If different types of marketing communications are used to support brand positioning, then they must work together in a synergistic fashion. The following BMW case study provides an example of an IMC campaign that set out to achieve this integrated creativity.

Case Study 1: BMW – creative integration

Companies that are confident about their marketing message have found that an integrated, creative approach to communicating it can bring real benefits. BMW employed an integrated marketing campaign in the launch of their Z3 roadster. By using their established agencies in a coordinated manner, BMW managed to explore a wider range of media opportunities than it had done previously. Central to the success of the campaign was ensuring that every agency understood the brand values of the car and the significance of the launch of the company's first smaller sports car.

Exploiting the car's product placement in the latest Bond movie, 'Goldeneye', three agencies worked together on a globally integrated marketing campaign that created a cult image of the product. Research had shown that targeted customers would be wary of any 'cheapening' or devaluing of the BMW brand, so it was essential that the feeling of exclusivity, quality and high status enveloped the vehicle's debut. The Bond link-up was seen as perfect for the launch of the 'hottest new sports car of the decade', as the secret agent was associated all over the world with driving exciting cars and pursuing a thrilling, exotic and glamorous lifestyle.

The marketing campaign featured television advertisements and posters that delivered news of the coinciding launches of both the film and the car. In addition, customized dealer brochures were sent in electro-static bags marked 'Top Secret', which, when opened, gave off a green flash similar to that experienced by Bond in the film. The special brochures were also sent to existing BMW customers in recognition of their expressed affinity with the brand. The dealer network was involved in local premieres of the film, which included champagne receptions attended by local BMW customers. Combined with an effective local and national PR campaign, the 'Goldeneye' launch of the new BMW sports car achieved a quality and consistent delivery of the marketing message.

Kate Wheaton, at Evans Hunt Scott, commented that a close alliance and working relationship with WCRS, the advertising agency, was possible because 'BMW is such a strong brand. There was no dissonance with any of the creative messages we all produced.' Martin Runacles, BMW Marketing Director at the time, concluded that the integrated marketing strategy achieved a greater increase in brand awareness and customer retention levels among existing customers than a non-IMC campaign would have achieved. BMW's UK order books were quickly filled and there was a six-month waiting list.

Strategic integration

As well as requiring creative synergy, there are also managerial implications to adopting an IMC strategy. Although IMC is now recognized as a distinct business process, the debate continues as to the role of IMC orchestrator. Should a client company place their entire marketing communications requirement with one agency, or should they instead engage a variety of specialists and retain control centrally?

The fact that agencies have been offering a range of communication services in-house is seen by many as a rush to diversify in order to retain profit margins as client spending shifts emphasis from advertising to 'below the line'. This trend has led some to argue that IMC is merely a re-packaging of the full service agency ideal of the 1960s, similar to BBDO's 'seamless communications' or Young & Rubicam's 'whole egg' approach. But these were really more of a 'one-stop shopping' strategy by the agency suppliers who understood that integration requires the overall marketing strategy, communication strategy and creative execution to be aligned. In the words of one commentator, 'When you hear that some agencies have separate floors for the "integrated" people, you begin to suspect that not everyone has got to grips with the subject.'

What is beginning to emerge is that clients are managing the marketing communications process in ways that better suit their own needs. Research indicates that a variety of management approaches are being used. Innovative agencies such as HHCL and St Luke's offer multi-disciplinary teams under one roof and focus on strategies for building dialogue with customers. One client practised what they called the 'virtual agency', putting together a team of marketing communications specialists while coordinating the communication strategy in-house. Another client had designated 'communication guardians'. These full-time representatives of the company's eight international agencies worked collaboratively to ensure the consistency of the marketing message across the world. The following case study, featuring the Whitbread Beer Company, illustrates the IMC approach used at brand level and involving a wide range of marketing communications specialists.

Case Study 2: Stella Artois – managing integration

Stella Artois is the gold standard of lagers in the UK. It is clearly established as the number one premium lager, and in 1996 it was included in the top 25 brands in the UK, bigger than Heinz and Kellogg's – with £103 million in retail alone. The marketing activities which took place in 1997 were designed to strengthen its market lead even more and enhance its brand identity.

The way the Whitbread Beer Company, the brand owner in the UK, decided to do this was through a programme of integrated marketing, whereby all the different aspects of promotion, advertising and so on were united under one main theme, in this case Stella Screen with its focus on film. The initial rationale for this integrated marketing approach in 1997 was to create an 'event' for the summer which Stella could attach itself to.

Tracy Darwen, the marketing manager, explained:

The previous two or three years had shown us that some of the bigger brands were getting into event marketing. For example Carling was getting into football and Heineken into rugby. But at the time we wanted to do that, there was no one big event, no Olympics, no football or rugby Word Cup or Euro '96. Therefore Stella Artois decided it would create its own major national campaign of activity.

An integrated approach would also mean it would be easier to control the consistency of communication at a time when the brand was becoming more widely available and, finally, would offer scale advantages.

With this in mind a brief went out to various agencies, some 12 months before the activity was due to start, asking them to come up with ideas. And the one they hit upon was 'film', which has a very high appeal to the Stella target consumers, men aged 18–34. Research showed that film was part of their lifestyle. As a group, they are more likely than average to go to the cinema once a month, and they rent videos at least once every two weeks.

Film has a big following and a quality image, plus all the associated glitter, glitz and sex appeal.

It was felt that the core idea of film would be appealing to all the different customers who drink Stella, as well as those the company was trying to win over. Film was a premium leisure pursuit and, importantly, was a relatively 'uncluttered' environment in which to market the brand as other beer brands were concentrated in the fields of sport and music. The agencies shared the view that with the right media territory, communications activities would have more impact. In other words, an ad in the right environment would be more influential.

Making integration work

From all the agencies invited to take part in the promotion, a lead agency was chosen and the core idea of film established. Below are shown the main agencies involved.

MAIN AGENCIES INVOLVED IN 1997

H H & S	Sales promotions agency – LEAD AGENCY
Lowe Howard Spink	Advertising agency
Motive	Media buying agency
Cohn & Wolfe	Consumer public relations agency
Bryant Jackson	Trade public relations agency

H H & S, a below the line agency, was selected for the lead role as it had come up with the Blockbuster idea, whereby all packs of Stella would win at least £1 off video rental from the video chain. All the other agencies were then tasked with coming up with ideas to work around this core theme.

Initially meetings were held once a month; these represented a big forum for everyone to get involved and contribute their ideas. Meetings then became fortnightly. It was important that all the agencies worked together well on this, setting aside the 'turf wars' which occasionally arise in less well managed campaigns. Agencies traditionally argue loudly for their particular medium to receive the lion's share of the communications budget. With an integrated approach, remuneration, in particular, could be a knotty problem if not handled decisively. (It is customary for UK advertising agencies to receive 15 per cent from media bookings.)

'All the agencies worked together in more of a learning and sharing information experience', explained Tracy Darwen. 'We wanted people to join in all the areas of discussion, so that they became more knowledgeable about both the brand and the film industry. They all had a valuable input to make.' Indeed, as the brand management team at the Whitbread Beer Company consisted of Tracy and a colleague, the agencies were also a useful means of outsourcing management resource.

Much later in the process, to make the meetings more fun, she devised some quizzes about Stella which not only helped people become more aware of the brand, but helped to break the ice and put them at their ease.

They also played a version of the 'hot air balloon game'. Each member of the team sitting around the table had to imagine they were in a balloon which was losing altitude. They were holding some 30 cards each bearing a statement about Stella, such as its brand name, packaging design, Belgian heritage and so on. Which 20 would they throw out and which would they keep? 'This may sound like a trivial exercise', said Tracy Darwen, 'but it actually helped people to focus on what was important about Stella in relation to this film promotion'.

'For example, initially we were talking in press releases about Stella being a number one beer brand, which was having so many millions of pounds spent on it. In fact people do not want to know that. They want to be told that it is an exclusive premium brand which not everybody is drinking; price is not an issue.'

She thought that working this way was effective, in that it challenged complacency among the team members and got them thinking, as well as being a bit of fun. 'There were some 10 to 12 people in the team, which is a good workable number, any more than that and people feel inhibited about contributing. But it means you gain more value out of what you have got.'

Summer of Stella

Stella Screen was the name given to the programme of activities being run by Stella Artois through 1997, and some £25 million was set aside to spend on marketing. The initiative aimed for as wide an audience as possible, being visible in newspapers, on billboards, on television and through live events such as film festivals and incentives such as ticket offers. The aim was to ensure all Stella drinkers saw or heard of Stella Screen.

On television and in the cinema the award-winning Red Shoes campaign appeared for the first time in March. In this particular execution in the popular 'Reassuringly Expensive' campaign, the hero spends his hard earned cash on a pint of Stella instead of a pair of new shoes for his grandmother. It aimed to keep Stella Artois in the forefront of customers' minds against competitors and reinforced Stella's 'Gold Standard' positioning. Consumer research indicated that this was the best Stella ad yet.

Media sponsorships would play a large part of the activity. On Channel 5 Stella was to sponsor 130 blockbuster movies on prime time television, from March to September 1997, aimed at the broader lager drinking audience. On Channel 4 a season of films brought together under the umbrella title of 'Cinema Extreme' was to run during July and August. These were classic 'cult' movies shown late at night at weekends, and aimed at the younger target audience. Radio sponsorship consisted of a Virgin Radio drive time movie review sponsored by Stella every weekday from March 1997 to February 1998.

Stella Screen was also to have a high profile in the press and magazines. A 32 page Stella Screen Film Guide was inserted in publications such as *Empire*, *Q* and *FHM*. More than 1.6 million film guides were distributed in this way in June 1997.

One of the major elements of the year's activities was the Stella Screen Tour which visited eight towns and cities: London, Brighton, Liverpool, Manchester, Oxford, Cardiff, Newquay and Nottingham. It spent two nights in each town, and included free outdoor movies and local radio broadcasts from the events. Additionally, student film clubs were operated in all these key towns during the summer and autumn terms. Every purchase of Stella Artois got a Stella Screen game card with the chance of getting at least £1 off video rental from Blockbuster, the UK's number one video rental and retail chain. There was also the chance to win a bigger prize, including a walk-on part in a Hollywood movie. All of these initiatives were creatively integrated and coordinated by the team.

Results

The Summer of Stella campaign was greeted with a lot of enthusiasm from inside Whitbread and outside among both trade customers and consumers. 'The benefit of giving it scale was that the sales force got really excited about it, and much more motivated', said Darwen. 'As a result we did a hard sales push and got a lot of new distribution points in the on-trade, and more in take-home sales.'

Sales volumes for 1997 increased by 28 per cent compared with 20 per cent in 1996. For the past few years the brand had been growing at a faster rate than the market and the gap continued to widen. As a result, by September 1997 Stella's share of the premium lager sector had grown to 18.4 per cent from 16.5 per cent in January.

'Research has shown that integrated marketing seems to be a good thing because consumers are becoming more demanding of the brands they like', said Darwen. 'Gone are the days when you could produce a good quality ad and rest on your laurels. You have to build consumer affinity and turn consumer like to respect. To do this you have to do more, and this "more" is rewarding loyalty; giving drinkers something more on top of just the drink. They are very sophisticated in terms of marketing. They know you are doing it, and they don't mind that, because it is still of benefit to them if they can go and see free films in London during the summer.'

Feedback from consumers showed that they approved of the idea of a long-term association with a particular theme, such as film. 'People said don't be fickle, give a long-term commitment to it', said Tracy Darwen. 'As our learning has increased over the first twelve months of this integrated marketing approach, we have refined our thinking and have shifted more towards what we call "association" marketing. By this we mean that we don't necessarily want everyone to know about every aspect of the campaign but we need to make sure that we offer something relevant for everyone. The campaign consistency will come through the quality of everything we do. Future activities will, therefore, be even more focused and targeted towards the right consumer groups'.

This case was written by Marion Cooper with Dr Susan Baker © Copyright: Cranfield School of Management, 1998. All rights reserved.

So, while marketers continue to come to grips with the managerial implications of IMC, it is evident that there are some general barriers to overcome.

BARRIERS TO IMC

Research has shown that marketers overwhelmingly believe that the orchestrating role has to be undertaken by the marketers themselves.[7] Indeed, 60 per cent of research respondents felt that they could manage an IMC programme more effectively than their agencies could. It was the view of some marketers that agencies' obsession with advertising creation has allowed new competition, in the form of management consultants, to enter the marketing communications field. One marketer suggested that marketing communications could be managed better by splitting up specialist agency input into the following three parts:

(a) marketing consultancy – strategic consultants such as PriceWaterhouse-Coopers or Andersens, who perhaps supply the strategic thinking;
(b) advertisement and marketing communications creation – specialist creative shops;
(c) marketing communications placement – media planning and/or buying agencies.

One major UK brewery has already placed a management consultant in the role of marketing communications orchestrator, with responsibility for overseeing the strategy of communications directed at all customers, in both consumer and business-to business markets. However, despite the advances some companies have made in adopting an IMC approach, most believe that the implementation of an IMC programme is a difficult and political process. When asked what they thought were the biggest barriers to IMC implementation, the brewery's client marketers identified several major obstacles. Each of these main barriers relates to the use of agencies, and they included the following areas.

• *Egos and value systems*: the seemingly entrenched attitudes and opinions of marketing agency staff are seen to restrict any progressive internal change. While marketing organizations are adapting to embrace IMC, agencies are persisting in maintaining an organizational structure and culture better suited to the dominance of mass advertising. For example, within the advertising industry, kudos is gained by the winning of creative awards, of which the most publicized and glamorous are those given for television and cinema work. By contrast, the status connected to the award for a direct mail campaign is minimal. The preservation of this apparently rigid and 'exclusive' value system among agencies has made it very difficult for marketers to implement IMC programmes.
• *Remuneration system*: historically, marketing agencies have been paid commission for 'above the line' (advertising) work and a negotiated fee for 'below the line' (all other forms of promotion) work. This remuneration system has often incentivized mass media advertising and only now does there seem to be evidence of a shift towards project fee payments. This development can only help in the adoption of an IMC approach.

- *Agency lack of expertise* – marketers feel that in using one particular agency, they might not be obtaining the best skills in every marketing discipline. An agency might also favour certain media that reflect its own area of creative expertise, rather than offering the client the best integrated solution.

The use of IMC can enhance marketing precision and effectiveness, if prevailing barriers to its implementation are recognized and resolved. In addition to the difficulties associated with agencies' resilience to change and clients' reliance on agencies, very few companies have managed to incorporate the feedback loop required for IMC into their technologies and operations.

Level of integration	The degree of integration
1. Vertical objectives integration	Do the communication objectives fit with the marketing objectives and with the overall corporate objectives?
2. Horizontal/functional integration	Do the marketing communications activities fit well with the other business functions of manufacturing, operations and human resource management?
3. Marketing mix integration	Is the marketing mix of product, price and place decisions consistent with the required communication messages?
4. Communications mix integration	Are all the communication tools being used to guide the customer/consumer/client through each stage of the buying process? Do they all portray a consistent message?
5. Creative design integration	Is the creative design and execution uniform and consistent with the chosen positioning of the product/service?
6. Internal/external integration	Are all internal departments and all external agencies employed by the organisation working together to an agreed plan and strategy with regular progress meetings?
7. Financial integration	Is the budget being used in the most effective and efficient way ensuring that economies of scale are achieved and that long-term investment is optimised?

Figure 13.6 Seven levels of integration (Smith, Berry and Pulford)

Source: Smith, Berry and Pulford, *Strategic Marketing Communications*, Kogan Page (1999).

One of the leaders in the use of IMC in the UK is Tesco, the supermarket retailer. With 10 million customers on its database, even Tesco admits that the implementation of feedback loops is very complex and costly. The company has piloted a one-to-one, micro-marketing programme with the top 10 per cent of spenders in each store, using information gathered from the loyalty card scheme. Customers are invited by store managers to share their thoughts and impressions of Tesco at special customer panels. Many of these panels have prompted Tesco to reward these loyal customers by offering them relevant and timely promotions, such as wine tasting evenings and 'privileged shopping' hours.

The successful implementation of an IMC programme involves the thorough fulfilment of all the requirements of the marketing communications process, from creative considerations to strategic management issues. The checklist in Figure 13.6 has been devised by Smith, Berry and Pulford to help managers successfully initiate and implement an IMC approach. It emphasizes the multi-faceted issues that managers need to consider to achieve full integration of their communication strategy.

THE FUTURE OF IMC

Recent developments in the IMC theory recognize that all communications are an integral part of a company's relationship with its stakeholders *and* that organizations need to reflect the importance of integration in *all* of their messages. Often, managers in separate departments control different communications and rarely see each other's input and output. Traditionally, a brand manager would be responsible for the communication and promotion of a brand, and a PR manager would be responsible for communicating with non-trade organizations. This spreading of marketing responsibility among non-collaborating parties gives rise to uncoordinated (potentially inconsistent and unsubstantiated) marketing messages. From a customer's, supplier's or employee's point of view, if they are imparting information to a company, then they expect that 'intelligence' to be acknowledged and assimilated into all their future dealings with the company. The model given in Figure 13.7 presents a new means of managing these communication flows within an IMC approach. This model emphasizes not only the corporate and marketing communications levels, but also the interactivity between the various sources of marketing messages, both internal (the organization) and external (its stakeholders).

There are *two* important points to highlight here. The first is the development of a cross-functional team to manage the marketing communications function. This organizational structure will make it possible to plan and monitor brand and corporate messages coming and going from all levels of the organization and to optimize their impact. Any communication with stakeholders can then be identified and used as relationship building blocks. In the past, corporate messages were not always strategically aligned to brand messages and, as a result, conflicting messages were sent to the company's stakeholders. This often served to undermine understandings and erode relationships. The management structure shown in Figure 13.7, aided by information databases, allows for

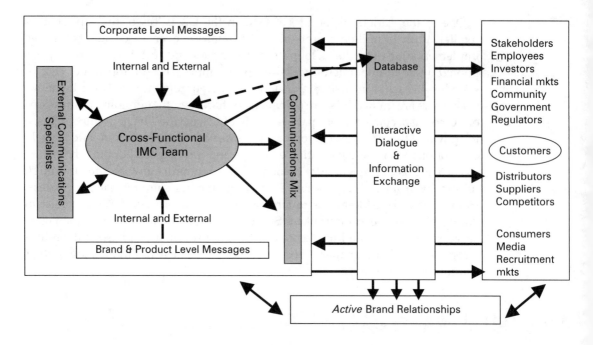

Figure 13.7 Model for managing communications

Source: Adapted from Duncan and Moriarty (1998).

the identification of stakeholder overlap so that conflicting or repetitive messages are not sent.

The second important point is that by managing information throughout the organization via a central team, resources can be allocated more efficiently and effectively. Employees can then be empowered to deliver messages that are timely and more relevant to the stakeholder concerned. Lexus, for example, has invested in the setting-up and daily maintenance of a database of all critical interactions with its customers, however small, so that everyone within the company has the same 'memory' and experience of the relationship as the customer. When a customer calls at a dealership, the Lexus representative they speak to can retrieve on-screen the customer's profile and detailed interaction history, making the current interaction more effective and the customer's experience more valuable[6]. It is then much easier to continue building the relationship with that customer.

SUMMARY

Business today is more communication dependent than ever before. The development of relationship marketing underlines this point. Relevant and individually targeted marketing communications have become a preferred and proven method of building stronger relationships with stakeholders. The marketer's ability to initiate and maintain dialogue with stakeholders using a range of communication tools is fundamentally (and crucially) based on the mutual exchange of information over time.

That investment and benefit must be 'mutual' is becoming increasingly evident to senior business leaders, as expressed by Niall Fitzgerald, chairman of Unilever, in an interview in *Marketing* (18 September 1997):

> The real value of interactive communications is that information flows both ways. It will be formidably difficult to learn how to use this well; to address each consumer as an individual person, not as a member of admass: and to use the information that flows back, but it means that we can focus, as never before, on potentially fruitful relationships.

Enhanced understanding of the dynamics of business relationships and advanced communication methodologies and technologies have meant that the marketing communications mix is increasingly complex, but also increasingly more important. Organizations today have the opportunity to manage their marketing communications in a way that delivers superior value to every customer as well as a competitive edge to the supplier. The key to successful marketing communications is curiously simple: marketing communications must be coherent, consistent and most importantly, *relevant*.

Notes

1. D. Schultz. and H. Schultz, 'Transitioning Marketing Communications', *Journal of Marketing Communications,* vol. 4 (1998), pp. 9–26.
2. *Marketing at a Point of Change* (HHCL & Partners: London, 1994), p. 25.
3. Chris Fill, *Marketing Communications, Contexts, Contents and Strategies,* 2nd edn (Hemel Hempstead: Prentice-Hall Europe, 1999).
4. D. Taylor and Altman 'Communication in Inter-personal Relationships: Social Penetration Theory', *Interpersonal Processes: New Directions in Communication Research* (eds Roloff and Miller) Newbury Park, CA: Sage (1987), pp. 257–77.
5. Stephen King, 'Practical Progress from a Theory of Advertisements', *Admap,* October 1975.
6. T. Duncan and S. Moriarty, 'A Communication-based Model for Managing Relationships', *Journal of Marketing*, vol. 69 (April 1998), pp. 1–13.
7. H. Mitchell. and S. Knox. 'A Client Perspective of IMC', *Proceedings of 28th EMAC Conference,* Berlin, 11–14 May 1999.

14

CUSTOMER SERVICE, PEOPLE AND PROCESSES

Moira Clark

In this chapter:

- The role of customer service in delivering competitive advantage
- The part that people play forms a valuable differentiation factor
- A case study illustrating the benefits of inverting the traditional 'top-down' management approach
- Internal marketing as a mechanism for integrated market-oriented management
- The role and remit of processes in securing strategic positioning

INTRODUCTION

Traditionally, marketers have considered the marketing mix as a combination of four basic components, or elements, namely: product, place, price and promotion. However, many marketers have long regarded the '4Ps' definition as too restrictive. Criticism has centred on its short-term transaction focus and its failure to concentrate sufficiently on the importance of building and maintaining long-term relationships with customers. Many authors have now suggested a modification of the existing 4Ps framework in an effort to capture the broader complexity inherent in relationship marketing.

Considerable support has also been given to the 7Ps suggested by Booms and Bitner.[1] They propose that the existing four elements of the marketing mix be extended to include three additional elements: physical evidence, people and processes. However, we would argue that 'physical evidence' should be replaced with 'customer service' (see Figure 14.1). While this substitution results in one element not being a 'P', it can be argued that a preoccupation with finding elements beginning with the letter 'P' may be counterproductive. For those fixated with 'Ps', we would suggest 'proactive customer service'.

Before moving on to a detailed discussion of the three additional marketing mix elements, it is worthwhile commenting briefly on why we feel they are particularly relevant.

1. *Customer service* – Customers are becoming more sophisticated and demanding better service from their suppliers. There is also an increasing need to build closer and more enduring relationships with customers through the provision of better service. Further, businesses now use

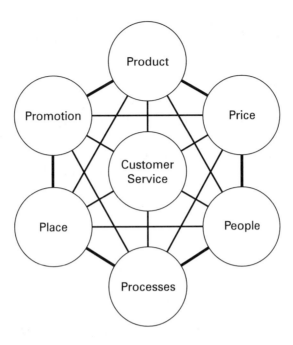

Figure 14.1 The expanded marketing mix

customer service as a competitive weapon to help them differentiate their product and service offerings from those of competitors.

2. *People* – The importance of managing internal customers was emphasized in Chapter 2. It is being increasingly recognized that people are an essential element in both product and service offerings since they are responsible for developing and sustaining long-term relationships with customers and, as such, they are part of the differentiation of organizations which provides competitive advantage.

3. *Processes* – Processes are the actual procedures, mechanisms, routines, and flow of activities by which the product and/or service is delivered to the customer. They can also involve policy decisions about customer involvement and employee discretion. Processes are seen to be worthy of inclusion in the expanded marketing mix because, if the processes supporting the product and/or service delivered to the customer fail, no amount of relationship building will overcome continued unsatisfactory process performance.

These three marketing mix elements (customer service, people and processes), along with the traditional marketing mix elements of product, place, price and promotion, are generally considered to be sufficiently robust to cover most situations. However, it is these three additional elements which are typically more concerned with keeping, rather than winning, customers and as such, they play a pivotal role in relationship marketing. Let us now examine these three key elements in more detail.

CUSTOMER SERVICE

Customer service has grown in importance in recent years for a number of reasons. First, more and more markets are becoming, in effect, 'commodity' markets, as the customer perceives little technical difference between competing offers. Thus the need to create differential advantage through added value has become paramount and customer service is a vital source of added value. Second, customers are becoming increasingly sophisticated and demanding in their service requirements and expectations. Third, companies are beginning to realize that increases in customer satisfaction and customer retention can have a significant impact on company profitability and corporate success.

Despite the fact that customer service can provide companies with such obvious advantages, customer care activities generally do not match either customers' expectations or organizations' aspirations. In many companies, customer care practices amount to reactive 'fire fighting', as opposed to any proactive attempt to systematically improve customer satisfaction. Customer service is often seen as the handling of customer complaints, rather than the managing of customer relationships.

This, of course, assumes that customers complain in the first case. Studies have shown that 98 per cent of dissatisfied customers never complain when they receive poor service, but, as a result, 90 per cent will not return to the disappointing supplier in future. Further, customers who are dissatisfied are likely to tell at least ten others about their poor service experience. This is quite extraordinary when you think that satisfied customers will tell only three people about their good service experience. This means that many companies face an uphill battle in trying to achieve a reputation for good customer service. If they get their service wrong, everyone will know about it, but if they get their service right, only three people will hear the good news. Therefore, the speed of response to customer complaints is a critical ingredient in managing customer satisfaction. If a complaint can be resolved quickly and effectively, then customers will generally be satisfied with the response given. Unfortunately, only 6 per cent of customers experience such an immediate response. Most customers have to wait for a response, which then drives up costs for the business, as shown in Figure 14.2.

The role of customer service

The provision of high levels of customer service involves understanding what the customer buys and determining how additional value can be added to an offer to differentiate it from competing offers. Thus customer service can be seen as an activity which provides time and place utilities for the customer; in other words, there is no value in a product or service until it is in the hands of the customer or consumer. It follows, therefore, that making the product or service 'available' to the customer is a key ingredient in the provision of customer service.

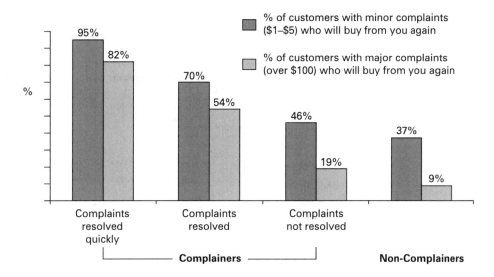

Figure 14.2 The implications of resolving customer complaints

Source: Technical Assisted Research Programme.

Availability is, however, a complex concept as it is affected by a range of factors that together constitute customer service. For example, availability may be influenced by delivery frequency and reliability, stock levels and order cycle times. In fact, it could be said that customer service is ultimately determined by the interaction of all those factors that affect the process of making products and services available to the customer.

In practice, there are many definitions of customer service. These range from 'All activities to accept, process, deliver and bill customer orders and to follow up on any activity that erred' to 'The timely and accurate delivery of products ordered by customers with accurate follow-up and enquiry response, including the timely delivery of invoices'. While a variety of perspectives exist on the subject, what all definitions of customer service have in common is that they are concerned with relationships at the buyer/seller interface.

For the purposes of this chapter, customer service is defined as being concerned with the building of relationships with customers and other markets or segments to ensure long-term relationships which are mutually trusting and profitable, and which reinforce the other elements of the marketing mix. Customer service, therefore, can be examined under three headings: pre-transaction, transaction, and post-transaction. Some of these key elements are shown in Figure 14.3.

Pre-transaction elements of customer service relate to corporate policies or programmes, involving written statements of service policy, and the planning of customer lifetime strategies and appropriate organizational structures. *Transaction* elements comprise the customer service variables that are directly involved in performing the physical distribution function, such as product availability, order cycle times, order status information, and delivery reliability.

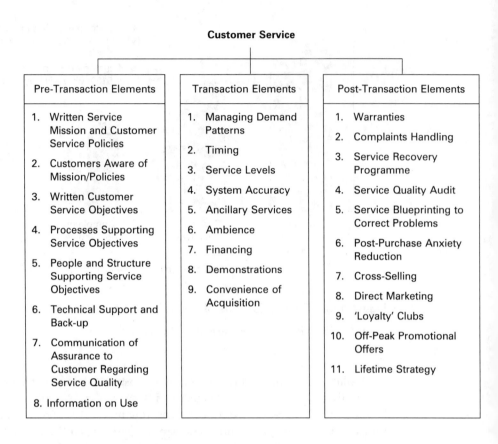

Customer Service

Pre-Transaction Elements	Transaction Elements	Post-Transaction Elements
1. Written Service Mission and Customer Service Policies	1. Managing Demand Patterns	1. Warranties
2. Customers Aware of Mission/Policies	2. Timing	2. Complaints Handling
3. Written Customer Service Objectives	3. Service Levels	3. Service Recovery Programme
4. Processes Supporting Service Objectives	4. System Accuracy	4. Service Quality Audit
5. People and Structure Supporting Service Objectives	5. Ancillary Services	5. Service Blueprinting to Correct Problems
6. Technical Support and Back-up	6. Ambience	6. Post-Purchase Anxiety Reduction
7. Communication of Assurance to Customer Regarding Service Quality	7. Financing	7. Cross-Selling
8. Information on Use	8. Demonstrations	8. Direct Marketing
	9. Convenience of Acquisition	9. 'Loyalty' Clubs
		10. Off-Peak Promotional Offers
		11. Lifetime Strategy

Figure 14.3 The elements of customer service

Post-transaction elements work to support product usage and include product warranties, parts and repair services, and customer complaint procedure. It is at this post-transaction stage that cross-selling initiatives and managing the customer relationship life cycle become essential to the establishment of long-term customer relationships.

In any product/market situation, some of the elements in Figure 14.3 will be more important and there may be factors other than those listed which will feature significantly in particular markets. Therefore it is essential to understand customer service in terms of the differing requirements of different market segments and to recognize that no universally appropriate list of customer service elements exists. A company may serve multiple markets that each have their own unique service requirements and priorities. The multi-variate nature of customer service and market segments means that it is essential to have a clearly defined customer service strategy.

Customer service strategy

There are four key steps to creating a customer service strategy, as outlined by Christopher.[2]

1. *Identifying a Service Mission* – the company should articulate its service pledge and values within its corporate mission, and/or in a separate customer service mission statement. This declaration should focus on the unique and distinctive elements of the company's offer while reflecting the company's philosophy and commitment to customer service.

2. *Setting the Customer Service Objectives* – the company's objectives, or goals, must be clearly defined and fully understood if effective strategies are to be developed. In terms of customer service, this involves answering questions such as:

   (a) How important is customer service compared with the other marketing mix elements?

   (b) With whom do we compete in the customer's mind?

   (c) Which are the customer service elements that contribute most to overall customer satisfaction and market share?

   (d) What dimensions of service are seen as priorities by customers when they choose suppliers?

   (e) How do we perform against the competition?

   In considering levels of performance in setting these customer service objectives, service providers must consider the importance of service quality variables such as:

   - *reliability* – the ability to perform the promised service dependably, accurately and consistently over time
   - *responsiveness* – prompt service and a willingness to help customers, (speed and flexibility are essential here)
   - *assurance* – knowledge and courtesy of staff and their ability to inspire trust and confidence
   - *empathy* – caring, individualized attention to customers
   - *tangibles* – for example, physical facilities, equipment, and staff appearance.[3]

3. *Customer Service Strategy* – most markets consist of market segments which seek different combinations of benefits. As all customers do not require the same level of service, segmentation can be a powerful means of creating appropriate service packages for each relevant market segment. Christopher's approach to developing a service-based strategy consists of four steps: identify the service segments and their specific requirements; identify the most important products and customers using Pareto Analysis; prioritize the service targets; and develop the service package.

4. *Implementation Programme* – once the most effective service package has been developed for each segment, the service package should then become part of an integrated marketing mix.

Competitive benchmarking

One technique used for measuring service performance and assisting in the setting of customer service objectives and strategy is competitive benchmarking. Competitive benchmarking seeks to understand the customer's perception of customer service and to monitor these perceptions market segment by market segment. It also seeks to measure customers' perceptions of the company's performance against other suppliers from within and outside the industry. Banks, for example, increasingly benchmark themselves not against other banks, but against excellent service providers such as Disney and Virgin. They believe that they can learn much more from comparing themselves with companies such as these, than from other companies in the financial services market. Figure 14.4 gives an example of competitive benchmarking for a manufacturing firm.

Figure 14.4 shows a list of components of service which have been elicited from earlier research with customers. The level of importance attributed to each of these service elements has also been identified. Against this data, on the right hand side of the chart, the company and its competitor are rated on each of these elements in terms of how their performance is perceived by customers. It can be seen here that the company profile more closely matches those elements that are perceived to be important for the customer. In contrast, the competitor's performance is poor in the areas that the customer values and good in the areas that are not so important to the customer.

Further profiles can be produced by analysing the data by market segment, customer type, area, and so forth. It is also quite useful to conduct competitive profiles for customers who have lapsed or who have defected to try to secure more satisfactorily their service requirements. Companies that use competitive benchmarking find that it provides them with a clear guide for helping to develop business strategy as it can often point to areas for improvement that have previously not been identified.

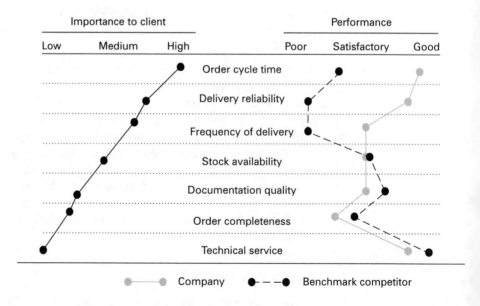

Figure 14.4 Customer service profile

Developing a customer service strategy is a logical extension of the RM concept. It is about recognizing the specific needs of the customer and developing a strategy that focuses the resources of the organization towards meeting those needs. However, in developing a customer service strategy, it would be a mistake to focus exclusively on the 'external' dimensions of service, or customer perceptions of service, and to forget the important role of the employee in shaping those perceptions. The next section of this chapter discusses the importance of the people 'P' of the marketing mix and how managing the internal market can have a significant impact on company success.

PEOPLE

People are increasingly becoming part of the differentiation by which companies seek to create added value and to gain competitive advantage. Employees play a pivotal role in customer acquisition and retention, by ensuring customer satisfaction and by developing and sustaining long-term relationships with customers. It is surprising, therefore, that not more companies recognize the strategic importance of managing the people 'P' of the marketing mix.

The significant role played by people in the marketing of products and/or services has led to a greater interest in internal marketing. Internal marketing is essentially a way of enabling organizations to recruit, motivate and retain customer-conscious employees in order to boost employee retention and customer satisfaction levels. Schneider and Bowen have found that when employees identify with the norms and values of an organization which reflect a commitment to customer service, they are less inclined to leave their jobs.[4] This reduction in employee turnover serves to strengthen the organization and to promote the transmission of service values to successive generations of employees. Furthermore, customers are more likely to be pleased with the service they receive from happy, experienced employees. Conversely, unhappy, poorly trained and inexperienced employees invariably lead to unhappy customers. Employee satisfaction in internal markets is, therefore, a prerequisite to customer satisfaction in external markets.

There are two basic rules to successful internal marketing.

1. Staff must work together across functional boundaries to ensure that the company's mission, strategy and objectives are served in both policy and practice. Cross-functional collaboration is particularly crucial in companies that operate high levels of direct interaction with customers.
2. Every employee fulfils the dual role of internal supplier and internal customer. To support and promote external customer satisfaction, every individual and department within the organization must provide fellow employees and departments with excellent internal customer service.

Differing roles of people

This second aspect of internal marketing, the idea of the internal customer, is the primary focus of the people 'P' for the purposes of this section. When viewing people as an element of the marketing mix, it is essential to recognize the different ways in which employees influence the marketing task and the customer relationship. Judd has developed a categorization scheme based on the degree of frequency of customer contact and the extent to which staff are involved with conventional marketing activities.[5] This scheme is shown in Figure 14.5.

The different roles fulfilled by employees are classified as set out below.

1. *Contactors* – Employees who have direct, frequent or periodic customer contact. They are typically involved with conventional marketing activities, (for example, customer service and selling). They are also responsible for building relationships with customers and, as such, they need to be trained, prepared and motivated to serve the customer well. Recruitment and selection processes should consider the person's potential to be responsive to customer needs, and appointees should be evaluated and rewarded on this basis.

2. *Modifiers* – Employees who have less direct, frequent or periodic customer contact. Their responsibilities usually do not entail face-to-face interaction with customers. Modifiers include people such as receptionists, credit department representatives and switchboard operators who are not involved with conventional marketing activities. Like Contactors, Modifiers also require excellent customer relationship skills. Here, training provision and performance monitoring are crucial.

3. *Influencers* – Employees who typically have no direct contact with customers, although they may take decisions that relate to customers as they are often involved with the traditional elements of the marketing mix. Influencers include people responsible for product development, market

	Involved With Conventional Marketing Mix	Not Directly Involved With Marketing Mix
Frequent or Periodic Customer Contact	Contactors	Modifiers
Infrequent or No Customer Contact	Influencers	Isolateds

Figure 14.5 Employee influence on customers

Source: V. C. Judd, 'Differentiate with Fifth P: People', *Industrial Marketing Management*, vol. 16 (1987), pp. 241–7.

research, and so forth. The recruitment of influencers should favour those with the potential to develop a sense of customer responsiveness. Influencers should be evaluated and rewarded according to customer-oriented performance standards.

4. *Isolateds* – Employees who have no customer contact. These people perform various support functions and do not have a great deal to do with conventional marketing activities. However, as support providers, their activities critically affect organizational performance. Isolateds include staff in the purchasing, personnel and data processing departments. They should be sensitive to the needs of internal and external customers.

This categorization suggests that people form an important part of differentiation, contributing to the creation of added value for the external customer. By viewing people as a separate element in the marketing mix, appropriate attention can be directed towards maximizing the impact of their activities through the provision of suitable and sufficient levels of support, incentive, and reward.

While Contactors are not the only people involved in service delivery, their ability to function effectively depends to a great extent on the support they get from other employees within the organization. Frequently, there are large numbers of support personnel who do not come into direct contact with the customer, but who nevertheless have a very important role to perform and who directly influence the service that is ultimately provided to the customer. They are often referred to as 'part-time marketers'. Systematic internal marketing, therefore, is a mechanism for developing and maintaining these part-time marketers as service-minded and customer-conscious employees. Through internal marketing, all employees can begin to understand how their tasks and the way in which they are performed affect customer satisfaction and contribute to a true marketing orientation.

Unfortunately, in many organizations, rules, regulations, practices and procedures are communicated from the CEO down through the organization to the front-line staff in an instructive manner: 'this is what you will do'. These front-line staff, or Contactors, usually have the first and most frequent contact with customers, but are often the lowest paid and least respected people in the organization. They include cashiers, van drivers and salespeople.

An alternative operational approach aimed at ensuring an internal marketing orientation is to turn the organizational pyramid upside-down, conceptually at least. Members of the front-line staff then become the most important people in the organization. They should be treated like internal customers, and more senior personnel should ask them instead, 'What can I do to help you do your job better?' When this change in attitude is adopted throughout the organization, employees will begin to regard themselves as internal suppliers and internal customers. Consequently, internal staff will be encouraged to recognize that if they are not serving the customer directly, they are probably serving someone who is, and therefore their contribution to enhancing the quality of internal service impacts the quality of service provided externally. An example of this approach is seen in the following mini case study.

Case Study 1: Felcro Electronics

A large engineering company's customer research showed that incoming telephone calls were rarely answered promptly. The usual response in this situation is to insist that telephones be answered within three rings. Instead, the company's management consulted the staff and asked, 'What can we do to help you do your job better?' The reply was very enlightening: 'Our job is pretty difficult. We are not only expected to answer the phones, but also to get drinks for visitors when they arrive and the tea and coffee-making facilities are two hundred yards away near the factory. We are also supposed to do photocopying for the offices'. At this point, many managers would have said, 'Well, this is what we will do for you', adopting the traditional top-down managerial approach.

However, in this instance, the employees were asked a further question: 'What would you like to do about it?' The staff responded by suggesting that someone bring them flasks of tea and coffee throughout the day so that they would not have to leave the reception area, and that the photocopying machine be brought into the reception area and placed behind a screen. These simple measures were taken and, not surprisingly, the telephones were answered promptly within three rings. As well as improving customer service, this incident also served to improve morale. The staff saw that their opinions were valued and that they contributed to shaping the service offering of the company.

Internal marketing, therefore, is essentially concerned with creating, developing and maintaining an internal service culture and orientation that assists and supports the organization in achieving its goals. The fundamental aims of internal marketing are to develop internal and external customer awareness and to remove functional barriers to organizational effectiveness. The idea is to ensure that all members of staff provide the best possible contribution to the marketing activities of the company and that all customer interactions are conducted in a way that adds value to the service encounter.

Developing internal marketing relationships

An increasing number of companies have recognized the need for internal marketing programmes and the implementation of such programmes has gained momentum in recent years. Perhaps the most famous examples of this are Scandinavian Airline System (SAS) and British Airways. In fact, some organizations have started to view internal marketing as a strategic weapon employed as a means of retaining customers through the achievement of high-quality service delivery and increased customer satisfaction. Yet, despite this, there is still no consensus on the implementation of internal marketing. What is clear is that internal marketing should not be solely the domain of marketers merely applying the same old traditional marketing concepts and tools. To do this would destroy the very nature of what is meant by relationship marketing and would not take into account the special needs of the internal market.

The model that would seem to offer the most in terms of enhancing the organization's capabilities is that proposed by Varey[6] which is given in Figure 14.6. This model of internal marketing acts as a process or mechanism for integrated market-oriented management. More work, however, needs to be undertaken to test this model empirically with organizations and to determine what it takes in operational terms to ensure internal marketing success. In the meantime, however, there is some agreement as to the range of interrelated internal marketing activities that are thought to be critical in helping to implement internal marketing.

1. *Organizational design* must be conducive to developing an internal marketing orientation. Market-facing, multi-disciplinary teams which are able to marshal resources to achieve market-based objectives are ideal for achieving an internal marketing philosophy.
2. *Staff surveys* are required on a regular basis to assess the internal service climate and culture to ensure internal and external service quality.
3. *Internal customer segmentation* by, for example, level of customer contact,[7] is necessary to target specific service provision and training to ensure service quality.
4. *Personal development and training* should be focused on core competencies for internal marketing. Research can help determine the internal and external customer requirements that will shape the nature of personal training and development.
5. *Empowerment and involvement* enable staff within clearly defined parameters to use their discretion to deliver a better quality of service to their customers.
6. *Recognition and rewards* based on employees' contributions to service excellence are critical to determining employee behaviour and should be based on careful consideration of their likely impact on behaviour, as well as their attractiveness or motivational factor for the individual.
7. *Internal communications* provides a mechanism for cross-functional participation in the coordination of activities within the organization. It helps to reinforce service quality and ensures that everyone knows what to do and the context of their role in the wider activity. Business television is now used in many organizations to facilitate communications, particularly in organizations that have branch networks. This medium ensures that all the employees receive news and information at the same time, and facilitates a greater organizational cohesion across the company.
8. *Performance measures* need to be visible and should measure each person's and department's contribution to the achievement of performance objectives for each key success factor.[8]
9. *Building supportive working relationships* for employees should be a key issue when developing an internal marketing approach. Employees should be able to provide each other with consideration, trust, warmth and support, all of which help to break down barriers within and between departments. This enhances internal communications and the likelihood of achieving internal and external service quality.

CUSTOMER SERVICE, PEOPLE AND PROCESSES

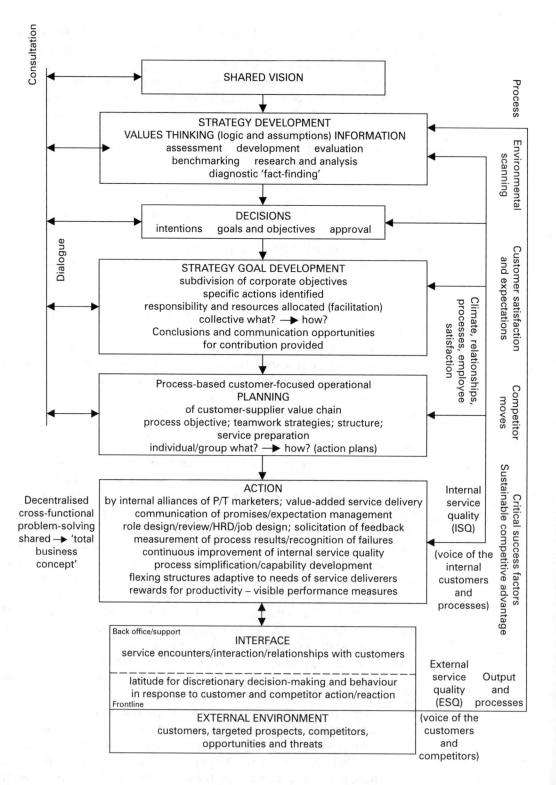

Figure 14.6 Integrated market-oriented management

The effective management of employees has become an increasingly powerful weapon in an increasingly competitive environment. However, while the people 'P' is a critical element of the relationship marketing mix, no amount of attention and effort from staff will overcome continued unsatisfactory process performance. If the processes supporting product or service delivery cannot, for example, provide an acceptable meal or repair a faulty machine within a defined period of time, an unhappy customer will be the result. The next section of this chapter, therefore, looks at the processes 'P' of the marketing mix and the key role it plays in determining customer satisfaction.

PROCESSES

The processes by which products and services are created and delivered to the customer are a major factor within the relationship marketing mix, as many customers will often perceive the service delivery system as part of the product or service offering. All work activity represents a process. Processes encompass the procedures, tasks, schedules, mechanisms, activities, and routines by which a product or service is delivered to the customer. They involve policy decisions about customer involvement and employee discretion. To reiterate, unsatisfactory process performance can diminish or destroy the strength of a customer relationship. This fact suggests that effective operations management is crucial to the success of marketing products and services, and that the close and continuous cooperation of marketing and operations functions is essential to business prosperity.

Processes as structural elements

Lyn Shostack has suggested that the structural nature of processes means that they can be engineered to help deliver a desired strategic positioning.[9] She argues that a process-oriented approach involves:

- Breaking down the process into logical steps and sequences to facilitate control and analysis
- Taking into account the more variable processes, which may lead to different outcomes because of judgement, choice or chance
- Deviation or tolerance standards which recognize that processes are real time phenomena which do not perform with perfect precision, but function within a performance band

Services processes can also be analysed according to their complexity and divergence. Complexity is concerned with the nature of the steps and sequences that constitute the process. Divergence refers to the 'executional' latitude, or the variability of the steps and sequences: for example, a surgeon's work is likely to be high in both complexity and divergence, whereas the services offered by the keeper of corner shop may be low in complexity and divergence. Further, the services provided by a hotelier may be low in divergence, but high in complexity.

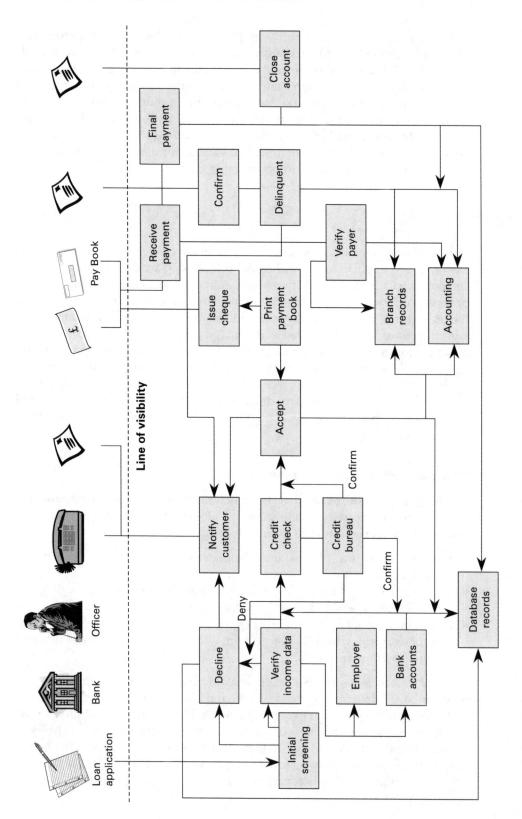

Figure 14.7 Service blueprint for instalment lending

Source: G. Lynn Shostack, 'Service Positioning Through Structural Change', *Journal of Marketing*, vol. 51 (Jan. 1987), pp. 34–43.

Processes can often be depicted as detailed maps, flow charts or blueprints. Such diagrammatic representations reduce processes to a series of interrelated steps and sequences as shown in Figure 14.7. This approach requires the portrayal of all the points of contact between the customer and the supplier. Possible weaknesses in the service encounter can then be identified and redressed, thereby improving service quality. When presented with a process blueprint, managers are often surprised at the complexity of the processes involved in the operation. Indeed, a major benefit of mapping processes is that resources can then be appropriately allocated towards the re-engineering of processes to simplify and streamline business activities.

Processes can be changed in terms of complexity and divergence to reinforce their strategic positioning or to establish a new positioning. The four options outlined by Shostack are as set out below.

1. *Reduced divergence* – this tends to reduce costs, improve productivity and make distribution easier. It can also produce more uniform service quality and improved service availability. However, its negative effects may include a perception of limited choice and a rejection of highly standardized service.
2. *Increased divergence* – this involves greater customization and flexibility which may command higher prices. This approach suggests a niche positioning strategy based less on volume and more on margins, enabling a more tailored relationship-building approach to be achieved.
3. *Reduced complexity* – this usually means a specialization strategy. Steps and activities are consciously omitted from the service process and this simplification tends to make distribution and control easier.
4. *Increased complexity* – This is usually a strategy to increase market penetration through the addition of further services. Supermarkets, banks and building societies are increasingly following this approach by providing a greater number and range of service offerings to their customers.

Each of these process management options has advantages and disadvantages, but they all provide opportunities to alter customers' perceptions and market positioning. These process characteristics constitute criteria by which customers can judge the quality of services. For example, Southwest Airlines in the USA and Singapore Airlines are both successful companies, but they follow very different process models. Singapore Airlines focuses on providing a customized service that is designed to meet the individual needs of the business traveller. As such, employees of Singapore Airlines are empowered to provide non-standardized services and to exceed performance expectations to satisfy customer requirements. In contrast, Southwest Airlines is a no-frills, low-priced carrier that offers frequent and relatively short-haul domestic flights in the USA. Its service does not offer in-flight catering or pre-assigned seating. The airline has adopted a totally standardized approach to service, although the fun in-flight atmosphere that is generated by the unique company culture compensates for the reduced divergence.

Processes have characteristics that can be deliberately and strategically managed within the context of the relationship-oriented marketing mix with the purpose of reinforcing or changing market positioning. Therefore, an organization needs to have a clear understanding of these process characteristics in order to maintain a competitive position in the market place and to determine the appropriate RM approach for its target market.

SUMMARY

This chapter introduces three additional marketing mix elements – customer service (physical evidence), people, and processes – to the previously discussed four elements of product, place, price, and promotion. These seven interactive and interdependent elements, known as the 7Ps, are managed together to achieve the best possible internal and external marketing strategies.

In developing a marketing mix strategy, managers need to understand the relationships between the different elements of the expanded marketing mix. It has been pointed out that there are three degrees of interaction between the marketing mix elements.[10]

1. *Consistency* – this occurs where there is a logical and useful fit between two or more elements of the marketing mix.
2. *Integration* – this involves an active, harmonious interaction between the elements of the marketing mix.
3. *Leverage* – this requires a more sophisticated approach and is concerned with using each element to best advantage in support of the total marketing mix.

Each of the elements of the marketing mix must be mutually supportive in terms of consistency, integration and leverage to reinforce the positioning and delivery of the quality of service that is required by the target market segment. In so doing, this relationship-oriented marketing mix should ensure a sound basis for creating, developing and enhancing long-term, profitable relationships with customers.

Notes

1. B. H. Booms and M. J. Bitner, 'Marketing Strategies and Organization Structures for Services Firms', in J. Donnelly and W. R. George (eds), *Marketing of Services* (Chicago: American Marketing Association, 1981), pp. 47–51.
2. M. Christopher, *The Customer Service Planner* (Oxford: Butterworth-Heinemann, 1992).
3. L. L. Berry, A. Parasuraman and V. A. Zeithaml, 'The Service Quality Puzzle', *Business Horizons*, vol. 31, no. 4 (September/October 1988), pp. 35–43.
4. B. Schneider and D. E. Bowen, 'Employee and Customer Perceptions of Service in Banks: Replication and Extension', *Journal of Applied Psychology*, vol. 70 (1985), pp. 423–33.

5. V. C. Judd, 'Differentiate with the Fifth P: People', *Industrial Marketing Management*, vol. 16 (1987), pp. 241–7.
6. R. J. Varey, 'A Model of Internal Marketing for Building and Sustaining a Competitive Service Advantage', *Journal of Marketing Management*, vol. 11 (1985), 41–54.
7. See note 5 above.
8. See note 6 above.
9. G. L. Shostack, 'Service Positioning Through Structural Change', *Journal of Marketing*, vol. 51 (January 1987), pp. 34–43.
10. B. Shapiro, 'Rejuvenating the Marketing Mix', *Harvard Business Review*, September/October (1985), pp. 28–33.

PART IV

PLANNING AND ORGANIZING FOR RELATIONSHIP MARKETING

PLANNING FOR RELATIONSHIP MARKETING

Lynette Ryals

In this chapter:

- When should marketing planning be done and who should be involved?
- How should it be done, and what process should be used?
- How should the plan deal with different market segments?
- How should planning for key accounts be done?
- Could decision support software help?
- What is the role of senior managers? Of the planning department?
- What is the relationship between operational (one year) and strategic (longer-term) planning?
- How can marketing plans contribute to building relationships with customers?

WHAT IS MARKETING PLANNING?

In this chapter we shall consider one of the most difficult aspects of the marketing task, which is actually making it all work in practice by means of a system within the company. This practical element, so crucial to marketing success, is often overlooked. Yet no investigation of marketing management can be complete without a fairly detailed consideration of how all the structures and frameworks presented in the earlier chapters are to be effectively implemented.

To make marketing work, it is necessary to have available a logical 'common format' for the implementation of strategy: that is, a *marketing plan*. In effect, the planner is attempting to manage the future by deciding *what to do about the possible different trading environments*. To best anticipate, influence and exploit future markets requires dedicated marketing planning.

Marketing planning is a logical and sequential series of activities leading to the setting of marketing objectives and the formulation of plans for achieving them. It is a management *process*. Formalized marketing planning employs a planning system to accomplish this process. The planning system is a structured way of identifying a range of options for the company, making them explicit in writing, establishing marketing objectives that are consistent with the company's overall objectives, and scheduling and costing the specific activities most likely to bring about the achievement of the objectives.

BENEFITS OF FORMALIZED MARKETING PLANNING

Formalized marketing is an institutionalized process designed to *work out* and *write down* in advance the particular competitive stance that the company plans to take. This system will ensure that the company's hopes for the future are, and remain, realistic, relevant and widely understood.

In one study, 90 per cent of the industrial goods companies involved did not, by their own admission, produce anything approximating to an integrated, coordinated and internally consistent plan for their marketing activities. Significantly, this majority included a substantial number of companies with highly formalized procedures for marketing planning. Marketing planning *procedures* are most valuable when they culminate in a marketing *plan*. Companies find that formalized marketing planning produces the following benefits:

- Coordination of the activities of many individuals whose actions are interrelated over time
- Identification of expected developments
- Preparedness to meet changes when they occur
- Minimization of non-rational responses to the unexpected
- Better communication among executives
- Minimization of conflict among individuals that might result in a subordination of the goals of the company to those of the individual

WHY IS MARKETING PLANNING ESSENTIAL?

'It is planning, not gambling, that produces profits and security.'

Marcus Aurelius

Organizations operate in increasingly fragmented, complex and fast-changing markets. Meeting the challenges presented by a highly fluid and competitive environment normally means experiencing conflicting pressures between business objectives, for example:

- Enhancing customer service versus increasing profitability
- Short-term profit versus long-term value creation
- Maximization of revenue versus minimization of costs

Marketing planning is an effective aid to management because of its integral role in identifying and clarifying the priorities for the business. Without a clear statement of priorities, the company is vulnerable to internal confusion and lost opportunities. The following list describes the most common symptoms of a reliance on traditional sales forecasting and budgeting procedure in the absence of a marketing planning system:

- Lost opportunities for profit
- Meaningless numbers in plans
- Unrealistic objectives
- Lack of actionable market information

- Interfunctional strife
- Management frustration
- Proliferation of products and markets
- Wasted promotional expenditure
- Pricing confusion
- Growing vulnerability to environmental change
- Loss of control over the business

An effective marketing planning system should offer more than an immunity against these operational problems: it should deliver clearer and more widely understood objectives and priorities, higher levels of usable market information, improved interfunctional coordination, less waste and duplication of resources, and greater overall business control. A *Business Week* survey in 1996 indicated that as few as 6 per cent of business people in the USA would rate their company as excellent at planning for the long-term future. Could this be because they have not mastered the art of planning, or because they suffer from a short-sighted business outlook, or because their organizations contain barriers to marketing planning?

BARRIERS TO MARKETING PLANNING

As a rule, formalized marketing planning results in greater profitability and stability in the long term and also helps to reduce friction and operational difficulties within the organization. When marketing planning fails, it is generally because companies place too much emphasis on the procedures and the resulting paperwork, rather than on generating information useful to, and consumable by, management. Also, when companies relegate marketing planning to a junior planner or outsource the task, it invariably founders for the simple reason that planning for line management cannot be delegated to a third party. The real role of the planner should be to help those responsible for implementation to plan. Failure to recognize this simple fact can be disastrous. Equally, planning failures often result from companies trying to do too much, too quickly, and without training staff in the use of procedures.

Barriers to implementing marketing planning may include:

- Weak support from chief executive and top management
- Lack of a plan for planning
- Lack of line management support (including hostility, lack of skills, lack of information, lack of resources, inadequate organizational structure)
- Confusion over planning terms
- Numbers in lieu of written objectives and strategies
- Too much detail, too far ahead
- Once-a-year ritual
- Separation of operational planning from strategic planning
- Failure to integrate marketing planning into a total corporate planning system
- Delegation of planning to a planner

If some or all of these barriers are an issue in your organization, you may find it necessary to combine the introduction of the planning process with a number of training sessions. It is *essential* to get buy-in from the top, early on in the process.

Let us now consider in more detail the key components of marketing planning: the preparation, the people, the plan and the process.

PREPARING TO PLAN

Preparation is an important part of the marketing planning process. Organizations that do not dedicate the time and resources necessary for planning can pay a heavy price. Inadequate preparation invites mistakes and careless thinking, and can allow important decisions to be made on the basis of insufficient or unreliable information. The typical planning cycle[1] is 12 months and, generally speaking, major market research projects should be commissioned in the first half of the planning cycle and plans and programmes should be formulated in the latter half of the planning cycle.

When preparing to plan, it is important to be clear *which* type of planning you are engaged in: strategic or tactical planning. The strategic marketing plan reflects what managers perceive to be their market position and competitive advantage, what objectives they want to achieve and how they intend to achieve them (strategies), and what resources they envisage will be required and at what consequence (budget). Tactical marketing plans are the detailed scheduling and costing out of the specific actions necessary to deliver the first phase of the strategic plan. Tactical plans should *never* be developed before strategic plans.

Who should be involved?

The people who are going to *use* the plan should be involved in the planning process, as should those within the organization who can contribute knowledge or information to the plan. However, everyone need not attend every planning meeting. A planning manager should be appointed to manage the virtual planning team, indicating who should be at which meetings and assigning whatever tasks need to be undertaken between meetings. It is also the planning manager's responsibility to establish clear communications and to ensure proper completion of the plan.

Criteria of a good marketing plan

The measure of a good marketing plan is *not* its 100 per cent accuracy in predicting the future. If you could foretell what is going to happen, you would not need to plan. The role of the marketing plan is to capture the essentials of the planning process and distil them down into a comprehensive working document. A good marketing plan should contain the following items, most of which are discussed later on in the chapter:

- Mission statement
- Financial summary
- Market overview (a *brief* summary of the marketing audit)
- SWOT
- Assumptions
- Marketing objectives and strategies
- Programmes, with forecasts and budgets

The written marketing plan is the background against which operational decisions are taken on an ongoing basis and thus it should not include too much detail. To be usable, the marketing plan has to be *well-written* and *short*. As Malcolm McDonald says: 'If it's quicker to weigh it than to count the pages, it's not a good marketing plan!' The marketing plan is central to the company's relationship management and revenue-generating activities, and from it flow all other corporate activities, such as the timing of the cash flow and the size and character of the labour force.

The marketing plan can be distributed to all those whom it involves directly or for whom it will have a significant impact. The distribution list should include the key account (or segment) director and manager, as well as each member of the key account (or segment) team.

Criteria of an effective marketing planning process

The success of the marketing planning process is determined by more than simply the production of a marketing plan. An effective planning process will yield a *usable* plan and, in so doing, will additionally identify insufficient or unreliable information, promote clarity of thinking within the team and recommend methods for better teamworking. The achievement of these criteria requires patient determination. Organizations usually take two to three years to install a planning process fully so if your plan is about 60 per cent of the way there in Year 1 and 80–90 per cent completed in Year 2, you are on track.

THE MARKETING PLANNING PROCESS

The marketing planning process has four phases made up of a total of ten steps. By seeking to answer fundamental questions, the phases work together to build a picture of the company's competitive position and commercial attitude. The phases are shown in Table 15.1.

Figure 15.1 illustrates the sequential relationship between the ten steps to creating a marketing plan. The adjoining broken lines indicate the reality of the planning process in that each of the steps is likely to be worked through more than once before being completed.

Although it is generally accepted that each of the marketing planning steps is applicable in most cases, the degree to which each of the separate steps in the

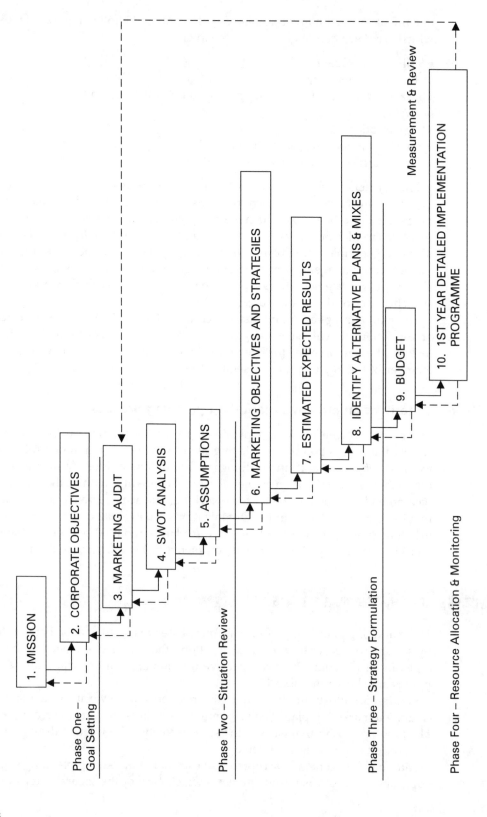

Figure 15.1 The ten steps of the strategic marketing planning process

Table 15.1   **The four phases of the marketing planning process**

Phase	Answers the question	Steps
One	Where are we going?	1, 2
Two	Where are we starting from?	3, 4, 5
Three	How will we get there?	6, 7, 8
Four	Who will do what, and when?	
	How much will it cost?	9, 10

diagram needs to be formalized depends to a large extent on the size and nature of the company. A large, diversified company will require much more formality than a small, undiversified company.

Phase 1: mission and corporate objectives

The mission statement is an enduring declaration of purpose, or vision. It encapsulates the organization's activities, values and beliefs, and its point of differentiation from competitors. The statement is intended to clarify the purpose of the organization, to inspire its people and to communicate its strategy; it should therefore be short, clear, unique and ambitious.

The UK sandwich retail chain, Pret A Manger, established by Julian Metcalfe in 1986 and now with 50 shops and turnover of more than £25 million, claims it is 'passionate about food'. The company has a particularly effective mission statement that genuinely defines its market position. The message is consciously reinforced, appearing on the shop windows and all product packaging (see Figure 15.2).

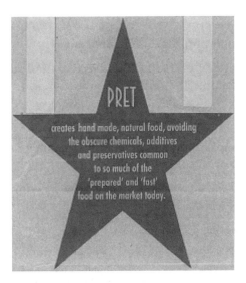

PRET

creates hand made, natural food, avoiding the obscure chemicals, additives and preservatives common to so much of the 'prepared' and 'fast' food on the market today.

(Reproduced by kind permission of the copyright and trademark owners Pret A Manger (Europe) Limited)

Figure 15.2   Pret A Manger's mission statement

Corporate objectives operationalize the mission by providing a means of measuring progress towards the achievement of the mission. The objectives set out specific goals in measurable terms such as monetary profit or percentage of market share gained within a defined period.

Phase 2: marketing audit, SWOT analysis and assumptions

Marketing audit

You may find it helpful at this point to refer back to Chapter 3, which deals with the marketing audit. To summarize the main points made there:

- It is essentially a database of all relevant company/market related issues
- It should be continuous/dynamic
- It should not hide behind vague terms, (for example, 'poor economic conditions')
- It should incorporate PLCs and portfolio matrices (see Chapters 3 and 9); diagrams and corresponding words should match
- It is a valuable 'transfer device' for incoming personnel

It is useful to produce a checklist of information requirements for the marketing audit, including suggested information sources and accuracy levels. A marketing audit checklist might resemble the format shown in Table 15.2.

Completing the SWOT analysis

To decide on marketing objectives and future strategy, it is first necessary to determine the business unit's *present* position in its market(s). This is

Table 15.2   **Example of a marketing audit checklist**

Information requirement	Possible source(s)	Accuracy level required (high/medium/low)	Urgent: yes/no
Economic growth forecast	DTI	Medium	No
Industry sales forecast	Financial Times Survey Trade Association	High	Yes
Supplier evaluation of us by customer	Customer's Logistics Manager	High	Yes

accomplished by summarizing the market audit in the form of a SWOT analysis which seeks to identify the business's *Strengths*, *Weaknesses*, *Opportunities* and *Threats*. In simple terms:

- What are the opportunities?
- What are the present and future threats to the business unit's in each of the segments that have been identified as being of importance?
- What are the business unit's *differential* strengths and weaknesses *vis-à-vis* competitors? In other words, why should potential customers in the target markets prefer to deal with you rather than with any of your competitors?

Guidelines for completing the SWOT analysis

The marketing audit will have identified what are considered to be the key markets, market segments and key accounts upon which the company should focus. For planning purposes, it is vital to prepare a SWOT for each segment or key account. Each SWOT should be brief and interesting to read.

Point 1 indicates how the *strengths* and *weaknesses* section of the SWOTs should be completed, while Point 2 concerns the *opportunities* and *threats* section.

1. *List of important factors for success in the business*. How does a competitor wishing to provide products in the same segment succeed? Relatively few factors determine success: the most important ones are often product performance, quality of software, breadth of services, speed of service and low cost.
2. *Summary of outside influences and their implications*. This should include a brief statement about the ways in which important environmental influences such as technology, government policies and regulations, and the economy have affected the segment. These external forces will no doubt represent both opportunities and threats.

A brief statement should now be made about the company's strengths and weaknesses in relation to those factors that have been identified as most important to success. To do this, it will probably be necessary to consider other specialist suppliers to the same segment in order to recognize why your company can succeed and what weaknesses must be addressed in the plan.

It is important that the SWOT analysis is carried out by segment (or key account) because it is possible that the critical success factors (CSFs) may be different for each segment, as may be the relevant competitors and the company's relative competitive position. Figure 15.3 shows how the information from the marketing audit feeds into the SWOT analysis.

It can be useful to present the SWOT analysis in the form of a grid or matrix, as shown in Figures 15.4 and 15.5.

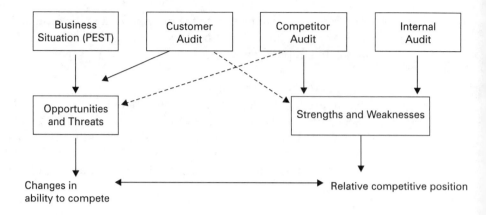

Figure 15.3 How the marketing audit feeds into the SWOT analysis

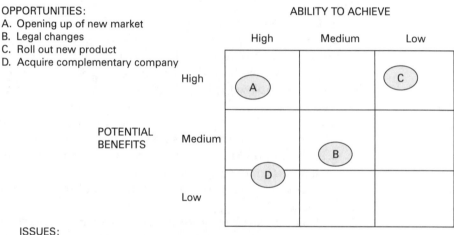

OPPORTUNITIES:
A. Opening up of new market
B. Legal changes
C. Roll out new product
D. Acquire complementary company

ISSUES:
- A. Need to identify channels
- B. Develop lobbying skills
- C. Need to reorganize to exploit this opportunity
- D. Borrowing costs may rise

Figure 15.4 Opportunities: worked example

Planning assumptions

In completing the marketing audit and SWOT analysis, assumptions will have been drawn and these now need to be explicitly written down. There are certain key determinants of success in all companies about which assumptions have to be made before the planning process can proceed. For instance, it would be of no use receiving plans from two product managers if one believed the economy was going into decline by 2 per cent while the other believed the economy was about to grow by 10 per cent. Assumptions should be relevant and few in number.

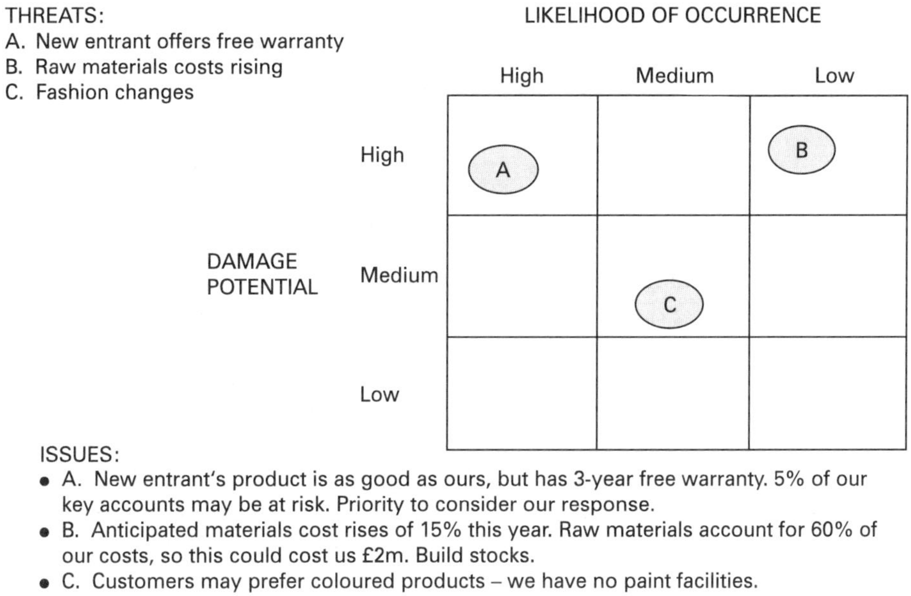

THREATS: LIKELIHOOD OF OCCURRENCE
A. New entrant offers free warranty
B. Raw materials costs rising
C. Fashion changes

	High	Medium	Low
High	A		B
Medium		C	
Low			

DAMAGE POTENTIAL (vertical axis)

ISSUES:
- A. New entrant's product is as good as ours, but has 3-year free warranty. 5% of our key accounts may be at risk. Priority to consider our response.
- B. Anticipated materials cost rises of 15% this year. Raw materials account for 60% of our costs, so this could cost us £2m. Build stocks.
- C. Customers may prefer coloured products – we have no paint facilities.

Figure 15.5 Threats: worked example

An example of presented assumptions for a European glass producer might be:

'With respect to the company's industrial climate, it is assumed that:

1. Industrial overcapacity will increase from 105 per cent to 115 per cent as new industrial plants come into operation;
2. Price competition will force price levels down by 10 per cent across the board;
3. A new product will be introduced by our Japanese competitor before the end of the second quarter.'

Phase 3: marketing objectives and strategies, and contingency plans

Marketing objectives and strategies

Following on from the initial phases of Goal Setting and Situation Review is the key stage in the whole marketing planning process, that of formulating marketing objectives and strategies.

(a) *objectives* are what you want to achieve;
(b) *strategies* are how you plan to achieve your objectives.

It is important to remember that marketing objectives are about *products and markets only*. Common sense will confirm that it is only by selling something to someone that the company's final goals can be achieved and that advertising, pricing and service levels are the means (or strategies) to this end. Thus pricing objectives, sales-promotion objectives and advertising objectives are subservient to, and not to be confused with, marketing objectives.

Marketing objectives are confined to one or more of the following:

- Existing products in existing markets
- New products for existing markets
- Existing products for new markets
- New products for new markets

Marketing objectives must be capable of measurement otherwise they are not objectives. The use of directional words such as 'maximize', 'minimize', 'penetrate' and 'increase' is only acceptable where quantitative measurement can be attached to them over the planning period. Measurement will be in terms of sales volume, monetary value, market share or percentage penetration of outlets (see Table 15.3).

Since marketing strategies are the means by which marketing objectives are achieved they are generally concerned with the marketing mix: product, pricing, place and promotion decisions. Customer service is constructed around these variables and underpinned by people, processes (including IT) and physical evidence, such as the outward appearance of personnel, buildings and documents. The marketing plan should set out for each objective:

(a) a statement of the *strategy* or *strategies* that will be used to attain the objective
(b) a detailed description of the *tactics* or *programmes* that will be employed, giving timings, responsibilities and an estimate of *cost*.

Table 15.3   Some examples of marketing objectives for a building company

Regional Project Management marketing objectives	Construction Management marketing objectives	Manufacturing Process Projects marketing objectives
To increase income from £1.2 million to £2.2 million by Year 3	To increase income from £2 million to £4 million by Year 3	To initiate this business in the first year and achieve a revenue of £2 million by Year 3
To increase average project size by 25% by Year 3	To increase market share of the commercial owner-occupier and developer market in the Southern Region from 3% to 10% by Year 3	To gain 5% market share of the small/medium project market
To add two new products each year	To add 3 new projects each year	
	To increase average project value by 10% per annum	

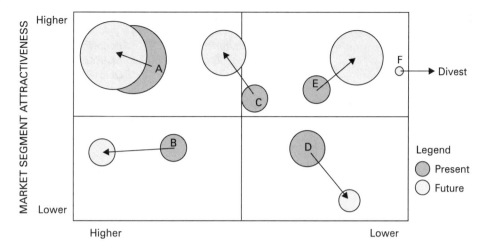

Figure 15.6 An example of a company's DPM

Portfolio matrix tools are extremely useful when developing marketing strategies. For example, consider the DPM in Figure 15.6. The diagram depicts the current and objective or desired position of this company's six product/market segments. Three product/market segments (marked A, B and C) have been targeted for improvement in relative business strengths (the arrows moving to the left). The marketing plan should explain how this would be achieved, referring back to the SWOT analysis and describing how the CSFs can be improved.

In segments D and E, the company's relative business strength is expected to decline. The plan should explain why this is happening; perhaps the market is becoming less attractive or a competitor is gaining relative strength. Segment F is very small and the DPM indicates that the business is intending to divest during the planning period: the plan should state the exit strategy.

Contingency planning

The marketing plan is thus far based upon a set of assumptions, and it is therefore wise to engage in some 'what if' thinking. Marketing plans that do not contain contingency or alternative plans are vulnerable to changes in circumstances.

Developing different scenarios or descriptions of possible futures is a helpful approach. Scenarios are best developed as a team exercise, even cross-functionally. It can be useful when developing contingency plans to involve a manufacturing and/or IT person to advise on possible technological developments and to invite the participation of 'independent' contributors from outside the industry.

To create scenarios, return to the market audit and think about what *might* happen. Choose two or three major themes and develop these into short

Table 15.4   An example of scenario development

	Scenario A (Base Case) 'RAPID GROWTH'	Scenario B 'MARKET COLLAPSE'	Scenario C 'TECHNOLOGICAL REVOLUTION'
Strategy:			
– Product	Range extensions, including low cost option	Low cost option	Low cost option, plus new product development
– Promotion	Extend advertising to new segments via specialist publications	Cut advertising budget	Switch to new media

qualitative descriptions. Then apply marketing strategies to each one. Strategies that appear to perform well across all scenarios are particularly robust. Strategies that perform well in only one scenario are vulnerable to changes in the underlying assumptions. An example of scenario development is given in Table 15.4.

Phase 4: research, allocation and monitoring

The final phase of the planning process is the production of a tactical marketing plan. This usually takes the form of a budget and a one-year detailed implementation plan. The tactical plan outlines *who* will do *what* and *when*, and *how much* it will cost. The tactical plan can be produced as a separate, but complementary, document to the strategic plan. Before issuing a tactical plan, it is important to check it against the strategic plan. In particular, the tactical plan should be consistent with the marketing audit to ensure that the planned implementation programme is feasible.

INTERNATIONAL PLANNING

The planning process described above works just as effectively across international boundaries as it does within national borders. However, an international market audit poses the following additional considerations:

- The product itself
  standardization
  adaptation
- Packaging and labelling
  protection/security
  promotional/distribution channels
  cultural factors
  package size
  language
  legal or regulatory requirements

- Brands and trademarks
  global or national
  legal requirements and ownership issues
  cultural factors
- Warranty and service
  international customers
  safety
  quality control standards
  usage
  promotion
  service networks

Some famous examples of not-so-successful international marketing initiatives include:

- The Mexican bread and cakes brand, *Bimbo,* has an image problem in the USA
- The Rolls-Royce *Silver Mist* ('mist' means 'manure' in German)
- The export of bacon flavoured crisps to Saudi Arabia (the entire planeload was incinerated at the side of the runway in Jeddah despite the manufacturer's protests that the product contained no pork)
- The Scandinavian vacuum cleaner manufacturer, *Electrolux*, ran a US advertising campaign with the slogan: 'Nothing sucks like an Electrolux'

Careful international marketing has much to offer, and not only in terms of increased sales. The successful international company is constantly on the look out for synergy and cost savings. Economies of scale can be found in production, product R&D and new technologies.

PLANNING FOR KEY ACCOUNTS

Key account management is a complex task, as is discussed later in Chapter 17. It often involves cross-functional teams and international planning issues, and can engender internal confusion over priorities where specially tailored products or services are required. When planning for key accounts, it is therefore useful to treat a key account as a segment (or several segments) in its own right and to prepare a separate sub-plan for each key account.

The purpose of the key account plan is to show how the supplying organization intends to build and strengthen its relationship with its key accounts. The plan should therefore address the following issues:

- The key account's decision-making unit and purchasing process
- The key account's objectives and drivers
- The market audit *from the key account's point of view* (the customer's market background competitive position)
- Opportunities and threats to the key account's business as well as to the relationship between the supplier and the key account

The strengths and weaknesses analysis should be based on the key account's CSFs while the strategies should deal with people and process issues as well as the 4Ps (product, price, place and promotion). It can still be appropriate to use the Ansoff Matrix ('new markets' become 'new parts of key account') and the DPM ('market attractiveness' becomes 'customer sub-segment attractiveness'). The other significant difference between key account planning and other forms of marketing planning is that key account planning may be a joint process in which both supplier and customer take part.

IT IN PLANNING

Various software packages are now available which assist with elements of marketing planning. These range from simple matrix generators to complex segmentation packages. There are even programs that will write your marketing plan for you (based on the data you supply, of course!).

The advantages of using planning software can be considerable. Benefits include the following points.

1. *Guidance* – on-screen prompts and access to 'Help' pages guide the user through the planning process, ensuring that it is thoroughly and correctly completed.
2. *Standardization* – the adoption of specific programs across large organizations or international divisions provides consistency and supports consolidation. Site licences and network versions may be purchased to allow planners in different locations to work on the same plan simultaneously.
3. *Presentation* – professional applications usually incorporate a choice of visual aids such as charts and tables to enhance clarity and interest value. Attractive graphics can help make essential points about segments or competitive positions (see the following examples).
4. *Contingency planning* – planning software is easier to manipulate than traditional 'paper and pencil' methods, affording a time and energy saving facility, especially in 'what if' type exercises.

The following three examples of marketing software output illustrate the diversity and flexibility of IT features. The first example, based on the experience of a German engineering company, is a CSF bar chart for a product-market segment that has been produced using the weighting and scoring system described earlier (see Figure 15.7). It is clear from Figure 15.7 that TopWidget surpasses its competitors on quality, shares similar product range and service levels, but performs least well overall because its prices are perceived to be less attractive.

The second example is the result of segmentation exercises using two different types of software. The following data shows the output from a cluster analysis of Europe-wide customer research data in a metal industry. Cluster 1

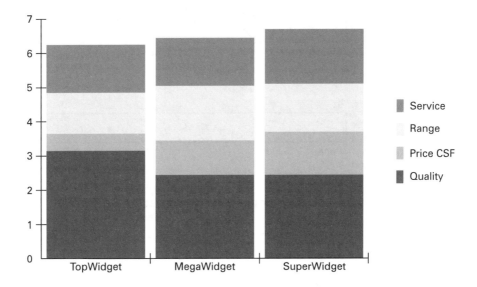

Figure 15.7 CSF bar chart

represents a group of customers for whom reliability of delivery and price are vital while cluster 2 represents a group of customers who are more interested in security of supply and consistent quality.

	CLUSTER 1		*CLUSTER 2*	
Reliability of Delivery	0.243	Security of Supply	0.237
Price	0.222	Consistent Quality	0.211
Security of Supply	0.189	Reliability of Delivery	0.184

Another segmentation program also uses cluster analysis but in addition produces the results as a bar chart. Market research by a South African insurance company indicated a number of different segments. One segment prefers to buy from a well-known company, preferably a company that is personally recommended. The insurance company labelled this segment 'Security Seekers'. A different segment was primarily interested in price and was called 'Economy'. Using this information, the insurance company was able to develop two different marketing propositions. It targeted the Security Seekers with an advertising campaign emphazising its history and track record, and introducing 'recommend a friend' incentives. The Economy segment was targeted with a new 'no frills' product and direct mailings were used to communicate the value-for-money message. Figure 15.8 shows the company's cluster analysis reproduced as a bar chart.

A word of warning: marketing software is a decision support tool, not a decision *substitute*. In the words of one experienced planner: 'The problem is not "garbage in, garbage out"; it's when you start to believe the garbage because it comes out of a computer. We call this "garbage in, gospel out." '

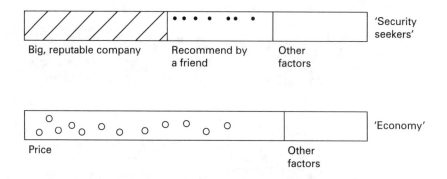

Figure 15.8 Cluster analysis reproduced as a bar chart

SUMMARY

There is a process for marketing planning, the formalization of which is a function of organization size and product market complexity. This process extends to an international context.

The planning process is vital and a good plan is unlikely to emanate from a poor planning process.

The typical planning cycle is 12 months, incorporating time for information collection and verification. However, where inadequate or unreliable information is discovered during the process, thorough completion of the planning process can take two to three years.

Key account planning differs from other forms of marketing planning in that it may involve the joint participation of both buyer and seller. Joint planning, in itself, can serve to strengthen the relationship.

Effective marketing relies on a *usable* written marketing plan that identifies and specifies objectives and strategies with the aim of creating sustainable competitive advantage. Marketing plans must take full account of the strengths and weaknesses of the organization and should never be prepared in isolation from other functions.

IT support software can assist marketing planning, especially where contingencies are being considered and where plans are being devised in a networked fashion.

Note

1. A *planning cycle* is the period from plan to plan, usually one year. This should not be confused with the *planning period*, the period considered in the plan, which might be three to five years.

ORGANIZING FOR RELATIONSHIP MARKETING

Lynette Ryals

In this chapter:

- A traditional organizational structure and the difficulties of implementing relationship marketing within it
- Other organizational structures
- How process organizations have an advantage in implementing relationship marketing

INTRODUCTION

Many organizations are convinced of the value of having a market orientation and understand the potential of RM, but are unable to implement RM because of their organizational structure. A large construction company, for example, could not say how much business it did with a major customer as the company was divided into several business units, each of which had its own independent accounting procedures. Further, records were based on projects, rather than on customers, and so profits were reported by project, rather than by customer. Consequently, each project was priced as if it belonged to a first time customer, leading the supplier to inadvertently make uncompetitive offers. Without a coordinated or relational approach, the company was unable to track and measure the transactions of an individual customer, and it missed valuable opportunities to fully develop and firmly retain existing customer relationships. Structural issues can be exacerbated by cultural factors such as resistance to change, fear of the unknown and confusion about what needs to be done.

This chapter sets out to review some of the difficulties with traditional organizational forms, to identify new types of organization and to explore how organizational structure can serve to enhance customer relationships. The concept of core processes is also discussed as it has a direct bearing on relationship marketing effectiveness. Finally, the transition from functional to process-driven organizations is examined in order to highlight inherent problems and offer potential solutions.

THE FUNCTIONAL STRUCTURE

Marketing is sometimes compared to warfare and similarly, organizations can be structured like armies led by a Field Marshal (the Chief Executive) and a series of Generals (the Directors). Such a traditionally disciplined organizational structure encourages specialization: one division deals with finance, another with manufacturing, another with purchasing, and so on. This is called a *functional* structure (see Figure 16.1).

Functionally structured organizations operate from the 'top down'. Significant decisions are taken by the main board and transmitted down to the relevant functional silos. Structural integrity and organizational efficiency are achieved by the hierarchical ranking of responsibility with reporting channels drawn upwards. The tendency for staff to reside within functional specialisms produces a workforce of highly skilled specialists. The management style is usually one of 'Command and Control', where information and instruction are given from above and compliance is expected throughout. Conformance to company culture is apparent in behavioural patterns: employees quickly learn what they have to say and do, and even the way they have to dress, in order to succeed in the organization.

Functional organizations have great strength and are especially effective where the business environment is either stable or changing very slowly and where competitors play by the same rules. In these circumstances, functional organizations can grow to a considerable size.

Functional organizations do, however, exhibit several serious weaknesses. Because they are governed from the top, their success depends upon the key decision-makers making the right decisions. Key decision-makers, however, often operate at a distance from the customer and can easily miss important signals of market change. Furthermore, many 'top-down' organizations have no mechanism for communicating information *up* or *across* the company. For these reasons, functional organizations can persist in inappropriate behaviour, even when those less senior in the organization know better. The functional organization finds it difficult to respond to requests for customized products or services because of its insistence on strict systems and procedures ('You can have any colour so long as it's black'). Staff may also be reluctant to embrace change, desiring instead to protect any personal investment in their functional specialism.

This inbuilt organizational rigidity and lack of customer responsiveness makes functional organizations less effective in flexible or hostile business environments, for example, where customers demand changes, or where competitors who do not play by the same rules enter the game. Consider UK

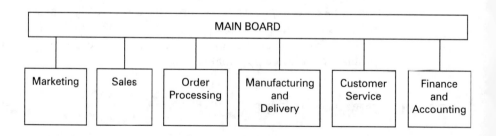

Figure 16.1 A functional organization structure

retail banking and the arrival of First Direct. For years, the retail banks had offered branch-based banking with limited opening hours. Their customer retention was high as there was little competitive differentiation. First Direct then entered the market, offering 24-hour telephone banking, which was quicker and more convenient for customers, and using IT systems to improve service levels. First Direct rapidly gained substantial market share and other banks had to follow suit by introducing telephone banking in order to stay in business.

THE PRODUCT/MARKET MATRIX STRUCTURE

The matrix organizational style, usually associated with product/market structures, represents one business response to changing markets. In matrix organizations, control runs in two directions: down, and across, the organization. The basic matrix structure might be designed around products, or groups of products and services, with a market structure superimposed upon it. The market might be based on geographical location, industry sector or even customer segment.

A typical matrix organizational structure might resemble that given in Figure 16.2, where a manager supervises a product group such as bearing assemblies, but has 'dotted line' responsibility for a market such as automotives.

Matrix organizations differ from functional organizations in their degree of decentralization. Functional organizations are highly centralized and tend to have a single marketing department. By contrast, matrix organizations delegate some responsibility to marketing departments further down in the organization, so that certain marketing activities may be carried out country by country while others may still be undertaken centrally. It is also common for matrix organizations to devolve managerial activities into individual markets which then establish their own replica board of directors.

The matrix structure introduces a degree of customer focus into an organization and facilitates information flow. It is effective where products require an element of technical selling and where products are specialized to an industry or market, rather than customized.

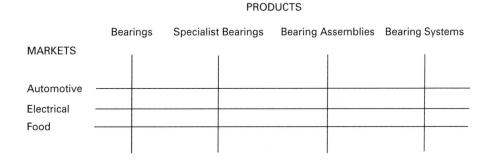

Figure 16.2 A product/market matrix structure

The drawbacks of matrix structures are confusion and duplication. The 'dotted line' reporting system leads to multiple reporting which can create conflicting priorities and confuse delineations of responsibility (either no one makes a decision or several people do). Matrix structures can also cause duplication of effort and, particularly, of information (everybody is sent a copy of the report just in case somebody needs it).

While matrix organizations are more customer responsive than functional organizations, they become progressively less able to cope as the heterogeneity of markets and customers increases. With today's industry concentration and greater access to information (for example, via the Internet), customers have become more powerful and more demanding. At the same time, suppliers have become better informed about the costs of acquiring new customers and the value of retaining existing ones. There is mounting interest in the customer *relationship*, as opposed to the commercial *transaction*. If we map the customer relationship on to the functional and product/market structures, it immediately becomes clear that neither structure will easily accommodate RM.

Functional organizations find RM difficult to implement because of inherent structural barriers, as indicated in Figure 16.3. Customers normally have contact with various parts of a supplying organization during the purchasing process and all of these interfaces must be managed effectively for the relationship to be a success. Functional organizations tend to view the customer in a piecemeal fashion, rather than as an integrated whole. This is because each organizational function deals with only one part of the relationship and, as we have seen, communication *across* functions is slow and inefficient. As a result, a functional organization is apt to send out conflicting messages to a customer. It is no good Sales treating a customer like royalty, if Customer Service ignores them and Finance sends them threatening letters!

In matrix structures, customers may span a number of products/markets. Figure 16.4 shows an example of a Scandinavian components supplier whose automotive customers buy products from across the entire automotive range. The same company also buys standard and specialized bearings for manufacturing electrical products. The diversity of the company's purchasing

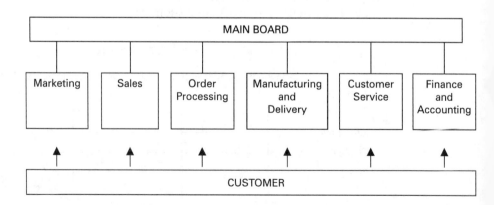

Figure 16.3 Multiple customer interfaces

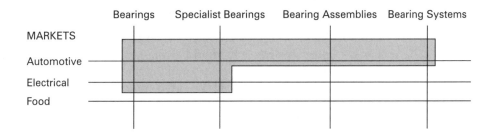

Figure 16.4 Mapping customers on to product/market structures

requirements may necessitate multiple visits to the supplier by different product sales people. The supplier will lose out if it is unable to recognize this situation and coordinate its offer so that the customer gets a better deal from purchasing across the product range, thus increasing the supplier's share of spend, than from buying products individually.

THE PROCESS ORGANIZATION

In the last few years, customer-focused organizations have been experimenting with a process orientation. The process-oriented company preserves its functional excellence in Marketing, Sales, Manufacturing and so forth, but recognizes that it is processes that deliver value to the customer. A business process may be defined as any discrete activity, or group of activities, that adds value to an input, as illustrated in Figure 16.5.

Processes create value for the customer as well as for the supplier. Organizational functions, by themselves, rarely generate much customer value. While Marketing may design 'the promise', it only assumes a value if Manufacturing delivers it. It is a rare customer nowadays who wants just the manufactured product with no delivery, no sales literature, no technical support and no guarantee. So a process is a set of *linked* activities that create value. Processes, therefore, tend to cross functional boundaries while remaining dependent on functional quality. They are often team-based and have strategic goals. The first step in building a process organization is to identify the core business processes.

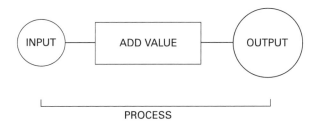

Figure 16.5 Definition of a business process

Identifying core business processes

Core business processes are likely to be those processes in which a company has a *relative strength*, which add *significant value* and which are regarded as *fundamental* to the business. A company should be unwilling to outsource its core processes as they can be used to provide additional customer and shareholder value. One American storage and distribution company, for example, identified 'distribution management' as a core business process and successfully managed to persuade its customers to sub-contract all of their warehousing and distribution functions to the company.

Relatively few processes genuinely contribute core value. Those that do include:

- New product development
- Consumer development
- Customer management/Key Account Management (KAM)
- Supplier development
- Supply chain management

Businesses which are not very complex generally have few core processes and even relatively large companies with comparatively straightforward businesses may be focused on just one or two processes. As the director of a European distribution company once commented: 'We have just two core processes – Key Account Management, and Distribution. They drive our business. We have to get these two right; everything else flows from that.' Process organizations identify the core business processes that deliver value to the customer and then build their frameworks around these processes (see Figure 16.6).

Intrinsic to process organizations are multi-functional teams that manage each facet of the customer relationship. For example, a company that has identified KAM as a core process might set up one or more cross-functional Key Account Teams, comprising:

- A key account director and/or manager to manage the overall relationship and discuss strategy with the customer's main board
- Marketing and Sales representatives to manage the day-to-day relationship
- R&D representatives to discuss potential customer needs and joint innovation
- Finance representatives to ensure that both parties benefit from the value that is created

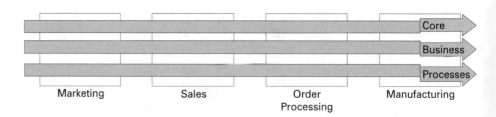

Figure 16.6 A process-driven organization

Managing core business processes

Once core business processes have been identified, they can be managed to create greater customer and shareholder value. Process management enables organizations to serve their customers *better, cheaper, faster, closer*. Process improvement, or re-engineering to offer better and/or less expensive products or services, is widely recognized as a source of value improvement. Value can also be created through speedier processes, by reducing time to market or customer response times, and through establishing more immediate connections to the customer.

Since they operate in a cross-functional manner, process organizations are better equipped to anticipate and respond to customer needs than are functional and matrix organizations. Therefore, process organizations are more likely to retain customers.

Reducing time to market is difficult in functional organizations where each department has to complete its own task before the next department can begin theirs. New car models, for example, can take years to develop. Figure 16.7 illustrates the total time to market in a functional organization.

Where 'new product development' has been identified as a core process, the process organization measures the efficiency of that process in its entirety, or in relation to the total time to market. This creates an incentive for different departments to work together to reduce the overall time involved, as shown in

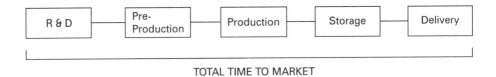

TOTAL TIME TO MARKET

Figure 16.7 Total time to market in a functional organization

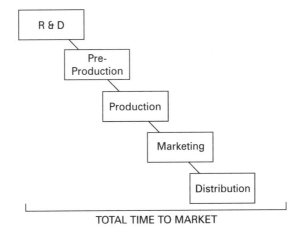

TOTAL TIME TO MARKET

Figure 16.8 Total time to market in a process organization

Figure 16.8. The cross-functional teams that are so typical of process organizations may facilitate this drive towards process improvement.

Opportunities for improving time to market can be identified by introducing a *process measure*: value-added time versus non-value-added time. A process measure assesses the amount of time a product spends having value added to it as a percentage of the total time it takes the product to pass through the entire process. Non-value-added time represents the time a product spends in storage, in transit or idle on a workbench.

'Consumer development' is another core process that can be successfully managed to create customer value by enhancing the closeness of the customer relationship. Tesco Stores, for example, rewards loyal customers with product discounts via its Clubcard scheme. Other organizations use customer data proactively to encourage custom. For example, a florist in the USA maintains a database on the orders it receives and then prompts customers the following year to remember anniversaries and special occasions. As mentioned in Chapter 13, Amazon.com, the Internet book retailer, uses the information it holds about past transactions to suggest to customers new books that might be of interest to them.

MANAGING MARKETING

Since process organizations are very customer-focused, they naturally view the customer relationship as an asset, rather than as a cost. Their marketing budget is considered an investment in the future of the business. Functional organizations, by contrast, often regard marketing as a cost tend to cut their marketing budget in times of difficulty; ironically, this is when investment is most needed.

In both functional and product-market structures, the temptation is to think that products, not customers, deliver profits. This misconception can have grave consequences. When profits are associated with sales volume, rather than with customer satisfaction, the objective is to maximize unit volume. Because each unit sold is seen to generate a set amount of profit, new customers are treated as if they are equally as valuable as existing loyal customers. Customers who buy *efficiently* are treated the same as customers who buy *inefficiently*, or in small amounts and with special requirements. Yet the profitability of those two transactions will be very different: a low cost to serve customer is more valuable to an organization than a high cost to serve customer.

Process organizations tend to view marketing rather differently. Because core business processes are cross-functional, process-oriented organizations are geared to managing and monitoring activities that span functional boundaries. Banks, for instance, talk about 'mortgage customers', 'current account customers' and 'deposit account customers'. These are not customers; they are products. Because banking systems are not designed to focus on the customer, banks can be completely unaware that it is the *same* individual or household which owns *all* three accounts. Of course, some functional or product-driven companies do manage to focus on the customer and not all process-driven organizations are as market-oriented as they should be. However, the process orientation to marketing does seem to reflect a better understanding of the value of the overall customer relationship.

Customer profitability

Customer profitability is a key control concept in relationship marketing and forms the basis of customer relationship management. Customer profitability may be defined as the identification of priority customers and the management of their lifetime relationship with an organization. An organization which realizes that profits come from customers, not from products, will establish systems to measure and manage customer profitability. To do this, customer turnover and associated costs need to be identified. Preferably, these calculations should be made in terms of the individual customer, but they can be done segment by segment. Most organizations begin this process by examining the profitability of a customer during a single period, using the model shown in Table 16.1.

Table 16.1 **Single-period profitability model**

	£	£
Gross sales value		80 000
Less discounts	8 000	
Net sales values		72 000
Less production costs	44 000	
Gross profits		28 000
Less sales and distribution costs:		
1. Selling cost	9 000	
2. Order processing	6 500	
3. Warehousing and order assembly	6 400	
4. Cost of holding stock	800	
5. Inbound freight	1 600	
6. Outbound freight	2 700	
7. Returns	250	
8. Merchandising	4 500	
9. Cost of credit	1 100	
TOTAL	32 850	
Net contribution		(4 850)

Notes
1. *Selling:* includes costs of sales force (including sales management) and sales administration.
2. *Order processing:* includes cost relating to credit rating, stock checking, processing the order, raising invoices, and the accounts and credit control departments, allocated according to turnover.
3. *Warehousing and order assembly*: includes warehousing, fixed costs, order picking, assembly and loading, allocated on the basis of work study measurements.
4. *Cost of holding stock:* includes cost of capital, credit, insurance, shrinkage, pilferage, staff.
5. *Inbound freight:* costs of transport from factory to warehouse, allocated according to order size.
6. *Freight out:* costs of transport from warehouse to customer. A standard unit of cost.
7. *Returns:* includes cost of returned goods, plus returns of packaging materials.
8. *Merchandising:* cost of merchandising (i.e., price marking, shelf stacking, displays, etc.).
9. *Cost of credit:* cost of credit over the average period of outstanding debts.

Single-period customer profitability analysis can, however, be misleading. A more accurate indication of customer profitability may be gained by understanding the lifetime value of the customer. The customer in this example was a large volume purchaser who was unprofitable this year. The customer's low profits could be explained in a number of ways.

1. It was a new customer, with customarily high acquisition (selling) costs. These costs will be lower in future years.
2. It was an investment customer, for whom the supplier is now producing customized products or greatly increased quantities. Consequently, production costs were higher this year, but will fall in future periods.
3. It was a strategic customer, who is unprofitable for the supplying business unit, but who generates massive profits for the supplier as a whole.
4. It was a valued long-term customer, who is normally profitable, but who has had a difficult year and thus has ordered in smaller amounts, which has had the effect of pushing up selling, order processing, warehousing and freight costs. Thanks to the support of the supplier, the customer expects to return to profitability next year.

Customer lifetime value

As discussed in Chapter 8, retained customers are more profitable. The lifetime value of a customer is the total value that a customer will generate for a supplier during the lifetime of their relationship. To determine the lifetime value of a customer, the supplier needs to know three things:

- Lifetime revenue
- Lifetime costs
- Appropriate discount rates

To calculate the lifetime revenue, the supplier must forecast the duration of the customer relationship and the amount of money that the customer will spend in each period of the relationship. The costs of securing that income from the customer must then be projected (see Table 16.2).

The customer represented in Table 16.2 is expected to stay with the company for seven years beyond the current period. Revenue is forecast to rise in each

Table 16.2 Calculating customer lifetime value

	t+1	t+2	t+3	t+4	t+5	t+6	t+7
Revenue	12000	12500	14000	16000	20000	21000	21000
Costs	8000	7750	7750	8000	8500	9000	9100
Profit	4000	4750	6250	8000	11500	12000	11900
Discountrate	15%	15%	15%	10%	10%	10%	10%
Discount factor	0.869	0.756	0.658	0.598	0.543	0.494	0.449
Present Value	3476	3591	4113	4784	6245	5928	5343

period. Costs will be high next year (t+1), but will then fall as the supplier learns how the customer likes to do business. Costs will rise again from t+4 as the supplier invests in the relationship and sales increase sharply.

These forecasts will allow the company to make a seven-year profit projection for the customer. However, profits in future years are worth less than profits in the current period and so the supplier has to apply a discount rate. The experience of this particular supplier has led to an interesting observation: customers are far more likely to defect in the first three years of the relationship than at any time thereafter. The company has, therefore, applied a higher discount rate to the profits from the more risky, early years than it has to profits from later years. Adding together the Present Value for each period shows that the net present risk-adjusted lifetime value for this customer is £33 480.

Customer relationship management

CRM refers to the management of the lifetime relationship with the customer. The term 'CRM' is usually associated with the use of IT in managing commercial relationships. To understand this marketing activity better, let us briefly review several aspects of relationship management that can be transformed, or enabled, by IT. These include data warehouses, sales force automation (SFA), call centres, websites and electronic commerce.

Data warehouses are big databases that contain information about customers. Data warehouses take data feeds from a variety of sources located both inside and outside the supplying organization. Transactional data, or information about purchases and sales, is considered to be the most important type of internal data, along with classification data, or names, addresses and dates of birth. External data feeds may include socio-demographic statistics, geographical information, or credit agency details. One of the functions of a data warehouse is to 'clean' the data (to identify any errors, missing data, or duplication). Data warehouses are extremely useful back-office tools for CRM. They are particularly valuable for identifying profitable customers and for enabling marketing campaigns to be made market-specific.

SFA refers to sales and marketing systems which are loaded on to laptop computers to link the salespeople in the field directly to their office via a modem and mobile phone. SFA enables rapid order processing and order status enquiring. SFA systems usually incorporate standard sales forms so that the salespeople can type up a report of their sales visit using their laptop. This will then be downloaded directly to headquarters.

Call centres facilitate communication with customers by telephone. The primary function of most call centres is to receive inbound calls such as customer orders, or to provide technical hotlines offering after-sales advice. However, some call centres undertake outbound calling to alert customers to relevant special offers. A call centre can be made more powerful by linking it to a data warehouse. A link to a postcode database, for instance, will make telephone order processing quicker and easier for new customers, as callers need only give their postcode and not their whole address. Where an existing customer's telephone number is known, calling line identification can flash up the customer's recent history on the computer screen before the call centre operative picks up the receiver.

For the growing number of customers who prefer to do business on-line, websites are an ideal CRM tool. Some customers may simply seek information on-line while others may wish to order products via the Internet. Electronic communication can be used by suppliers to help attract and retain customers through the provision of on-line services such as tailored websites, e-mail and e-commerce facilities.

The multiple markets model of relationship marketing may explain the sudden upsurge of interest in CRM and the availability of new software tools to support it. Successful implementation of CRM relies very heavily on internal markets; both the cross-functional working between departments and also the willingness of individual employees to work with new technologies. Process organizations are quick to involve their suppliers and customers in new collaborative ways of working. This collaboration can promote closer relationships between supply chain companies and even lead to the formation of strategic alliances. Influencers are changing as IT enables customers to meet on-line to talk about products and services. Many companies facilitate these discussion groups in order to invite customer feedback and solicit market information.

Despite the availability of sophisticated marketing tools and techniques, the road to becoming process-oriented and customer-focused is not an easy one. Let us next consider how traditional functionally organized companies can make the change to being process organizations.

MANAGING THE TRANSITION FROM FUNCTIONS TO PROCESSES

Experience suggests that there are three key issues to be considered when moving from a functional orientation to a process orientation. These concern organizational *structure, behaviour* and *culture*.

Structural issues

The first problem that organizations encounter when making the transition from functions to processes is how to manage the tensions between functional excellence and customer orientation. In functional structures, the individual functions may be cost centres or profit centres. In process organizations, the cross-functional customer management team usually assumes some responsibility for customer profitability. The customer management team may wish to make a portfolio offer to the customer to increase the overall profitability of the customer relationship. This portfolio offer might require the agreement of one function to cut its prices or customize its products, thereby driving up its costs. If the function is also a profit centre, it may be reluctant to do so. Such conflicts of interest between functions and the organization as a whole will need to be resolved.

Behavioural issues

The traditional behaviours and practices of a functional organization may not be appropriate in a process organization. Resistance to change is not necessarily due to personal reluctance; it may be that existing performance measures are no longer suitable. Altering the organizational structure without amending the reward system accordingly can result in a situation where people are instructed to act in one way, but are encouraged to act in another. A familiar example is the sales team that is told to maximize customer profitability while being rewarded on the basis of unit sales. The team will still be tempted to offer discounts and inducements to customers, as the overriding message is 'maximize volume, rather than profits'.

The adoption of new performance criteria may involve additional staff training. For instance, an organization that wishes to maximize lifetime customer profitability will need to teach its people the difference between short-term profit maximization and long-term value creation. With an emphasis on customer retention, as opposed to customer acquisition, employees will have to learn new skills such as how to handle customer complaints effectively, or how to conduct customer exit interviews.

Cultural issues

Research has shown that vested interests can be particularly difficult to overcome. Functional managers, for example, may be reluctant to release their staff to work in cross-functional teams. In one study, the functional silos of a bank were so strong that not a single employee interviewed had ever worked outside his or her current department, and the average employment contract lasted ten years! In an extreme case, an employee who expressed an interest in working in another department was viewed as 'disloyal' and was ostracized by his functional manager.

Attitudes that could inhibit a smooth transition towards a customer focus should be identified and anticipated. Potential reluctance to change can be reduced by selecting the team leader of the cross-functional customer management team from within the function or department which previously had the closest relationship with that customer segment, or the most to gain from efficiency in that process.

OTHER ORGANIZATIONAL STRUCTURES

While functional, matrix and process organizations are the most common organizational forms, a complete review of how companies organize for RM must also include three emerging types of organization: informal alliances, formal joint ventures and networks. These organizational newcomers, like their more traditional relatives, are collections of processes, but they have the popular merits of affording more flexibility and requiring less commitment.

Supply chain collaborations and informal alliances

The idea that entire supply chains compete with one another, as mentioned in Chapter 10, has prompted a new type of organization: the supply chain collaboration. This is a long-term informal or semi-formal alliance between cooperating organizations. It is founded on a process of supply chain management with the aim of increasing customer and shareholder value through enhanced customer responsiveness.

Evidence of supply chain collaboration is seen in the change from brand management to category management. Brand management, as a technique, was developed in the 1930s by P&G whose brand managers would compete with one another for shelf space in the supermarket. The Tide manager would compete with the Ariel manager, even though they both represented P&G laundry detergents. Since the P&G move from brand management to category management, not only do the Tide and Ariel managers now work together to find ways to grow the whole category, but P&G now manages the whole category of washing products for some of its supermarket customers. As a dominant supplier, P&G manages the shelf space for competing products (for example, Persil), as well as for its own products. If it is successful in growing the whole category, everyone gains.

Formal joint ventures

Formal joint ventures are contractual alliances, where two or more parties seek to limit their collaboration to a single project or market and so set up a separate company to exploit the opportunity. Such companies are sometimes called special purpose vehicles, or SPVs. The act of establishing an SPV serves to clarify the respective responsibilities of each partner and to limit individual risk should things go wrong.

Car manufacturing, for example, is a set of processes requiring various competencies, including chassis construction, engine building, interior fittings, security systems and so on. Each process is vital to the customer's enjoyment of the finished product and combining the expertise of different specialist organizations can create even greater value. This is exactly what Mercedes and Swatch tried to do through their joint venture to manufacture the SMART car.

The SMART car also represents how formal joint ventures and informal alliances can work together. The project was initiated by Mercedes and Swatch, who formed a joint venture company called MCC. The car is produced at a site in France where eight different companies are located; one is MCC, while the others are suppliers with whom MCC has an alliance. Each of the suppliers provides sub-assemblies, rather than individual parts, and this enables a complete car to be assembled in just 4.5 hours.

Networks

In addition to supply chain management, 'consumer development' is another key process around which organizations can create greater value through alliances. Consumer development seeks to build loyalty and share of spend. For an organization operating on its own, there is a limit to the share of a customer's spend it can gain without moving outside its area of core competence. A network is an alliance of complementary businesses that can create greater customer loyalty by working together than they can working apart.

The alliance between McDonalds, Coca-Cola and Disney is an example of a hybrid network alliance: hybrid because parts of it are formal while other parts are informal; a network because the parties are all linked. McDonalds and Disney have a formal 10-year alliance to promote Disney films with a tie-in to McDonalds through special film plus meal ticket offers and related theme meals. Coca-Cola supplies McDonalds and informally collaborates with it on equipment design and financial arrangements. Coca-Cola is the sole supplier of cola to Disney theme parks and it also has a marketing alliance with Disney.

The advantages of informal alliances are that they are quick and easy to establish, and the individual partners keep their existing brand names. In fact, the stronger the individual brand names, the more the other partners in the alliance benefit. Networks can easily be broken up because the degree of commitment is minimal.

SUMMARY

Organizing for RM may take many forms: individual companies, supply chain alliances, joint ventures and networks. However, they all share common themes, including:

- Customer focus, not product focus
- Commitment to deliver customer value
- Identification of the core processes that deliver value
- Willingness to reorganize and to change appraisal and reward systems
- Acceptance of the need for cross-functional collaboration and even for joint working with other organizations

As discussed in the previous chapter, pursuing a customer focus has implications for planning. It was suggested that plans should be drawn up for each customer segment/key account and that customers might be involved in the planning process. When an organization adopts a process approach, this should likewise be mirrored in its planning. In particular, alliance partners should have an input in the planning process where joint objectives, strategies and marketing programmes are being developed.

The barriers to implementing a process structure can be intractable, but not insurmountable. Problems can be resolved, or avoided altogether, if companies are able to identify core processes early and to organize their frameworks accordingly.

MANAGING KEY ACCOUNTS

Malcolm McDonald

In this chapter:

- The origins of Key Account Management (KAM)
- The observable phases of KAM
- Determining the KAM relationship
- Implications for the Key Account Manager
- Developing key account professionals

INTRODUCTION

KAM is a natural development of customer focus and relationship marketing in business-to-business markets. It can offer critical benefits and opportunities for profit enhancement for both the seller and the buyer if it is managed with integrity and imagination.

The scope of KAM is constantly widening and at the same time becoming more complex. The skills of those involved both at a strategic and operational level therefore need to be continuously developed and updated.

This chapter, based on unique research carried out at Cranfield School of Management, puts KAM relationships under the microscope. The Cranfield study tested and advanced some groundbreaking research carried out in 1994 by Professor Tony Millman and Dr Kevin Wilson, which found that the relationship between buyer and seller moved through observable phases. By conducting in-depth interviews with suppliers and customers alike, Cranfield established the nature of the challenges faced by key account managers and their directors in their quest to maximize the full potential of the KAM business approach. These insights provide a practical framework for better understanding and practising key account management.

The chapter is in three sections. The first section describes how key accounts can develop over time. The second section discusses how key accounts should be selected and categorized for the purpose of setting objectives and strategies. The third section recommends how people and material resources should be allocated to get the most out of key account relationships.

THE ORIGINS OF KAM

The roots of KAM can be found in various fields such as industrial marketing, sales management, purchasing management, the psychology of customer behaviour and relationship marketing. These disciplines all share a marked emphasis on relationship-building within a transactional context, a quality characteristic of (and crucial to) effective KAM. The development of KAM has been gradual and successive, evolving over time to meet changing needs and altered thinking. This evolution is reflected in the KAM process as a progression of five distinct stages of relationship maturity as illustrated in Figure 17.1.

As the nature of the customer's relationship with the selling organization deepens from that of an 'anonymous buyer' to more of a 'business partner', the level of involvement between the two parties becomes correspondingly more complex. We have labelled the typical stages of relationship maturity as Exploratory KAM, Basic KAM, Cooperative KAM, Interdependent KAM and Integrated KAM. Our research showed that each stage of KAM is clearly distinguishable by the issues impacting on the relationship at the time.

Although Figure 17.1 shows an upward or positive development of the business relationship, a selling company should not always expect this to be the case. As with personal relationships, the business partnership can founder for a number of reasons, ranging from a relatively minor misunderstanding to a massive breach of trust. Additionally, the market position and priorities of the buying or selling company can change in ways that negate the strategic necessity for a close relationship.

Recognizing that the KAM relationship can break down at any time, Figure 17.1 nonetheless provides an overview of what can happen if all goes well. This model represents a useful tool in implementing KAM and is therefore worth studying in more detail.

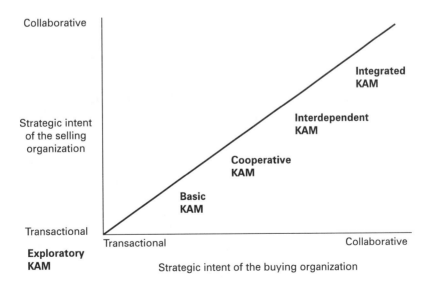

Figure 17.1 Evolution of the KAM relationship

Source: Adapted from a model developed by A. F. Millman and K. J. Wilson (1994).[1]

Exploratory KAM

Exploratory KAM can be described as the 'scanning and attraction' stage. Like a spaceship seeking its mother craft, both seller and buyer are sending out signals and exchanging messages prior to taking the decision to get together.

Broadly speaking, the aim of both parties is to reduce costs. The supplier prefers customers who are leaders in their respective markets and can offer high volume sales over lengthy periods. The buyer is looking to safeguard the quality and quantity of supplies it purchases in future. Both parties instinctively know that any form of lasting commitment will be superior to *ad hoc*, tentative arrangements. Thus commercial issues such as product quality and organizational capability feature strongly in KAM. Expert selling and negotiating skills are also paramount in the inevitable discussions that take place about price.

As depicted in Figure 17.2, the key account manager and the purchasing manager must be capable of interacting effectively and on a regular basis in order to bring the two organizations closer together.

Successful bonding relies heavily on the key account manager's ability to encourage his or her company to become more customer-focused by improving production processes or internal procedures accordingly. All too frequently other managers block proposed changes by putting their individual interests before those of the company. The key account manager must have high level status (or top level backing) to overcome such adversity. Moreover, the implications of KAM must be made blatantly clear throughout the supplying organization.

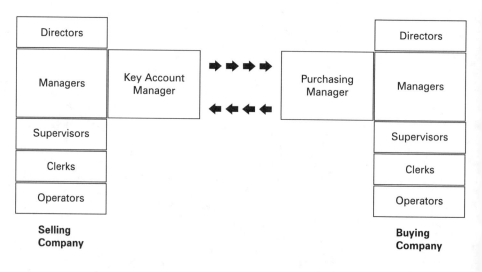

Figure 17.2 The Exploratory KAM stage

Source: From the Cranfield Research Report: 'Key Account Management: Learning from Supplier and Customer Perspectives' by M. McDonald, A. Millman and B. Rogers (1996).

At this early stage, it is unlikely that either party will disclose confidential information as no basis of trust has yet been established. A careful and concerted effort is required to protect and cultivate the fragile relationship.

Basic KAM

At the Basic KAM stage, transactions have begun and the supplier's emphasis shifts to identifying opportunities for account penetration. This means that the key account manager needs to have a greater understanding of the customer and the markets in which the customer competes.

The buying company, meanwhile, will continue market testing other suppliers for best price as it seeks value for money. It is, therefore, essential for the selling company to concentrate on packaging the core product or service and its surround into a customer-specific offer. Actions such as the simplification of 'paperwork' systems can contribute to a customer-friendly appearance.

At this primary stage, although there may still be a lack of trust, the relationship undergoes a subtle change structurally. The key account manager and the customer main contact are closer to each other with their respective organizations aligned supportively behind them, as shown in Figure 17.3.

The single point of contact presented by the key account manager is a powerful benefit to the buying company in getting things done. To provide an effective customer interface, the key account manager must not only be highly skilled and approachable, but he or she must have the status to demand and

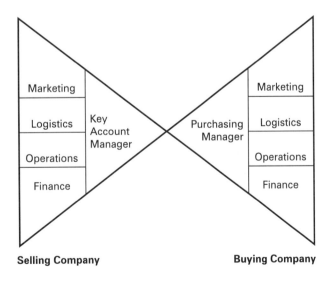

Figure 17.3 The Basic KAM stage

Source: From the Cranfield Research Report: 'Key Account Management: Learning from Supplier and Customer Perspectives' by M. McDonald, A. Millman and B. Rogers (1996).

obtain speedy responses from the selling company whenever it becomes necessary. Without such status, the key account manager will be bypassed and, for example, a more senior figure will be sought who can deliver the buyer's requirements.

Cooperative KAM

By now an element of trust has developed and the selling company may be a 'preferred' supplier. However, the buying company is rarely prepared to put all of its eggs into one basket and will periodically test the market to check alternative sources of supply.

With increasing trust comes a greater preparedness to share information about markets, short-term plans and schedules, internal operating systems and other issues. Employees of the selling company enter into discussions with their counterparts in the buying company and vice versa, forging links at all levels from operations to the boardroom. This collaboration transforms the business relationship into a network with the key account manager and the purchasing manager at the core, as shown in Figure 17.4.

The multiple relationships portrayed in Figure 17.4 often extend beyond the workplace into the social arena. Interactions may take the form of organized events (such as golf) days or be less formal affairs (such as small dinner parties).

This network arrangement brings new strength to the relationship, highlighting the fact that customer service operates on many levels and is driven by a desire not to disappoint personal contacts. It is this trust between people which gets results, rather than the somewhat patronizing statements of intent or customer charters favoured by many companies.

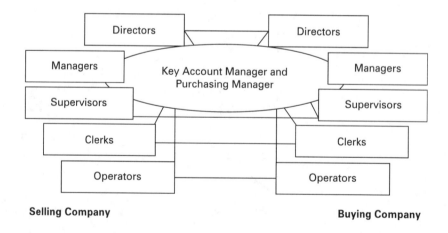

Figure 17.4 The Cooperative KAM stage

Source: From the Cranfield Research Report: 'Key Account Management: Learning from Supplier and Customer Perspectives' by M. McDonald, A. Millman and B. Rogers (1996).

However, as the willingness to cooperate is voluntary, not contractual, the relationship is vulnerable to breakdown caused by staff turnover or random management.

Interdependent KAM

At this stage, the buying company regards the selling company as a strategic external resource. The two companies are sharing sensitive information and engaging in joint problem-solving. Such is the level of maturity of relations that each party allows the other to profit from the partnership. Consequently, pricing is long-term and stable, perhaps even fixed.

There also exists a tacit understanding that expertise will be shared. Collaborative programmes to improve products or to simplify the administrative systems which support the commercial transactions provide evidence of this interdependence. The selling and buying companies are now jointly communicating at all levels, as shown in Figure 17.5. It should be noted that the main customer contact is by now not necessarily the purchasing manager, but may be someone more senior.

Here, the corresponding organizational functions communicate directly. The key account manager and the customer main contact adopt a more supervisory role, ensuring that the various interfaces are effective and that nothing deters or disrupts the working partnership.

The partnership agreement is long-term, extending to perhaps three or four years. Some buyers in our study asserted that in practice there is no limit. Even

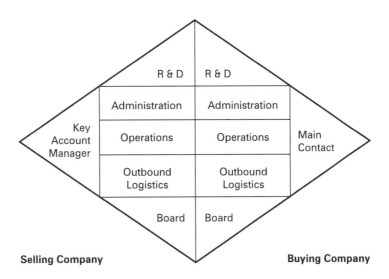

Figure 17.5 The Interdependent KAM stage

Source: From the Cranfield Research Report: 'Key Account Management: Learning from Supplier and Customer Perspectives' by M. McDonald, A. Millman and B. Rogers (1996).

so, performance stipulations contained within partnership agreements may affect the longevity of commitment. The selling company will strive to uphold the 'spirit of partnership' by meeting all performance criteria consistently and to the highest possible standards.

However, as there are no exit barriers in place at this stage, it is still possible for both parties to end the relationship.

Integrated KAM

Integrated KAM refers to the companies relating so strongly and pervasively that they create a value in the market place over and above that which either could achieve individually. In effect, the two companies operate as an integrated whole while still maintaining their separate identities.

At this stage, the key account manager's role changes fundamentally. The multiple linkages now function in a way that is largely independent of the key account manager. This is not to say that the role is redundant but that the incumbent can take a far more strategic approach than before. Figure 17.6 illustrates arrival at the integrated stage.

The borders between buyer and seller become blurred. Focus teams made up of personnel from both companies assume responsibility for generating creative ideas and overcoming problems. The key account manager and the customer main contact merely coordinate the efforts of these teams.

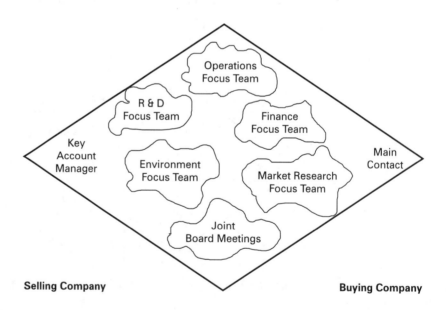

Figure 17.6 The Integrated KAM stage

Source: From the Cranfield Research Report: 'Key Account Management: Learning from Supplier and Customer Perspectives' by M. McDonald, A. Millman and B. Rogers (1996).

The reason for constructing focus teams may be to tackle operational, market or project issues or to introduce motivational forces. The respective teams will meet on a regular basis, setting their own agendas and objectives. Special project teams may be short-lived, existing only long enough to serve their intended purpose.

At this advanced stage, the companies' electronic data systems are integrated, information flow is streamlined, business plans are linked, and the erstwhile unthinkable is now willingly explored. About the only issue that remains sacrosanct for the selling company is its brand. Any requests from the buying company that might undermine the brand should be rejected.

DETERMINING THE KEY ACCOUNT RELATIONSHIP

No one KAM stage is better than another; they are just different. The main question concerns the appropriateness of the relationship with a particular customer at a particular time. To illustrate this point, let us consider some of the relationships we experience in our personal lives.

Our relationship with passing acquaintances may not extend beyond an acknowledgement of familiarity such as nodding 'Good morning!' At the other end of the scale are our close family and friends with whom our relationship is warmer and stronger. The degree of intimacy in a relationship reflects the level of personal investment.

A reversal of our behaviour with these two groups would be seen as highly inappropriate, verging on insane. Similarly, we do not seek intense friendships with everybody we meet. To do so would not only be unsuitable but impossible, for we do not have unlimited emotional reserves.

In the same way, organizations do not possess the resources to have all of their KAM relationships at the integrated level, even if it were deemed appropriate. Like people, organizations have a range of relationships that can be intensified, maintained or subdued. Naturally, investments of time, energy and resources must be justified and guided by strategic considerations.

As stated at the beginning of this chapter, the development of the KAM relationship is an evolutionary process. The speed of progress through the five typical stages is largely determined by the rate at which the buyer and seller can develop the necessary levels of trust. While some relationships may appear to 'stick' at one particular level for a long time, it is also possible for relationships to be held in a transitional phase, somewhere between any two consecutive KAM stages. It is therefore likely that an organization will have key accounts at different stages.

The significance of identifying the present position of key account relationships is that it allows us to anticipate the development requirements of individual accounts as well as the collective demands of the account portfolio. Such knowledge and understanding is intrinsic to the setting of key account objectives and strategies, as is explained in the next section of this chapter.

Developing key account objectives and strategies

A little thought will quickly expose the inadequacies of systems that classify key accounts into just three categories such as A, B or C.

As most companies are judged on the basis of profit, key accounts should be classified in accordance with their potential for growth in profits over, say, a three-year period. The Cranfield research showed that the criteria used by companies to measure potential profit growth are:

- Available size of spend
- Available margins
- Growth rate
- Purchasing policies and processes

When these criteria are each weighted and scored appropriately for each key account, the accounts can be evaluated in terms of profit growth potential on a 'thermometer' scale from low to high. The obvious problem with this simple analysis is that it does not consider the maturity or business strength of the key account relationship. As discussed earlier, the KAM relationship can be anywhere between the Exploratory stage and the Integrated stage.

In order to define and select target key accounts accurately, a full profile of each account must be obtained. This is achieved by measuring profit growth potential in combination with relationship maturity. A comparative guide using these two dimensions, as given in Figure 17.7, is helpful in setting realistic objectives and strategies for key accounts.

Taking the boxes in each quadrant in Figure 17.7 in turn and starting with the bottom left quadrant ('low potential/high strength'), it is possible to work out

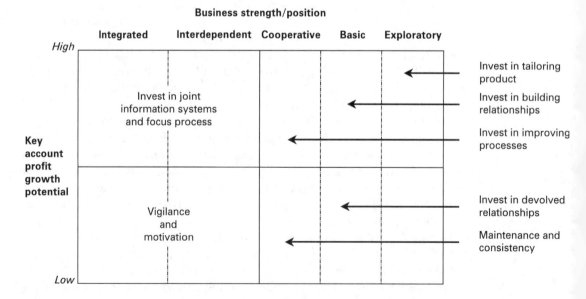

Figure 17.7 Identifying target key accounts, objectives and strategies

sensible objectives and strategies for each key account. Accounts meeting the profile of the bottom left quadrant are likely to continue to deliver excellent revenues for some considerable time, even though they may be in static or declining markets. Good relationships are already enjoyed and should be preserved. Retention strategies are therefore advisable, incorporating prudence, vigilance and motivation. More importantly, as the supplying company will be seeking a good return on previous investment, any further financial input here should be of the maintenance kind. In this way, it should be possible to free up cash and resources for investing in key accounts with greater growth potential.

The boxes in the top left quadrant ('high potential/high strength') represent accounts with highest potential growth in sales and profits. These warrant a quite aggressive investment approach, providing it is justified by returns. NPV calculations may be used as a basis for evaluating these returns, using a discount rate higher than the cost of capital to reflect the additional risks involved. Any investment here will probably be directed towards developing joint information systems and collaborative relationships.

Accounts situated in the boxes in the top right quadrant ('high potential/low strength') pose a problem, for few organizations have sufficient resources to invest in building better relationships with all of them. To determine which ones justify investment, net revenue streams should be forecast for each account for, say, three years, and discounted at the cost of capital (plus a considerable percentage to reflect the high risk involved). Having made these calculations and selected the promising accounts, under no circumstances should financial accounting measures such as NPV be used to control them within the budget year. To do so would be a bit like pulling up a new plant every few weeks to see whether it had grown! Achievement of objectives should instead be monitored using terms such as sales volume, value, 'share of wallet' and the quality of the relationship, enabling selected accounts to be moved gradually towards partnerships and (in some cases) towards integrated relationships. Only then will it become more appropriate to measure profitability as a control procedure. Accounts which the company cannot afford to invest in should be managed in a similar way to those residing in the final boxes to the bottom right.

Accounts found in the boxes in the bottom right quadrant ('low potential/ low strength') should not occupy too much of a company's time. Some of these accounts can be handed over to distributors while others can be handled by an organization's sales personnel, providing all transactions are profitable and deliver net free cash flow.

All other company functions and activities should be consistent with the goals set for key accounts according to the general categorization given in Figure 17.7. This rule includes the appointment of key account managers to key accounts. For example, some key account managers will be extremely good at managing accounts in the Exploratory, Basic and Cooperative KAM stages where their excellent selling and negotiating skills are essential, whereas others will be better suited to the more complex business and managerial issues surrounding interdependent and integrated relationships. The implications for key account managers are examined in the third section of this chapter.

IMPLICATIONS FOR THE KEY ACCOUNTS MANAGER

The fundamental challenge of the KAM task is to succeed in a matchmaking exercise: that is, to marry the manager of most compatible and complementary qualities with a specific account in order to maximize the return on investment. The correlation between the development of the account relationship and the development of the account manager's role is summarized in Table 17.1. Of course, real life is not quite so predisposed as to split conveniently into neat boxes and the table merely encapsulates what Cranfield found to be the general experience.

Clearly, the key account manager must be adept at balancing the growing expectations of both selling and buying companies. The roles and responsibilities of key account managers, and their ability to fulfil them, are critical to the success of any KAM strategy. So what is the personal specification of a key account manager?

As part of the Cranfield research, key account managers, their managers and their buying company contacts were all asked the same question, 'What essential skills/qualities does the key account manager need?' Surprisingly, there was little agreement among the three groups of respondents.

Table 17.1   Strategy, role and skills progression

	Exploratory KAM	Basic KAM	Cooperative KAM	Interdependent KAM	Integrated KAM
Selling Company Strategy	Invest in tailoring product	Invest in building relationship	Invest in improving administrative processes	Invest in sharing information and expertise	Invest in joint planning and development
Buying company Concerns	Does supplier have product knowledge and industry expertise?	Does Key Account Manager demonstrate integrity?	Does Key Account Manager possess authority?	Does emphasis on key account teams mean loss of direct relationship?	Does autonomy of key account teams mean loss of direct control?
Key Account Manager's Role	Identify prospective customers	Identify opportunities for account penetration	Facilitate formation of a network	Supervise relationship interactions and collaborations	Coordinate focus teams
Key Account Manager's Skills	Technical knowledge, 'scouting' ability and communication skills	Product knowledge, selling and negotiation skills	Management skills, especially interpersonal skills	Full range of financial, marketing and consultancy skills	Full range of business skills, plus general management capability

The selling companies involved in the study were unanimous in rating selling and negotiating skills as the chief essential attributes of successful key account managers. The buying companies, on the other hand, voted trustworthiness and strategic decision-making ability as the principal traits. Furthermore, the buyers so intensely disliked being sold to that they would not permit a salesperson to lead the key account team!

The disclosed discrepancy between the comments of managers of key account managers and those of customer contacts is particularly alarming considering that these senior managers are responsible for appointing key account managers to valuable accounts.

The skill area that prompted most dramatic disagreement is that of 'selling/ negotiating'. While selling companies put great store on these skills (62 per cent and 67 per cent respectively), only 9 per cent of buying contacts rated them as important. In simply repeating old patterns, selling companies show their perspectives to be more outdated than perhaps they care to admit.

Developing key account professionals

Training

The selling companies stated difficulty in designing appropriate training for key account managers, especially for those operating in global markets. Problems centred on the need to develop a range of competencies in traditionally specialist areas, such as:

- technical/product knowledge
- relationship-building skills (interpersonal skills)
- finance
- marketing/strategic thinking
- business management
- project management
- creative problem-solving

According to respondents, the training of key account managers mainly consists of attending a number of short courses when deemed appropriate. On average, key account managers receive 5–10 days training per year excluding induction. Because recruits generally have a background in sales or marketing, training must deliberately extend their skill bases in order to develop 'all rounders' rather than better specialists. It seems unlikely that the *ad hoc* and limited approach to training identified here could ever create outstanding key account managers.

In terms of succession policy, selling companies do endeavour to ensure that the handover of a key account is managed with a sense of continuity. Where possible, new account managers are introduced to contacts by their predecessors, who then gradually pass over responsibility to the newcomers. Our study found that buying companies profoundly appreciate this smooth transition and do not expect the new contact to be a clone of the old one. In fact, it was recognized that a new face can sometimes revitalize a flagging relationship.

Authority and status

'We don't want to be dealing with a postman who has to trot back [to their boss] every time we ask a question' was the graphic view offered by one buyer on the autonomy of key account managers. The perception of key account managers as lacking status and authority, especially in the early stages of the KAM relationship, was a recurring theme among the buying companies. Selling companies would be wise to address this concern. Key account managers, it seems, are well aware of expectations and feel the pressure to make decisions and commit their company, even when they do not have the authority to do so. Paradoxically, although the KAM relationship is intended to develop unique arrangements with the buying company, it is on decision-related matters that account managers most often have to refer back to their company.

It was generally agreed that the one area in which the key account manager has least room for manoeuvre is on prices and margins. Any discretion that is allowed constitutes a 'freedom' to operate within carefully defined bands.

When dealing with key accounts, it is important to remember that the position of the key account manager can easily be undermined if the buying company is allowed to gain the ear of someone higher up in the selling organization. Therefore, more senior managers and directors should always be seen to defer to the account manager.

Reporting channels

The Cranfield research revealed that 36 per cent of key account managers reported to directors within their companies. Reporting at a less senior level usually meant being accountable to a sales manager, sales and marketing manager, or business unit manager. All of the key account managers interviewed were, in effect, national account managers. Only four also held some global accounts, with responsibility for results achieved in other countries.

In most of the selling companies studied, key account managers did not have formal – or, for that matter, informal – teams assisting them. Working alone, they were expected to fulfil customer requirements solely by influencing their colleagues to mobilize the necessary resources, which would clearly make progression to interdependent or integrated stages extremely difficult, if not impossible.

Best practice KAM seeks to redress this operational weakness. As the KAM relationship matures, 'dotted line' project teams develop. Comprised of functional staff, these teams report to the key account manager on specific matters of interest, while remaining responsible to their functional manager throughout the working day. Not surprisingly, this duality of duty can be a source of tension. However, problems are not normally about questions of loyalty, but about confusion over priorities. Where project teams are more formalized, team members are set specific objectives and timeframes. In this team environment, it is imperative that the key account manager, as the main customer interface, keeps team members fully updated on all operational and strategic issues relating to their accounts.

Appraisal and reward

The majority of key account managers interviewed received a basic salary plus a bonus related to generated earnings, although a significant minority was employed on the basis of a straight salary. The level at which bonuses were set was a contentious issue.

Managers receiving 10–20 per cent of their income as bonus felt that it was too low in relation to the importance placed on the volume of key account business. Other managers felt it unfair for bonuses to be closely linked to volume, since matters in the buying company such as market shifts over which the key account manager has no control could influence business volume.

In some of the selling companies, share options figured as a form of bonus, providing an incentive related to overall company performance.

Many managers remained sales driven by a remuneration package based on 50 per cent salary and 50 per cent commission. Targets were either set by KAM directors or, more usually, were the outcome of negotiations between the director and the key account manager.

In addition to sales volume, the key account managers identified other performance criteria, including:

- customer satisfaction ratings
- market share
- account profitability
- accuracy of forecasts
- debt recovery
- handling of complaints
- number of new contacts
- new opportunities identified

Where products were project based, key account managers were judged by the achievement of milestones and deadlines. In businesses marked by cyclical sales such as capital equipment, the performance of key account managers was assessed against the total value of the selling company's product portfolio. This relative approach avoided the situation of having excessive bonuses one year and none the next.

SUMMARY AND CONCLUSIONS

The purpose of the Cranfield research was to advance understanding of KAM by finding out how selling companies actually operate, how their operations are perceived by buying companies, and where there may be scope for improvement. From the evidence gathered, the following conclusions can be drawn:

- Business success depends upon excellent processes as well as excellent people and products
- KAM is not a 'quick fix' management process and thus companies need to think in terms of long-lasting, ongoing relationships

- Despite the attraction of KAM, businesses have difficulty implementing it
- The KAM relationship is particularly vulnerable in the early stages of development
- Not all accounts can be developed beyond Cooperative KAM (preferred supplier) even though sellers may aspire to interdependent or integrated relationships
- Higher level KAM relationships can only be achieved in customer-focused companies
- Organizing to meet the demands of global key accounts is particularly challenging
- The key account manager is critical to the KAM relationship and requires skills considerably greater than those of a salesperson
- The key account manager is likely to require ongoing training throughout his or her career as the role and inherent relationships increase in complexity
- In addition to training, selection, appraisal and remuneration policies influence the performance of key account managers
- Buying companies place a high value on the status and authority of key account managers and expect to deal with someone who can get things done
- Account teams can enable a commitment to key accounts that transcends what key account managers can deliver working alone

Like all good research, our study clarified many issues, but also raised some new and potentially far-reaching questions.

1. If the KAM relationship is evolutionary, what is the next developmental stage likely to be?
2. What is the best way to build key account teams?
3. What are the special problems for key account managers who operate in complex supply chains or on a global basis?
4. What are the organizational implications of global key account management?
5. What kinds of decision support systems are required for key account management?
6. How should the relationship between key accounts and non-key accounts be managed?
7. How should the relationship between key accounts and non-key accounts be measured, particularly financially?
8. At what level might the KAM relationship be seen to be a barrier to competition and fair trade?

While Cranfield's research provides a practical framework for understanding how to progress key account management, marketing professionals and business academics are not left unchallenged: the quest to maximize the potential of KAM is as long as the scope of KAM is wide.

Note

1. The original Millman and Wilson labels were: Pre KAM; Early KAM; Mid KAM; Partnership KAM; Synergistic KAM. The labels were changed by the Cranfield KAM Best Practice Club as the members felt the new labels were a more accurate reflection of the duality of the relationship.

    A. F. Millman and K. J. Wilson (1994) 'From Key Account Selling to Key Account Management', Tenth Annual Conference on Industrial Marketing and Purchasing, University of Gronigen, The Netherlands.

PART V

MEETING THE CHALLENGE THROUGH RELATIONSHIP MARKETING

RELATIONSHIP MARKETING: TAPPING THE POWER OF MARKETING

Martin Christopher and Susan Baker

In this chapter:

- The formidable challenge to marketers
- The importance of an integrated approach to marketing
- The imperative of making marketing better understood

INTRODUCTION

This brief chapter concludes the book by drawing together the preceding four parts with a focus on two themes: the importance of employing an integrated marketing approach as exemplified by RM, and the imperative for marketers to communicate more effectively within their organizations the message of marketing's potential to drive sustainable competitive advantage. Marketers today, like so many professionals, face the formidable challenge of envisaging and enabling the future. RM offers marketers a valuable and viable perspective with which to see their way to success; it is a means of accessing and realizing the true power of marketing.

THE CHALLENGE

'As for the future, your task is not to foresee, but to enable it.'

Saint-Exupery, 1948

In our efforts to create organizational vision and mission, the only certainty is that things will change and experience tells us that change will happen even faster in the future. Within the business arena, this climate of ongoing modification and accruing momentum presents unprecedented challenges for marketers, especially where marketing is viewed as a matching process between customer demand and business delivery.

Marketers today are confronted with turbulent shifts in demographics that have resulted in the emergence of new consumer groups, including the mature consumer aged 55 plus, and new types of household and time-pressured consumers possessing higher levels of disposable income. Converging technologies in the telecommunications industries are leading us into an era of the totally connected consumer and opening up a new generation of marketing opportunities.

Wider changes in the marketing environment are being driven by greater globalization, where the focus has moved away from the question of whether being a worldwide community is considered a good or a bad thing, to what form globalization should take, and what are to be its economic rules and its political guidelines and constraints.

Perhaps most crucially, the dynamics of the relationships between buyer and seller are evolving, illuminating changes in choice and influence criteria. As discussed in Chapters 5 and 10, supply chains are becoming the discriminators of success in the market place. Mutual trust, benefit and value are paramount in this age of unparalleled competitiveness and opportunity.

Such key trends in the make up of the consumer, the market place and the buyer-seller relationship significantly impact consumer expectations and behaviour, and thus the role and relativity of marketing. Given this challenge, how should marketers proceed to firmly secure their identity and successfully perform their function?

One of the foremost issues confronting both academics and practitioners is that the fundamentals of marketing theory and practice were developed and first promulgated in a bygone age. The major foundations of marketing were established in the 1950s, in a competitive environment (primarily the North American market place) that contrasts starkly with the global market place of the new millennium. While the fundamentals of the marketing orientation hold fast no matter what changes occur in markets and the competitive framework, there is now a widespread realization that marketing must do more than merely create customers and generate sales; marketing must also seek to retain customers and to develop enduring, mutually beneficial relationships with them. We are operating in an era of in-depth understanding of customer needs and customer retention.

The thematic thrust of marketing, therefore, needs to switch from the blind pursuit of quantity of market share to an emphasis on the quality of that share. In other words, are we doing business with customers who make money for us and who stay with us? Answering these questions lies at the heart of RM.

As suggested throughout this book, the role of RM is to forge long-term and profitable relationships with targeted customers. These relationships are built upon the consistent delivery of customer value. Hence successful RM relies on understanding what constitutes customer value in any given market (see Chapters 6 and 7), and how that value can be created and delivered in a way that is perceived by the customer as superior to competing offers (see Chapters 9–14 about creating customer value through the expanded marketing mix).

THE IMPORTANCE OF AN INTEGRATED APPROACH

The premise of this text has been that an integrated approach to marketing will best enable the organization to meet head-on the current challenge of determining and delivering sustained, superior value to customers. To integrate is variously defined as to combine and amalgamate, to make up as a whole. RM exemplifies integration in that it actively seeks and unites the interests/contributions of all those involved in the marketing activity, be they internal or external players. Indeed, the total value of the marketing process is deemed a culmination of all the constituent elements described in the 17 preceding chapters of this book.

RM requires that organizations work across multiple markets, not just one customer market, as a means of delivering superior value for customers and shareholders. In order to achieve this output, processes and not products must take precedence. (Chapter 16 is specifically dedicated to the issue of organizing around processes.) As we have seen, leading edge companies are organizing internally around the key processes of market understanding, relationship management, innovation, supply chain management and knowledge management. These processes are the capabilities through which firms compete and they share one vital characteristic: they all cut across functions. They are, in fact, horizontal, rather than vertical.

The organizational implications of cross-functional, or integrated, marketing are profound. In the past, responsibility for marketing, in the widest sense, belonged to the marketing 'department'. Marketing plans were based on the classic 4Ps of product, price, promotion and place, and the execution of the plans was delegated to brand or product managers. Now, in the process-oriented business, there is recognition that marketing needs to become a pan-company concern, with cross-functional teams taking responsibility for the development and implementation of process strategies aimed at creating and enhancing customer value. Thus three other elements – people, processes and customer service – are added to the conventional marketing mix.

MAKING MARKETING BETTER UNDERSTOOD

With the growing popularity of the process-oriented, cross-functional approach to marketing, as advocated in relationship marketing, it has become an imperative to make marketing better understood throughout the organization. The traditional functional hierarchies are no longer so rigidly applied, and managers of various disciplines will find that they assume some responsibility for aspects of marketing or need to work more closely with marketing colleagues. Managers must thus develop and improve their understanding of marketing in order to contribute more effectively to their organization's marketing strategy. Figure 18.1 illustrates how such a process-oriented business might look and highlights the participation of different disciplines in completing the marketing process through the delivery of stakeholder value.

As can be seen from Figure 18.1, the source of inspiration, impetus and instruction is the CEO, who is charged with being the ultimate keeper of the organization's marketing orientation. The authors of a forthcoming book[1] on this subject have described the need for this person to be 'The Value-Driven CEO'. Their task is to rethink business strategy, processes, organization and culture in order to win customer preference by ensuring that the organization offers customers consistently superior value. The multidimensional quality of

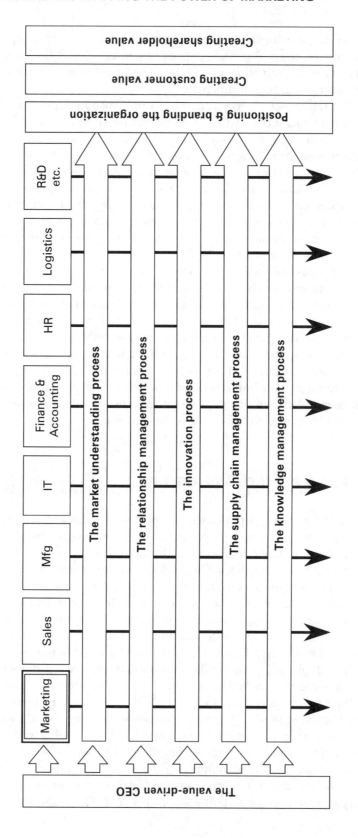

Figure 18.1 A process-oriented business

marketing and the complexity of communicating its comprehensive role do not make fulfilling this responsibility easier.

As discussed in Chapter 1, the problems surrounding the meaning of the word 'marketing' arise from the fact that it is generally referred to in a number of ways within an organization. Most people recognize *promotional literature* (brochures, posters, and so on) or advertising campaigns as 'marketing'. But this is only the *tactical end* of the marketing process, occurring at the level of implementation and being very much the remit of people with the word 'marketing' in their job title. If these visible manifestations of marketing activity are viewed as the tip of the iceberg, as depicted in Figure 18.2, then the bulk hidden beneath the surface can be described as *marketing as a management process*, involving the *allocation and management of resources*. This larger aspect of the marketing task is also generally carried out by people with the word 'marketing' in their titles.

The deepest level of marketing is that of the *marketing orientation*. This describes a *philosophical approach to doing business* that puts the customer at the heart of business matters. The keeper of the marketing orientation is not necessarily someone with the word 'marketing' in their title and the responsibility is frequently assumed by senior management, but everyone within the business has a role to play to uphold it.

These three levels or dimensions of marketing (tactics, management processes and orientation) describe what marketing is in total, yet the outputs at each level are very different. This complexity explains why use of the word 'marketing' leads to so much confusion. Seeking to understand the contribution of marketing to a business by continual reference to the tactical outputs (the brochures, posters, and even products as suggested in Chapter 3) can only give a shallow appreciation of the enormity of marketing's full potential.

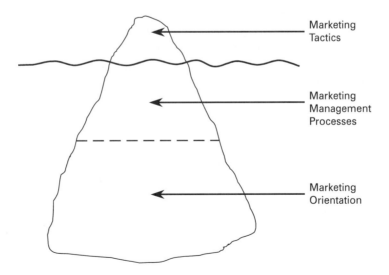

Marketing Tactics

Marketing Management Processes

Marketing Orientation

Figure 18.2 The deeper dimensions of marketing

It is hardly surprising that many managers, working in areas other than marketing, are unclear about what marketing is when marketers themselves cannot agree on an acceptable definition or find more adequate ways of communicating the distinction between the three levels. Over the last few years, disagreement among the marketing profession has focused on whether marketing is going through some form of mid-life crisis and now finds itself at a crossroads. This debate is based largely on discussions about marketing's effectiveness and what it actually delivers. Signalling the extent of disillusion and disappointment that exists, some organizations have gone so far as to consider doing away with their marketing department. Is this sort of talk an indication of the fact that marketing is losing its way or rather, is it, as in the view of Malcolm McDonald, Professor of Marketing Strategy at Cranfield School of Management, a reflection of organizational growing pains – or, in some cases, the very birth pangs of marketing?

Recent articles in the marketing press have discussed the assertion of Hugh Davidson, author of *Even More Offensive Marketing*, that there is a need to find a new name for marketing to distinguish the substance of marketing from its abuse, which, he believes, 'stems from its association with spin doctoring, manipulation and the flashier end of selling'. Davidson's suggestion is 'demand management', and hence the marketing director would become 'the director of demand'.

With the name and nature of marketing in a state of uncertainty, how can a better understanding of the potential of marketing be developed? We would argue that the priority is not to argue semantics, but instead to get on with the job of bringing true relevance and meaning to the marketing discipline. Making marketing meaningful involves communicating effectively with colleagues of other disciplines, and selling the philosophy and benefits of marketing in a more confident and considered manner.

In its relatively short history as a recognized discipline, marketing has matured from being a business bolt-on to becoming the integral force that empowers, expresses and enables overall business strategy. This transition from 'latent' to 'potent' reflects profound changes generally in our needs, capabilities and aspirations as people. Where marketing will go from here and how it will get there is an open question, but surely its enormous capacity to both connect us and content us deserves our focused attention and full commitment.

CONCLUDING REMARKS

This book set out to provide the reader with a firmer grasp of what marketing means and an enhanced perception of the potential of relationship marketing as a possible marketing solution. It is hoped that the insights and information provided will enable both marketers and non-marketers to manage their business tasks better by removing confusion surrounding the role of marketing and offering a marketing approach consistent with today's requirements.

Clearly, doing business in way that harnesses the organization's strengths and addresses its weaknesses to deliver superior customer value is a winning formula. The pursuit of prosperity through relationship-based objectives and operations exploits the holistic nature of buying and selling, an integrity born of integration. Marketing through the effective management of multiple markets acknowledges the composite structure of creating and nurturing custom, encompassing both internal and external factors. As progress is a process, so successful marketing relies on building profitable, long-term relationships; adopting an RM perspective could be the answer.

Note

1. M. McDonald, M. Christopher, A. Payne and S. Knox, *Building a Company for Customers* (London: Pitmans, 2000).

INDEX

Note: **bold** type denotes a figure or table.